CENTRAL ASIA.

CENTRAL ASIA

AND THE

ANGLO-RUSSIAN FRONTIER QUESTION:

A SERIES OF POLITICAL PAPERS

BY

ARMINIUS VAMBÉRY,

Ordinary Professor of Oriental Languages and Literature in the Royal University of Pesth.

TRANSLATED BY F. E. BUNNÈTT.

LONDON:
SMITH, ELDER, & CO., 15 WATERLOO PLACE.
1874

SG

PRINTED BY BALLANTYNE AND COMPANY
EDINBURGH AND LONDON

PREFACE.

— o —

THE following reasons have induced me to collect and publish my political writings, chiefly relating to Central Asia, which appeared in the columns of *Unsere Zeit.*

In the first place, hitherto in Germany, and in fact throughout Europe, so little has been written during the last ten years on the events going on in the Oxus territory, and recent events have so greatly astonished every one, that, for the sake of the information and explanation necessary, the remotest recesses of travel-literature have been ransacked and investigated, and the following pages may therefore perhaps be of use to many. In the second place, these papers contain a chronological and somewhat detailed delineation of those events which have produced, in slow but sure course, the question at issue between England and Russia—a question which has already become a subject of general attention, and will in future be certainly still more so, as, in the advancing course of events in these very districts of Central Asia, that die will soon be cast on which is inscribed, not the words Oxus and Indus, Etrek and Herat, but the significant motto—" Dominion over Asia."

In the third place, apologising for my want of modesty, I must myself produce evidence in these pages, by referring to Count Schuwaloff's mission and the controversy waged between the English and Russian press, that the political opinions which I have expressed since my return from Central Asia were not based on chimeras and empty visions, and were, moreover, not the emanation of any Magyar, and consequently anti-Russian feelings, but were founded on facts, and on perceptions resulting from long study and practical experiences. My political opinions were in nowise too bold and fanciful, as my adversaries asserted, but just the contrary, as has now been proved; for what, nine years ago, I still doubted, namely, Russia's designs upon India, recent events have convincingly proved to me.

Gladly, after the course of another ten years, would I be convicted of having entertained erroneous views, and be designated as a false prophet; yet, with the present political circumstances in the Mussulman East, and with Russia's feverish thirst for territory and boundless ambition, possessing as she does scope enough for her mission of civilisation, and yet ever desiring conquest, it is indeed difficult to foresee how the convulsing collision in Asia of the two Christian colossal powers is to be avoided.

A. V.

PESTH, *May* 8, 1873.

CONTENTS.

—o—

CONTENTS.

CENTRAL ASIA

AND THE

ANGLO-RUSSIAN FRONTIER QUESTION.

———◆———

THE RIVALRY OF RUSSIA WITH ENGLAND IN CENTRAL ASIA (1867).

GENERAL SURVEY FROM 1864.

IT is now three years since, in the concluding chapter of my "Travels in Central Asia," I expressed my astonishment and disapproval at the indifference of England to the advance of the Russians in Central Asia. I pointed both to the Russian line of operations on the Yaxartes, and to the ever-increasing influence of Russia on the territory adjacent to British India. Intentionally refraining from all intricate political sophistries, I was as brief and concise as possible, and I scarcely imagined that the unpretending words of a European just returned from Asia would be deemed worthy of closer attention. Nevertheless, almost every organ of the English and Indian press, from the *Times* to the *Hirkaru Bengalu*, repeated and discussed these few lines. Only a small number of these different

A

journals sympathised more or less with my ideas; the majority rejected my good advice; and without exactly making my remarks ridiculous, a loud Hosanna was proclaimed on all sides at the happy change in English politicians, who, no longer so short-sighted as they had been thirty years before, when the advance of the Russians had been regarded only as a hostile event, now awaited it even joyfully, and wished them good speed on their march to the south over the snow-covered summits of the Hindukush and the Himalaya.

Much has changed, however, within these three years. Far from wishing to exult at the fulfilment of my prophecies, I cannot forbear pointing out the line to which the Russian forces had advanced at the time that I drew attention to their position. When I was in Central Asia, the furthest outposts of the Cossacks were at Kale-Rehim, thirty-two miles from Tashkend. Forts 1, 2, and 3 on the Yaxartes had not yet passed into certain possession, though they had been actually conquered. In the north of Khokand, and in the west of the Issikköl and the Narin, the Court of Petersburg had but small traces of success to show. The Kirghises were exasperated and provoked at the foreign intruder, and the Özbeg population of the northern frontier of Khokand might even at that time have regarded a Russian occupation as synonymous with the end of the world, so thoroughly were the infidels hated and repudiated. Three years have passed away, and what has happened in the interval? Not only in Hazreti-Turkestan has Khodja-Ahmed-Yesevi, the most holy patron of the Kirghises, become a Russian subject; not only has Tashkend, the most important trading town

and emporium of the commercial intercourse between
Russia and Central Asia and China, become incorporated
in the Northern Colossus; not only does the Russian
flag float on the citadel of Khodjend, the second city
of importance in Khokand, but the Russian standard is
apparent also on the small fortresses of Zamin, Oratepe,
and Djizzag. The dreaded Russian has established
himself as patron saint in the Eastern Khanate of
Turkestan; and the Hazret, the Khan, no less than the
Hazret, the high-priest of Namengan, strives to acquire
the favour of a power which a few years ago even
to dream of would have excited deadly fear. In fact
not only Khokand, but the Tadjik population of
the whole of Bokhara and Khiva, the greater part of
both the free and subject Sclavonians, as well as the
richer merchants of Moultan and other parts of India,
who once trembled before the Özbeg power, now proclaim from ear to ear with joyful satisfaction the fact
that Russia is slowly advancing, and that Özbeg
supremacy and arbitrary rule is near its end.

It is three years ago since these changes in the
oasis-lands of Turkestan were conducted with a sure
and certain hand from the banks of the Neva. Having travelled in these countries formerly, and having
from my youth felt great interest in them, I had
always, even though from afar, kept a watchful eye
upon all that was taking place on the banks of the
Yaxartes. I devoured the statements in the papers,
as well as the scanty notices which were sent me by
my Hadji friends in Turkestan, through their brethren
travelling westward. It will not surprise any one that
I took a warm interest in everything, nor that the

expressions of the English press during these events, and the steps of the Indo-British diplomatists, claimed my full attention. Neither of these parties called to mind my prophecies; the tone of satisfaction begun three years before was uninterruptedly continued; they were now no longer contented with the bare assertion that the advance of Russia in Central Asia was a thing to be desired, but they ventured to prove this assertion by representing the success of the Muscovite arms as increasingly advantageous to the interests of England.

In order to solve this problem still more surely, and to convince the thinking world in England still more unanswerably of the advantages of Russian success, the question for discussion was placed in a light which must have been acceptable to each different class of society. The scientific world heard from the learned President of the Royal Geographical Society what extraordinary service would be rendered to our cosmology by the Russian trigonometrical, geographical, and geological societies. Russian voyages of discovery were extolled above all others, Russian scholars were deified, and even the great gold medal was recently bestowed on the Vice-Admiral Von Butakoff for his discoveries on the Sea of Aral. Social reformers were led to compare Tartar rudeness with Russian civilisation, and the picture which I had myself sketched of Central Asia was placed in contrast to that of the young Russia of the present day; the emancipation of the serfs, the efforts of Russia for the enlightenment of her people, the great change in customs, the Russian ideas of civilisation in their approximation to the English, were brought prominently forward, and in every thread of the fabric thus woven, expression was given to the great utility of Russian supremacy in Asia. The commercial world was shown the advantages which must result from safe roads of communication, such as Russian arms are about to level to India through the inhospitable steppes of Turkestan. Indeed, certain papers in their eagerness went so far as to prove to the honest manufacturers of Birmingham, Sheffield, Manchester, &c., that on the new Russian commercial highway to Central Asia none but English wares would be exported, and nothing but English capital would return. Even the military profession caught the whisper of a friendly word ; Russian aggression in India was represented to the sons of Mars as a ridiculous bugbear. Such an aggression was declared an impossibility in a strategical, physical, and moral point of view. How was Russia to overcome the great bulwark of the vast unwatered steppes ? How was she to subdue the warlike Afghan race, or to traverse the dreaded Bolan or Kheiber Pass ? And if she even succeeded in all this, what reception would she meet from the British lion calmly awaiting the foe in its luxurious palankeen ! Even the Church, that almighty lever in England, was lulled to rest by a cradle song. The desire of the Russian orthodox Church for union with the Anglican was pointed out. Dr Norman Macleod's appeal, " The Greek Church is not yet lost!" awakened hopes in the hearts of many ; and learned ecclesiastical dignitaries looked forward with delight to the moment when the Greek triple cross on the Neva would extend a fraternal embrace to the proud dome of St Paul's in London, and when these united Churches would become one mighty defence against the ideas of the Papacy.

Independent pamphlets and stormy newspaper articles repeated in turn the arguments mentioned. The warning voice of the small minority could not venture to appear against the optimists—against these apostles of the new political dogma. Sir Henry Rawlinson, indisputably the best versed in the affairs of that country—a man who combined practical experience with theoretic judgment—alluded, it is true, here and there, in able articles in the *Quarterly Review*, to the erroneous mode in which matters were viewed; and although doubting any actual aggression upon India on the part of Russia, he advised against all active interference, and only blamed the indifference above mentioned; yet his words passed away without effect upon the multitude. I might, indeed, assure myself, that where such an authority has little weight, I should gain but little with my present words. I have for this reason long delayed to speak; still, having studied this important question in all its phases—having tested it on all points with an impartial eye—I have felt myself able to prove, not only to English politicians, but to the whole of Europe, that the Cabinet of St James has fatally erred in its mode of viewing the matter, and that the indifference so cherished is not only injurious to the interests of England, but is in truth the deadly weapon with which Great Britain is committing an act of suicide unprecedented in history.

Why I, who by birth am neither English nor Russian, should take up the subject with such warmth, rests principally in the fact that I regard the collision of these two colossal powers in Asia less from the point of their mutual rivalry, than from that of general European interest. Whether England or Russia has the advantage in Asia—which of the two will be the great arbiter of the destinies of the Old World—can never be indifferent to us; for just as much as these two powers differ from each other in their character as channels of Western civilisation, just so much do they vary also in their future appreciation of the fruit of the contest. A hasty glance on the one side at the Tartars who have been under Russian rule for two hundred years, and on the other at the millions of British subjects in India, would be sufficient at once to inform us on this point. We will, however, set this comparison aside for subsequent examination, and for the present only authenticate the fact that the question of the rivalry in Central Asia between these two north European powers concerns not only Englishmen and Russians, but every European, and that in truth it deserves to be watched with interest by every thoughtful man of the present century.*

I. THE CONQUESTS OF RUSSIA IN CENTRAL ASIA WITHIN THE LAST THREE YEARS.

In the first place, we will mention the historical facts of the Russian scheme of conquest within the last three

* Up to the present day the *Revue des Deux Mondes* is the only journal of the whole Continental press that has alluded to the subject, and this has produced two special articles on Central Asia. The first, without betraying any partisanship, points only to the critical circumstance of the approaching collision ; the second, which is pervaded with Russian feeling, sings the song of the English optimists, and I should not find fault with it if the writer had not quoted several passages from my book on Central Asia as his own property.

years. Instead of entering into the details of Peroff-sky's, Tschernajef's, and Romanoffsky's campaigns, which have been discussed in Mitchell's book, "The Russians in Central Asia," and also in several able articles in the *Quarterly* and *Edinburgh Review*, or into the scanty notices which find their way to the public from the Russian State Cabinet, or into the still more scanty statements made by the dearly-paid English spies in Central Asia, we will only cast a hasty glance on the events generally, in order to make the reader acquainted with the present condition of the Russian forces in Central Asia.

The Russian operations in Central Asia began most successfully by the apparent subjection of the Kirghises. The conquest of Khokand was then immediately begun in order to secure a firm footing in the three khanates. In this eastern part of the three oasis-lands of Turkestan there had always prevailed, comparatively speaking, the least social order, the feeblest religious culture, and the greatest repugnance to warlike undertakings. With this were combined great internal disturbances; for while the Khodjas, by their inroads into the Chinese terri-tory on the east, always exposed the khanate to the danger of a collision with China, which had, indeed, fre-quently ensued in the past centuries, the covetous emirs of Bokhara on the west had ever cruelly laid waste the land in their desire of conquest. The advancing columns of the mighty Russian in the north had, until the cap-ture of Ak-Mesjid, but little occupied all tongues at the bazaars of Namengan and Khokand; for the con-test for the crown, which Alemkul, the Kiptchak chieftain, was carrying on with Khudajar-Khán, had at

that time absorbed the general interest. At the period
of the unsuccessful Peroffsky expedition, Mehemmed-
Ali-Khan was on the throne. He was beloved and
extolled; and the infatuated multitude were far better
pleased with the ideas of conquest than in contemplat-
ing a defence against the threatening enemy in the
north, or in considering Conolly's projected alliance
with Khiva. It was not till after Mehemmed-Ali's
death that the fall of Ak-Mesjid took place—that first
dangerous wound in the existence of the khanate; and
success was all the easier to the Russians, as, just at
that time, on the one side, the most violent contest was
going on in the interior of the khanate between the
Kirghises and the Kiptchaks; and on the other, the first
attempt of the Weli-Chan-Töre against Kashgar was
paralysing the warlike powers. The columns of the
Russians which advanced against the Khokand fortresses on both banks of the Yaxartes could scarcely be
accused of cowardice, although the thousands of Khok-
and warriors, of which Russian reports speak, seem to
argue a somewhat exaggerated measurement.

After the taking of the last-named place, or, to speak
more correctly, after the systematic establishment of
the chain of fortresses along the Yaxartes, on the waters
of which the steam-vessels of the Aral fleet could now
freely move, the Russian power increased with the same
giant strides as that of Khokand retrograded, owing to
the continuance of the causes before mentioned. The
line of forts afforded not only security against Turke-
stàn, but it was also a powerful defence against the
Kirghises, who, now surrounded on all sides, would find
some difficulty in upholding an Izzet, as the last anti-

Russian chief during the Crimean war was styled. The work of occupation was therefore carried on by the Court at Petersburg with its wonted energy ; and not until the two forces united which were carrying on operations from the Chinese frontier towards the Issik-köl, and from the Sea of Aral along the Yaxartes, extending, therefore, from the north-east and north-west southwards to Aulia Ata (Holy Father, a former resort of pilgrims) — not until then did the Russian diplomatists consider it necessary to state in a despatch, signed by Prince Gortschakoff, on the 21st November 1864, that the Government of the Czar had now fulfilled its long-cherished desire of removing the boundary line of the Russian possessions from the uncertain soil of the Sandy Desert to the inhabited part of Turkestan ; that all aggressive policy was herewith concluded ; and that the behaviour of the Government would have but one aim in future—namely, to prove to the neighbouring Tartar states, with the utmost respect for their independence, that Russia was free from all hostility and all designs of conquest, &c.*

It is readily imagined that the Cabinets, with the exception of the English, placed as little reliance on these assurances as did the Russian minister himself. The history of states impelled into ever new conquests is sufficiently known—we have examples of it in every page of the history of the world, in every age in which any single power has been on the increase. Just as the English exculpate themselves in vain respecting the annexation or incorporation fever of Lord Dalhousie, so

* See the original text of the despatch in question at the close of this paper.

all the Russian memoranda, drawn up in the same spirit, are superfluous. It is the natural progress of things; and the Court of Petersburg was right, and in fact could not have acted otherwise than to follow the southern course of the Yaxartes after the establishment of the gubernium of Turkestan; and as the inhospitable steppes had been before no tenable frontier, the thinly-peopled neighbourhood of Ichemkend and Hazret were scarcely a better one. A well-cultivated region was needed, in order not merely to be dependent for provisions on the highway of communication from Orenburg to Semipalatinsk. For this reason it was absolutely necessary to incorporate Tashkend—the rich and fertile Tashkend—in the Russian territory.

It would therefore be a useless waste of time were we to attempt to allege as the main cause of the Russian occupation of the last-mentioned town on the 25th June 1865, the touching story of the petition of the Tashkend merchants, and of the numerous deputations who came imploringly into the Russian camp in order to entreat the shelter of the two-headed eagle, called by the tribes of Central Asia the Ashder dragon, or the Karakush vulture, a bird not otherwise held in much favour. Tashkend, which since time immemorial had lived in feud with the rulers of Khokand, had been latterly especially indignant that its favourite, Khudajar, should have been twice expelled from the throne. It was very agreeable, therefore, to its authorities to damage the prevailing influence of the Kiptchaks by Russian supremacy; still it is not quite probable that the latter was generally desired.

Russia took possession of Tashkend because it

seemed indispensable to her as a strong basis for further operations, and not in order thus to acquire a protecting barrier for possessions already gained. Through Tashkend, however, the Court of Petersburg had entangled itself in hostilities with the Khanate of Bokhara. As is well known, the Emir, by his campaign of 1863, had gained the nominal right of sovereignty over the western parts of Turkestan; and although after his departure everything returned into the old track of Kiptchak despotism and party strife, he imagined, nevertheless, that he had vindicated his right over the whole of Khokand. He wrote, therefore, a threatening letter to the commandants of the newly-conquered town, demanding the evacuation of the fortress. This troubled the Russian general but little; and as he heard that Colonel Struve, whom he sent to Bokhara to arrange the matter amicably, had been taken prisoner there, he set out on the 30th January, crossed the Yaxartes at Tashkend with fourteen companies of infantry, six squadrons of Cossacks, and sixteen cannons, intending to proceed direct to Bokhara, and to punish the Emir for having ill-treated his envoy.

This project, however, failed. The Russians were obliged to retire, but they did so in the greatest order; and although countless masses of Bokhariots swarmed around them on all sides, their loss was, nevertheless, too inconsiderable to agree with the bombastic accounts of victory which the Bokhariots trumpeted forth throughout the whole Islam world, and which even found their way to Europe through the Levantine press. General Tschernajef exculpated himself by asserting that his hasty advance was alone intended to impede the steps of some secret English emissaries who were eagerly engaged in forming an alliance between England and Bokhara, and who had been, moreover, the chief cause of the imprisonment of his envoy, Colonel Struve. Nevertheless, the authorities in Petersburg could not pardon his military error; he was suspended from his high command, and General Romanoffsky succeeded to his post. The latter advanced forwards with slow but all the more cautious steps. On the 12th April a flock of 15,000 sheep, guarded by 4000 Bokhariot horsemen, was captured; and a month afterwards there was a warm engagement in the neighbourhood of Tchinaz, generally called "the battle of Irdjar," in which the Tartars were totally defeated. On the 26th May the small fortress of Nau fell into the hands of the Russians, and soon after Khodjend, the third city in the Khanate of Khokand, was taken by storm, and that after a hard contest, in which the Russians left 133 dead and wounded on the field, and the Tartars certainly ten times as many. Nevertheless, the prize was well worth the hard contest, for this place had better fortifications than Tashkend and all the other towns in the khanate. It was the second resting-point of the Russian arms on their progress towards the south; and although the Russian *Invalide* asserted, in an official statement with regard to further plans, that the conquest of Bokhara, separated as it was by steppes from all other possessions, could not be the object of the Russian operations, but, on the contrary, was utterly fruitless, still the forces advanced over Oratepe, through the small towns of Djam Zamin, as far as Djizzag, leaving important garrisons behind everywhere.

The events that were passing in the Khanate of
Khokand itself during the victorious march of the
Russians are no less worthy of our attention. The
inhabitants, consisting of nomad tribes, Özbegs, and
Tadjiks, or Sarts, were just as much divided in their
Russian sympathies and antipathies as they differed
from each other in nationality, rank, and occupation.
The warlike, powerful, and influential Kiptchaks, the
old enemies of the often-intruding Bokhariots, who
wanted to force upon them the hated Khudajar-Khan,
were not signalised by any special opposition. Their
friendship was an important acquisition for the Russians,
and the approximation must have begun as early as the
time that the north-east army corps, marching from
Issikköl, came into contact with them ; for if this had
not been the case, the advance on this line would certainly have been more dearly purchased. The Özbegs,
as the ruling race, defended themselves as much as
possible; yet, with their well-known lack of valour,
decision, and perseverance, they could effect but little,
and as it was a matter for consideration whether Russian
supremacy was after all a worse evil than the everlasting
war with Bokhara or internal disturbances, they did
well to submit to their unavoidable fate. Only a few
exasperated Ishans and Mollas were driven by an
unfounded fear to Bokhara, as, for example, the descendants of Khodja-Ahmed-Yesevi in Hazreti-Turkestan, who, however, will probably soon return to the
bones of their sacred forefathers, as the Russians will
certainly not hinder them in gathering in the pious
gifts of their pilgrims. The Russian occupation appeared, however, desirable and advantageous only to the

rich merchants of Tashkend, to the Sarts or Tadjiks, and to the small number of Persian slaves; for as the former expected considerable benefit from the incorporation of their native city into the Russian territory, so the latter hoped to be freed from their oppressed position by the decline of Özbeg supremacy. As we see from a correspondence addressed by General Krischanofsky to a Moscow paper, it was these very Sarts who were most helpful to the Russians. Their Aksakals, and not those of the Özbegs, were the first who were presented with posts of importance by the Russians. They appear in public always at the side of the Russian officers; they harangue the people; and while Russian churches are being built, they have disseminated the report that his Majesty, having been converted to Islamism by a nocturnal apparition, is on the very point of making a pilgrimage to Hazreti-Turkestan. For a long time in commercial intercourse with Russia, many of the Tadjiks, especially those at Tashkend, are familiar with the Russian writing and language; they act as interpreters and mediators; and as several of them have attained high positions in the Mehkemes (courts of justice) and other offices, the main inducement for their adherence is easily understood.

Such is the state of things on the main line of operations in the Khanate of Khokand. At the adjacent points, also, east as well as west, the work of transformation has been silently going on. Of Chinese Tartary we hear that since the year 1864 the Chinese garrisons have been removed, and have been replaced by a national government. First there were the disturbances of Tunganis, then followed the emancipation of Khoten,

Yarkend, Aksu, and Kashgar; and although the traditional love of pillage that distinguishes the Khokand Khodjas may lie at the foundation of these disturbances, yet many know with certainty that the Court of Petersburg favoured these revolutionary movements, and indeed that the Kiptchaks, who are now in possession of Kashgar, acquired it with Russian arms. This is the usual prelude to Russian intervention. For some time these independent towns are allowed to be hostile and to make war upon each other; yet it is easy to foresee that their hostilities will appear dangerous to the repose of the Russian frontier, remote as it may be; and if the Court of Pekin does not hasten to restore order, the Russians will certainly anticipate their proceedings. The English press consoles itself with remarking that the insurmountable barrier of the Kuen-Luen range renders a further advance toward Cashmere impossible, and that this Russian diversion at any rate would be advantageous to the commerce of Central Asia. We will, however, defer the discussion of this question for the present, and rather cast a glance at that part of Central Asia lying to the west of Khokand. Although entangled in the war with Bokhara, Russia, up to the present time, has not attacked the real Bokhara territory; for Djizzag is the lawful boundary between the former and Khokand. Nothing but a few diplomatic skirmishes have as yet shown themselves, and foremost among these stands the revolution of Shehri-Sebz, that notorious focus of the contests with Bokhara. For if the Russian press were to deny a thousand times all interference in it, the appearance of the Shehri-Sebz Aksakal in Tashkend cannot be regarded as devoid of meaning, and this all the more as Djuna-Bei, the prince of the country, is at the present moment at war with Bokhara. Comparatively speaking, we are least aware of the Russian plans in Khiva. Russian influence has not yet affected the inhabited part of that khanate, and in the north alone, since the destruction of the fortress of Chodsa-Nijaz on the Yaxartes, a few wandering hordes of Cossacks and Karakalpaks along the eastern shore of the Sea of Aral have been made Russian subjects.

2. THE FUTURE POLICY OF RUSSIA.

The sketch of the proceedings of Russia in Central Asia shows in itself in what manner the policy of the Petersburg Court will pursue its plans in the immediate future.

The most southern, and therefore most advanced, outposts are at Djizzag. This word signifies in the language of the country a hot, burning place, and its position in the deep valley of the Ak-Tau range perfectly justifies the name. In consequence of its extremely unhealthy climate and the great lack of water, the number of the inhabitants in this station on the highway to Khokand is very small, and I cannot believe that the Russians have chosen it as a place of permanent abode and as a halting-point, in spite of the assertion in the Russian *Invalide* before mentioned, or the opposite opinion of the learned writer of the article "Central Asia" in the *Quarterly Review* of October 1866. Not only is it an unhealthy and scarcely tenable post, but any lengthy sojourn there must be considered extremely unpolitic. The gentlemen on the banks of the Neva know well what Bokhara is in the eyes of the whole Central Asiatic world, and indeed, I might say, of the whole Mohammedan world. They know that on the Zerefshan is to be sought the true source of the religious ideas and thoughts, not only of all Central Asiatics, but also of the Indians, Afghans, Nugai Tartars, and other fanatics. To accomplish any grand *coup*, therefore, the Emir, who styles himself Prince of all orthodox believers, must be brought to acknowledge the supremacy of the white Czar; and the sacred and noble Bokhara, where the atmosphere is perfumed with the aromatic odour of Fatihas and Koran recitations, must do homage to the power of the unbelievers; and the multitude of frantic fanatics and religious enthusiasts must acknowledge that the influence of the saint resting beneath their soil is not strong enough to blunt the Russian bayonets. The fall of Bokhara will be a frightful example to the whole Islam world, and the dust of her ruins will penetrate into the far distance as a mighty cry of warning. This must, and will most certainly be, the aim of the Court of Petersburg.

From this point of view it is therefore very probable that the greatest attention will be directed in future to the line of operations extending through Tashkend, Khodjend, and Samarkand. The conquest of the whole Khanate of Khokand may indeed follow in time, for such a scheme presents no special difficulties; but the main interest is the maintenance and security of those highways of communication, which will afford the advancing army a road provided with an uninterrupted succes-

sion of springs, with strong garrisons in the now strongly-
fortified Tashkend and in the more northern forts,
besides the guberniums of Orenburg and Semipalatinsk. The Emir may use all possible means to acquire
the friendship of Russia, a matter which he has not at
present done ; he may send to Constantinople as many
messengers of bad news as he will; he may despatch as
many friendly invitations as he likes to the Vice-Regent
of India, but it will all avail nothing. The town of
Bokhara must, either without him or with him, be
governed by an Isprawnik ; for the Russians dare not
and cannot rest until the old Samarkand and Nachsheb
(Karshi), or the entire right bank of the Oxus, are
incorporated with the gigantic possessions of the house
of Romanoff. That this catastrophe, this final hour of
the independence of Transoxania, will not be brought
about with such ease as the former military achieve-
ments in Central Asia is indeed obvious. I see already
in imagination the frantic hordes of the Mollas and the
Ishans, and of thousands of students, preaching the
cause of the Djihad (religious war), and wandering
with holy fury through the khanates, among Afghans,
Turkomans, and Karakalpaks, calling down the curse of
God upon the intruding stranger, and presenting spec-
tacles of the deepest and most devout contrition. The
fatal contest will be a mighty though not a useless one.
So far as I know the Khivans and the Afghans, I consider the idea of a common alliance with Bokhara as
utterly impossible; for if they were inclined for such
a thing, it must have been formed sooner. No selfish
feeling, no political combination, nothing but the utmost
want of character and the absence of all calculation for

the future, will keep them in repose till Hannibal no longer stands at the gates. Not only in Central Asia, but among all the other peoples of the East, we look in vain for an effort after a common aim. As the warlike Afghans could combine in forming a well-ordered auxiliary force, so also it would be possible for the Khan of Khiva to join the army of the Emir with 20,000 or 30,000 horse; yet neither the one nor the other will do this. To unite them under one command would alone be possible to a Timur or a Djengis, and even then the smallest booty might awaken rancour and discord in their ranks. The hundred thousands also of well-mounted Turkomans who inhabit the great steppes on the other side of the Oxus as far as the Persian frontier, are of no use at all as regards the safety of the holy city. Their Ishans will indeed do their utmost, if summoned by the Emir or by the members of their order in noble Bokhara, to induce the wild sons of the desert to join in the holy contest. Yet I know the Turkomans too well not to be aware that they will only take part in the Djihad so long as the Emir gives them good pay and the prospect of still better booty; and just as they have occasionally entered the Afghan-Persian service, it is highly probable that the Russian imperials will speedily make them the best comrades of the Cossacks. Enthusiasm for the religion of the Prophet, in my opinion, only existed for the first century—in fact, I might say, only for the first fifty years. All that Islamism subsequently achieved in Anatolia, in the empire of Constantine, in the islands of the Mediterranean, in Hungary and in Germany, was the result of a wild thirst for booty and treasure, and of an inclination for adventure. Where these motives are lacking, zeal is also lacking; and I repeat, that though the contest will be a hard one, there is not the least doubt of the speedy victory of the Russian arms in Bokhara.

With the fall of this most influential and strong part of Turkestan, Khokand will of itself exchange apparent sovereignty for the protection of the white Czar. Khiva, however, to all appearance, not intimidated by the example, will nevertheless resume the contest. The conquest of Khahrezm, moreover, although easier than that of Khokand, is subject to important difficulties. With the exception of two cities, the inhabitants of which are better acquainted with Russia through commercial relations, the Özbeg population of this khanate already abhor the name of Russia. They stand far higher than the Khokands and Bokhariots in valour, and, assisted by the soil of their country, they will give the Russian troops a good deal to do with their Turkoman mode of warfare. I must, as before, oppose the opinion maintained by many geographers and travellers, that the Oxus will form a highway for the expedition. This river, from its great irregularity, and from the sand which it carries with it, is difficult of navigation to small vessels, to say nothing of ships of war. Not a year passes that it does not change its bed for some miles in the loose soil of the steppes, and if the Russians were not accurately convinced of this circumstance, the small steamers of the Aral Sea fleet, built for river navigation, would have begun their advance into the interior of the country on the Oxus rather than on the Yaxartes. For although the smaller fortresses, such as Kungrat,

Kiptchak, and Mangit, which are built on fortified heights on the left bank of the river, might do damage to an advancing fleet, they are scarcely to be taken into consideration in the deplorable condition of the Khiva artillery. Attempts to navigate the river from the mouth as far as Kungrat, where the stream is deepest and most regular, have been also already set on foot; yet that they have been attempts only is an excellent proof that the navigation of the Derjai Amu (Oxus), although not quite impossible, is a difficult task.

These are, however, only secondary hindrances; and as in Bokhara, so also in Khiva, the white Czar will contrive his elevation to the throne of the Khahrezm princes—not, indeed, by the greybeards of the Tchagatai race, but by his own bayonets and cannons.

When once the acquisition of the entire right bank of the Oxus is secured, when the whole tract of land from Issikköl to the Sea of Aral has passed into the possession of Russia, richly provided with excellent commissary stores, then the diplomatic game will begin with Afghanistan. The Court of Petersburg will not suddenly appear among the Afghans with an armed force, and this not because of the warning given by the failure of England in 1839, but because such a proceeding is once for all not the custom of the Russians. Such an act, moreover, would be partly superfluous and partly injudicious, with the proverbial dissension prevailing among the descendants of Dost Mohammed; where brother rages against brother in the bitterest feud, where intrigues are ever arising from covetousness and vanity, a secret agent, a wise word, a few friendly lines are of greater use than any armed invasion. Up to the present time, Abdurrahman-Khan, in his family dispute with Shir-Ali-Khan, has entered into no communication with Russian agents, although he made a semblance of so doing, in order to intimidate the English Munschi (agents) in Kabul. That he would be much inclined to such a step, I do not doubt in the least; yet the Russians have given him no occasion for doing so. For if the Afghan party adverse to Shir-Ali-Khan, the Emir accredited by England, had received even the slightest sign from the Neva, they would certainly have held no parleying with Sir John Lawrence in Calcutta. Not only chiefs and princes, but every Afghan warrior and every shepherd on the Hilmend is familiar with the idea of Russian commerce, and I have convinced myself a hundred times how readily, and indeed how gladly these people would enter into a Russian alliance against the nobles of Peshawur. Whether the result of this friendship would be salutary, and would promote the interests of Afghanistan, never occurs to any one. The Afghan, like every other Asiatic, only perceives the interest of the moment; he only sees the evils which his race has suffered in Cashmere and Sindh from English supremacy; he vividly remembers the last occupation of the red coats in Kabul and Kandahar, and although every one knows that the Muscovite Kafirs are not much better than those of Western Europe, still, impelled by feelings of vengeance, he prefers, and ever will do so, the alliance with the north to any English approximation.

Hence nothing but friendly sentiments, nothing but an alliance, supported not by treaties, but by a strong power on the Oxus, can be the future aim of the Russians in Afghanistan.

The same state of things is also to be aimed at in Persia. Here also the Court of Petersburg has played a very successful game within the last few decades. Russian influence has passed through various phases in Iran from the appearance of the Muscovite ambassador at the brilliant Court of the Sefevis, at the time of Chardin, until the present day. Formerly ridiculed and despised, the Russians have risen to be the most powerful and dangerous adversaries of Iran. While England and France in the time of Napoleon I., desirous of asserting their influence at the Court of Teheran, rivalled each other in rendering service to the Shah and some of his grandees, Russia, as " inter duos certantes tertius gaudens," silently made the way for the conquest of Transcaucasus, and achieved the advantageous treaties of Gulistan and Turkmantshaj. And while the two Western powers were persisting in their policy, the Northern Colossus had taken up such a position both on the Caucasus and on the Caspian Sea, that the shadows of it stretched not only over the northern edge of Iran, but far into the interior of the country. At the time of Sir Henry Rawlinson's embassy, English influence was on the point of gaining the ascendancy, but from that period it has been gradually sinking ; for the English policy in Iran was just as lavish in Malcolm's time in gold and favours, as it has been cold and indifferent from M'Neil downwards. The Shah as well as his ministers seemed constrained by necessity to receive the Russians as their Mentor. It is from no conviction of a better future that they have cast aside the embraces of the English lion and thrown themselves into the arms of the northern bear ; and the Shah, whether he likes it or no, has to dance to every tune which the latter growls to him.

Having thus depicted the condition of Russian power and policy in Central Asia, if we now cast a glance upon the frontier line stretching for 1300 wersts from the Sea of Japan to the Circassian shore of the Black Sea, along which Russia is in constant contact with such various races of different origin and different religion, over whose future her aggressive policy hangs like the fatal sword of a Damocles, we shall soon see that although the most southern outposts in Asia are on the Araxes, yet the point at which they meet a European power in their further advance is alone to be found in Central Asia. Twenty years ago, separated from the northern frontier of British India by the great Kirghises hordes and by the three khanates, the present distance between Djizzag and Peshawur, though the laborious pass of the Hindukush lies between, amounts to no more than fifteen days' journey and scarcely 120 geographical miles. This pass, difficult indeed, but not insurmountable to an army, is peculiarly adapted to the furtherance of political influence; and however much England may regard the snow-capped summits of the Hindukush as the mighty bulwark of her frontier, she forgets the ease with which a Russian propaganda from the shores of the Oxus might make a way from here to the northern Sindh; in fact, from the moment that the Russian flag floats over Karshi, Kerki, and Tchardjui, England may regard this power as her nearest neighbour.

3. RUSSIA'S DESIGNS UPON INDIA, AND THE ENGLISH OPTIMISTS.

Does Russia, then, really entertain serious designs upon British India? will she attack the English lion in its rich possessions? does her ambition really go so far that she desires to wave her mighty sceptre over the whole continent of Asia, from the icy shores of the Arctic Ocean down to Cape Comorin? This is a question which must be of interest not only to an Englishman, but to every European. The statesmen on the banks of the Thames, as well as those in Calcutta, have of late answered this question negatively; for their official and non-official journals perceive in the extreme danger of approximation nothing but a vicinity of frontier and no aggression —a vicinity which, far from endangering the interests of England, will be even advantageous to them. Unhappily these gentlemen are much mistaken; for the spirit of the traditional policy of Russia, the tenacious adherence to preconceived plans, the boundless ambition of the house of Romanoff, the great resources which stand at their disposal for the success of their designs,—all these proclaim a certain prospect of the prosecution of an object once conceived. Russia's designs on India are of three kinds: in the first place, in the far future to insert these rich pearls in the splendid diadem of her Asiatic possessions—these pearls, for the acquisition of which she so long and with so much expenditure has been making her way across the most inhospitable steppes of the world; in the next place, as the possessor of India has attained in the eyes of the Mohammedans the *non plus ultra* of power and greatness, her design is to increase to the utmost, by this very acquisition, her influence over the whole world of Islam, whose greatest and bitterest foe she now is; and lastly, by subduing the British lion on the other side of the Hindukush, to be able with greater ease to realise her intentions on the Bosphorus, in the Mediterranean, and indeed throughout Europe; for no one at the present day will any longer doubt that the Oriental question can be solved with greater ease on the other side of the Hindukush than on the Bosphorus: and had Russia had her present position on the Yaxartes at the time of the Crimean war, when Nana Sahib's brother was worshipped at Sevastopol, the designs of the Emperor Nicholas upon Constantinople would not so easily have been buried under the ruins of the Malakoff.

These vast plans are perhaps not the work of the next ten years, and especially not that of the reign of the peaceful and good-natured Alexander; yet who can assure us that the latter may not be succeeded on the throne by a Nicholas, or by a still severer type of autocrat, who will oppose the desire of a Timur or a Nadir to appear as the conqueror of the entire Asiatic world? Every one knows well enough, and the English statesmen among the rest, what a Russian autocrat can do in the present constitution of Russia, and in the present social condition of her subjects, which is likely, moreover, to be a permanent one. It is therefore all the more striking that these very statesmen allow themselves so readily to disregard the contingencies just mentioned, and will dispute with such superficial arguments the question of the possibility of a Russian invasion of India. They gener-

ally bring forward the inaccessible glaciers of the Hindukush and the Himalaya range, and the multitudes
of hostile tribes who would impede a power advancing
from the north in its way to the south.   They console
themselves with the great distance, which would bring
an invading army weary and exhausted to the frontiers
of India, while the English troops, stronger in military
tactics and ardour, calmly expecting the foe and ready
for battle, would be eagerly awaiting the encounter.
Do these gentlemen, however, believe that Russia, if she
really entertained such designs, would despatch the
invading army direct from Petersburg, Moscow, or Arch-
angel?   Of what use are the southern Siberian forts? of
what use are Tashkend, and Khodjend, and subsequently, we may be sure, also Bokhara and Samarkand?
and what is the good of the Persian-Afghan alliance?
What have the Cossacks and the Russian troops of the
line done at Gunib and in the rugged mountains of Circassia?   Did they in these instances arrive exhausted at
the station?   And these mountains are not so much
further from the capital on the Neva than Peshawur is
from the above-mentioned cities of Transoxania!   And
why should it even be assumed that Russia would select
alone the difficult road across Belkh to Kabul, and from
thence over the Kheiber Pass, in preference to any other?
Apart-from the fact that this might have been so fatal
only to the English army of 1839, when fleeing in fear
and disorder, for the march thither had cost no special
sacrifice, the route across Herat and Kandahar, the real
caravan-road to India through the Bolan Pass, is far
more convenient.   The latter, 54 or 55 English miles
long, has indeed cost the Bengal corps of the Indus

army several days' labour, still we learn from a reliable English author that the transport of 24-pound howitzers and 18-pound cannons caused no special difficulties. Or why should not the Russians take the Gomul or Guleri Pass, which the Lohani-Afghans use as the main route of communication to Burnes, and which presents no peculiar difficulties at all?

It is truly too difficult to share the sanguine views of the English optimists with regard to the strength of their imagined bulwarks. The road by Kabul, they assert, must be taken only in case of necessity; for the main points at which Russia can conveniently approach the frontiers of India are Djizzag and Astrabad—by the first in a southern, and by the second in an eastern direction. Both routes from time immemorial have already frequently led armies to the object of their desires; for both, although bounded by great deserts, pass through well-cultivated and indeed fruitful lands, which could feed without difficulty several thousands of soldiers.

In fact, even the issue of a possible war is greatly over-estimated in England. It is true their present army in India, which numbers 70,000 British troops besides the strong contingent of the Sepoy, is not to be compared with their former military forces in that country. To transport an equally strong number across Afghanistan into the Punjaub would certainly be a difficult task for Russia; still we must not forget what firm support an invading army would find in a Persian-Afghan alliance, and in the great discontent which prevails in the Punjaub, in Cashmere, in Bhotan, and especially among the fanatical Mohammedans of India. The railway network

gradually extending over India may indeed expedite
and assist in a concentration of forces, yet the main
source of military support on the Thames or in the
islands of the Mediterranean is not much nearer for
India than that of the Russians, especially when we consider that more than 300 vessels which pass up the
Volga considerably facilitate all transport to the southern shores of the Caspian Sea. A great army could be
brought in a short time to Herat and Kandahar by this
route, through the well-peopled part of Northern Persia
—on the one side through Astrabad, Budjnurd, and
Kabushan, and on the other by the railway to Meshed,
which as yet is only in prospect. The Czar is construct-
ing this railway nominally to facilitate the pilgrimage to
the tomb of Imam Riza, yet other non-religious plans
appear in the Russian promise of the subsidies. Or
does England consider the political arrangements which
the above-mentioned power has made in its own favour
in the field of European diplomacy, in connection with
the scarcely doubtful possibility of a Russian design
upon India? The Russian-French alliance of Napoleon
I. and Alexander I., which left behind such sensible
traces in Teheran, would be far more easy to enter
into now than then, owing to the preponderating influence of France in Egypt and Syria on the formation
of the Suez Canal. And apart from this, may not the
ever-increasing *entente cordiale* between Washington
and Petersburg be of importance in the designs of
Russia? We laugh at the idea of the Republican cap
of the Yankee being entwined with the Russian knout;
yet are not the banquets on the Neva, at which
American brotherhood is stoutly pledged—the journey

of the Czar's son to New York—the powerful appearance
of America in China and Japan, where she threatens to
transform the quiet ocean into an American lake,—are
not these causes enough to discover symptoms of the
greatest danger to England in a Russian-American
alliance? In fact, in the decisive moment of action,
Russia will be able to make use of so many ways and
means, which in the eyes of English statesmen have
scarcely been considered worthy of attention, but which
have been carefully and noiselessly prepared.

Nevertheless, we will allow that the effective collision
will take place in a very distant future, and we are ready
to submit to the designation of a false prophet; how,
however, will English statesmen explain as harmless the
now undoubted approach of their northern rival? how
will they conceal and palliate the threatening danger of
her intentions?

The political party in England which is friendly to
Russia is wont to answer, so often as this question is
brought on the *tapis*, that the vicinity of a well-ordered
state is more agreeable to them than that of wild
nomad races living in anarchy and rapine. An Englishman once even asked me, whether I should not prefer
sitting by the side of an elegantly-dressed and refined
man than of a rough and dirty peasant. We wish success
with all our heart to the Muscovite vicinity, yet it is
never clear to my mind why those gentlemen should
wish a crafty and powerful adversary as a neighbour,
instead of a barbarous, but, in truth, powerless foe? The
events that once took place in America, in the south of
Africa, and even on Indian soil, between the growing
power of England on the one side and the declining

power of Holland and Portugal on the other, have often
been repeated on the pages of history, and will be
repeated still oftener. Just as in ordinary life two strong
egotistic individuals seldom prosper on one and the same
path of life, so is it utterly impossible with two states ;
and this fact is well proved by the long war between
France and England for superiority in India. Even if
guided by the best intentions, will Russia, supported at
the back by the gigantic power of the entire Asiatic
continent, and having pursued with such persistency and
expenditure her policy of a hundred years' standing, will
she be able to resist following out her own plans, and
listening to the insinuations of her abettors ? Will she
have forbearance enough not to wish to use the favourable opportunity which places in her hand more than
thirty millions of the Mohammedan population of India ?
The last-named—the most fanatical of all the followers
of Islam—are filled with inexpressible hatred against
British rule. Their religious zeal, fostered on the one
side by Bokhara, and on the other by the Wehabites,
goes so far that in order to quaff the cup of martyrdom
they often murder an innocent British officer walking in
the bazaar, and then give themselves up to the axe of
the executioner. In India, where religious fanaticism
has at all times found the most fertile soil, Islamism dis-
plays itself in the most grotesque forms. The fraternities
introduced in the time of the Timurides are here more
vigorous and of greater importance than elsewhere ; and
not only Swat, but every place can produce its Achond,
whose summons to the Djihad is readily obeyed by
thousands. In spite of the various benefits which the
English Government has bestowed on the Mohamme-

dans, it is nevertheless they alone who form the focus of revolutions—they alone who in the late disturbances most supported the rebels—they alone who chiefly delight in the combinations of a Russian occupation, and who everywhere proclaim the advantages of Muscovite supremacy.

And who can help also calling to mind the Armenians, who, scattered over Persia and India, form separate rings of the chain by which the Court of Petersburg conducts the electric current of its influence from the Neva to the Ganges, and indeed to the shores of Java and Sumatra? The rich aspiring Armenians, who in their religious feelings are more Catholic than the Pope, and are more Russian and orthodox than the Russian Czar himself, will certainly not commend the Protestant Church and Protestant power to the natives of India, to the injury of the most Christian Russia. How many zealous subjects of the British rule in Calcutta, Bombay, and Madras are registered at Petersburg as still more zealous promoters of Russian interests? Every member of this Church in Asia may be considered a secret agent of the Muscovite policy; and were the decisive moment to appear, the English would be astonished to see into what this religious, moral, peaceful, and industrious people have developed.

How, therefore, can England regard the fact with indifference, to say nothing of desiring it, that in a country where such easily inflammable elements exist, a great and certainly not friendly power should be her neighbour? Trade will increase, I hear said on all sides; yet it seems to me that the prospects of the commercial advantages which the British statesmen see in the approach of Russia, and in the removal of

c

the anarchical condition in Central Asia, is rather a
feigned consolation than a true conviction. It is
indeed striking enough that people of such practical
minds as the English, can even for a moment indulge
in the hope that any good can result for England
from the designs which Russia has for years pursued
with labour, cost, and sacrifice, and that English wares
will carry the day in the markets of Central Asia
as soon as they are under Russian rule. Mr Davies,
with his commercial reports, may point to the considerable sum which the export trade with Central Asia,
through Peshawur, Karatchi, and Ladak, can show within
the last few years; he must, however, confess that it
would be ten times larger if it were supported by
English influence on the other side of the North Indian
frontier. And so also it will decrease again in the same
proportion as the Russian eagle spreads its wings
over these countries. The Petersburg Cabinet gave its
apparent consent to the plan of Lord William Hay to
make a commercial highway through Ladak, Yarkend,
Issikköl, and Semipalatinsk; but in reality no one would
support the plan, and it will not occur to any Russian
statesman to do so. The Chinese are far superior in
mercantile spirit, not only to the Russians, but even to
the English, and nevertheless they trade along the
great commercial highway from Pekin through southern
Siberia only as far as Maimatchin, and from Kiachta
most of the Chinese exports pass through Russian
hands to Petersburg and Europe. And how was it with
the Italian silk-traders, who repaired to Bokhara under
Russian protection, and were arrested there and deprived of their property? One of them (Gavazzi)

allows it to be strongly felt in his report that he could never give full credence to the Russian letters of recommendation, in spite of all the subsequent intercession from Petersburg. The productions of the English manufacturing towns are wont everywhere to drive Russian fabrics out of the market. The merchants of Khiva and Bokhara bring even now Russian articles with them from Nishni-Novgorod and Orenburg, which they sell in Central Asia under the name of Ingilis mali (English goods), as the preference is always given to these. It is forgotten in England that candour will long be wanting to Russian policy, and that on the commercial highways opened by Russian arms, equal hindrances, though not of the same nature, will be placed in the way of foreign interests as those now encountered on the highways to the Oxus through Afghan rapacity and Özbeg anarchy. In the years 1864–65 America sold in India alone more than fifteen million ponnds sterling of linen and cotton goods, which of course was possible alone under the free institutions of England. Do the gentlemen in Calcutta expect perhaps similar conduct on the part of the Russians?

Unfortunately the measures are but temporary which are taken in England with respect to the future policy of Russia as regards India. Just as the fabric of security which the present statesmen in Downing Street weave in their imagination may be thoroughly shattered, so the arguments also of a future *entente cordiale* are very shallow. Instead of useless refutation, we would rather point to errors committed, and we would rather mention the means by which the danger might be avoided, even now, of a direct collision, and of beginning a game so fatal to the interests of England.

4. THE ADVANTAGES OF THE RUSSIAN POLICY, AND THE DISADVANTAGES OF THE ENGLISH.

In order to understand accurately the errors of the English politicians with regard to their Russian rivals, it is necessary that we should state the advantages which the latter have always possessed in the field of action, and which they possess still. In Europe we are wont to look with astonishment at the gigantic empire of Russia in Asia, yet the means essentially used in its acquisition occur to no one. The Russians are Asiatics, not so much in consequence of their descent, as of their geographical position and their social relations; and it is only because they combine the *laisser-aller* of the Asiatics with the perseverance and resolution of Europeans, that they are for the most part a match for the Asiatic tribes. In their contact with Chinese, Tartars, Persians, Circassians, and Turks, they have always shown themselves Chinese, Tartars, Persians, and so forth, according to the circumstances of the case. An English historian says, if not without rancour, at any rate with some justice, that the advance of the Russians was always like that of a tiger, " first crawling cautiously and creeping along cowardly in the dust, until the favourable moment permits the fatal spring. With the peaceful smile of friendship, and with the smooth and sweet words of their emissaries, they have often lulled all fear and all precaution, until the security of their plans have made all fear useless and all precaution vain. Infatuated and perfidious must that Government be which can slumber as the Russians approach its frontier,

however slow this approach may be, and however great
may be the distance between the conqueror and the
aim of his endeavours." As Asiatics, they are not wont
to stand in such harsh contrast to their neighbours in
manners, customs, and mode of thought as the English
do, to whom, with their higher degree of culture, such
a renunciation would be a sacrifice, and would be
incompatible with their efforts at civilisation. They
offend but rarely against the notions of the different
tribes, and they adapt themselves to them with the
utmost ease when their interests demand it. In England
the Government has until now considered it beneath its
dignity to place itself in direct communication with the
Emir of Bokhara, for all that has hitherto passed between the capital on the Zerefshan and the British
Cabinet has been through the medium of the Governor
of India. In Russia the feeling has been different, and
even the proud Nicholas, that strict autocrat, who long
refused to give the French Emperor the title of " *mon
frère*," demeaned himself in his dealings with the Tartar
princes in Central Asia, not as an Emperor of all the
Russias, but as a Khan on the Neva. The consequence
of this conduct is, that we find at the present day, all
along the frontier line of Russia in Asia, nomads or
settled tribes, Buddhist or Mohammedan races, in such
a degree of intimacy, if not even friendship, with the
Russians, as is the case nowhere else in the foreign
possessions of a European power.

These advantages of Asiatic feeling—the appropriation
of which we may indeed designate as special cunning
and craftiness—are, however, in political intercourse also
of far greater use than the language of openness and

justice, which the English have on principle always employed. None but the enemies of Great Britain in Europe, none but the enviers of her power, can reproach the English for their conduct in India ; yet any one who is accurately acquainted with their political collisions with the native princes and with the frontier tribes, or any one who is thoroughly familiar with the character of the Asiatics, will see that in the utter want of these faults lies the error of the English statesmen.

From the great territory on the Amur to the smallest possessions which Russia has recently acquired on Asiatic soil, we find ever the same proceedings of intrigues and artifices, the scattering of the seeds of discord, and all the bribery and allurement by the lowest means which precede an invasion. They first come into contact with the foreign elements in their commercial relations ; the smallest disputes are easily converted into *casus belli.* Where these fail, the soil is undermined by emissaries, the chiefs are allured by presents, are intoxicated by a rich distribution of wodki (Russian brandy), and are drawn into the fatal magic circle. A well-founded cause for war and invasion would nowhere be readily discovered, and the gigantic empire of the house of Romanoff has been certainly raised more by the artifice of its Asiatic politicians than by the power of its arms. Moreover, Russia, in consequence of the last-mentioned quality, is far better acquainted with the relations of Asiatic tribes, and far better informed of everything that is passing in the frontier states than the English are, or any other Europeans. It is owing to the great watchfulness of her emissaries, and to the unwearied zeal of her diplomatists, that her cabinet is informed of the most secret events in the adjacent countries, often more speedily and more thoroughly than the Government of the country itself. Apart from the fact that in Petersburg a society of the most able men can turn to account their experiences respecting the different parts of Asia, here and there a Khirghise, a Buriate, a Circassian, or a Mongol, after having been trained in Russian principles, is converted into the most useful instrument with regard to his subjected native land.

In England we meet everywhere with the greatest contrast to all this. Any one who knows the great ignorance of public opinion in England respecting events in India, respecting the relations of the neighbouring states to these vast possessions—any one who, during the course of a year, has registered the absurd and ridiculous reports and telegraphic dispatches of the English press, which are sent through Bombay and Calcutta to Europe and England—any one who knows the limited number of the English statesmen who, accurately informed on Asiatic matters, can pronounce a sound judgment on the questions of Eastern policy—must truly be astonished how Great Britain established her foreign possessions, to say nothing of how she has retained them up to the present day.

Just as, among the English public, even those who have sojourned for some time in Asia, have, in consequence of their national character, kept aloof from the natives, and are but rarely acquainted with their language and habits, so the English Government has not been able to assign to Englishmen, but only to naturalised Levantines, such important posts of legation as, for example, that of dragoman at Constantinople, that essential organ of mutual intercourse. . While Russia, France, and Austria have long had oriental academies for embryo diplomatists, England, with her rich endowment of colleges, schools, and universities, has never yet thought of an institution of the kind. Thus even in the Legislature as well as in the Ministry, where often the smallest questions have each their own department, only a very few men are competent as regards the important affairs of Asia ; and even these men are rarely allowed, in consequence of the nepotism that prevails, to bring their experiences forward.

This indifference must surprise every stranger ; yet still more astonishment is excited when we hear men of the Liberal party exclaim, " What does Asia concern us ? that mass of barbarous tribes, who bring us more trouble than good, and that rich India, the revenues of which do not cover the expenses, to say.nothing of the cost of the conquest !" I have often heard remarks of this kind made by the most famous heads of this party ; the sincerity of their confession is indubitable ; nevertheless I have never received an answer when I have inquired what would compensate for the loss of the political influence arising from the great colonial empire. They seem wholly to forget that a great number of young Englishmen of all classes find a political and military career in India ; they seem to ignore the fact that many of' the sons of the clergy and officers, to whom the narrow scope of their insular home affords no sphere of activity, grow rich on the Ganges and Indus in lucrative appointments, and consume at home in their peaceful old age the earnings of their youthful years ; they seem to leave wholly out of account the enormous number of

merchants who live on their large Asiatic estates, and
carry on the most extensive commercial interests, in
whose hands English capital is increased by millions.
Short-sighted indeed are these Liberals, to whom the
possession of such a colony as India appears indifferent
and even unnecessary. That they prefer to see the greatness of their country based on the flourishing condition
of her inland manufactories, and not on the dominion
over foreign races, cannot in the present day, when
more than £60,000,000 sterling are expended on Indian
railways, be any longer regarded as the general feeling
prevailing in England; for that the industry of the
manufactories, as well as the enterprising spirit of the
English merchants abroad, flag when not supported by
English sovereignty, is a fact plainly to be perceived
from the British commercial relations in Algiers, Central Asia, and other non-British possessions.

It is these erroneous views which place all the excellences of the English character at a disadvantage when
compared with that Russian policy which ever works on
with perseverance and consistency. To this it is to be
ascribed that Russia has in an incredibly short time
grown into a powerful rival, and has approached so close
to the Achilles heel of Great Britain. With her position
on the Aral and Caspian Seas, with her entire conquest
of the Caucasus, with her enormous advantages in Central Asia, it would be useless at the present time to try
to repel the monster power. It is far too late now to
attempt all that could have been done twenty years ago
with no especial difficulty; and if England wishes to
avoid the common lot of commercial states, the fate of
Carthage, Venice, Genoa, Holland, and Portugal, there

is but one way left—namely, a policy of strict watchfulness, and a speedy adoption of the measures still standing at her disposal.

5. ADVICE TO ENGLAND FOR THE AVERTING OF THE DANGER.

To advance in open hostility to the increasing Russian power would, at the present day, be as great an error on the part of the English as the striking inaction which England has for the last twenty-five years shown in all events taking place on the other side of the Hindukush. Russia will establish herself on the right bank of the Oxus, she will incorporate into her territory the three Khanates, and perhaps also Chinese Tartary, and everything which is Özbeg will be obliged to acknowledge her supremacy. This is no longer to be prevented; yet only so far and no further must the English allow their rivals to proceed.

All that lies between the Oxus and the Indus must remain a neutral possession. Afghanistan, from its physical condition, from the warlike character of its inhabitants, and more especially from their diplomatic inclination, would be thoroughly suitable for the purpose of forming a military and political barrier, thus rendering the collision of the two colossal powers impossible. This land would cost the conqueror, whether he came from the north or the south, a tenfold harder contest than the Caucasus. The possession of it, moreover, would not for a long time compensate for the expensive war, and although the constant disturbances which prevail in the mountainous home of the Afghans can be of little advantage to the two neighbours, the danger is nevertheless not so great as to justify designs of conquest on one side or the other.

How, then, shall England preserve the neutrality of Afghanistan, if Russia continues her aggressive policy? What must she do, without coming forward as a conqueror, in order, by her influence, to present a firm check to her rival?

This is the work of a skilful diplomatic transaction, the work of an uninterrupted communication by means of agents, who, well acquainted with the Afghan character, and avoiding the English mode of thought, can assume an Asiatic demeanour if necessity requires it.

The error which Lord Auckland committed in 1839 in actually interfering in Afghan affairs, may on a far greater scale be laid to the charge of his successors in their utter abstinence and indifference with regard to the affairs of the neighbouring state. The English are like a child, who, when it has once burnt itself at the fire, will not for a long time venture to go near the warmth. The catastrophe of the Afghan campaign, and the thirty millions sterling which it cost, are even at the present day, after the lapse of the quarter of a century, still so terribly alive in the memory of every Briton, that he trembles even at the idea of political influence beyond the Hindukush. Are not these two opposite extremes? First of all, armed to the teeth in order to support the cause of such an unpopular prince as Shah Shedja, and then, after the annexation of the Punjaub, to think scarcely more of Kabul! And why should the boundary line beyond Peshawur be such a dangerous barrier to all Englishmen and Europeans? If yearly some thousands of the Kakeri, Luhani, Gilzi, and Zusufzi tribes of Afghanistan cross the northern frontier of Hindostan, either for mercantile purposes or to graze their flocks, why should not the British traveller also be allowed to venture over the Hindukush, and even wander a few hours' distance beyond Peshawur? Afghan merchants carry on a flourishing trade with Moultan, Delhi, and Lahore; why should not one or another English house of business repair to Kabul for the same purpose?

In truth, this state of things has always surprised me, and still more so when I heard that the officer whom Sir John Lawrence sent to Kabul to congratulate Shir-Ali-Khan, could only show himself accompanied by a strong division of troops, in order not to expose himself to the fury of a fanatical populace. This is truly an erroneous as well as ridiculous attempt to instruct Asiatics in European magnanimity and in European love of justice. England, who has long dealt with Asiatics in this manner, is like a man endeavouring with all his might to make a blind man perceive the beauty of one of Raphael's cartoons. In this respect Russia is far more practical. She knows that such proofs of magnanimity and humanity are only ridiculed by the Orientals; that far from taking example from them, they only misuse them for their own aims; and instead of lavishing moral sermons upon them, England would do more wisely to make use of the same weapons, and to treat Orientals in Oriental fashion.   •

At the time that the martyrs Conolly and Stoddart were languishing in cruel captivity, from which they

were subsequently to be freed only by the headman's
axe, there were Bokhariots, Khokandians, and other
Asiatics to be found on the British territory, by whose
arrest the lot of the English officers in Bokhara might
have been alleviated and their lives saved. Russia is
wont in such cases to extricate herself at once from the
dilemma by the right of retaliation. England does not
do this. She prefers to do the magnanimous—yet what
is gained by it? When I was in Bokhara, I heard how
this very act of British generosity had missed its object.
The Bokhariots asserted that England did not venture
to arouse the anger of the Emir of Bokhara, and that
weakness impelled her to moderation.

Do the gentlemen in Calcutta imagine that the
Afghans think otherwise? No, no; they, too, say—
" Protected by the power and greatness of Islam, our
indigo and spice traders and our camel-owners may
repair unhurt to British soil, while not a single soul of
the unbelievers dares show himself among us !"

In truth, this unpardonable weakness was again shown
in 1857 by the Viceroy of India (Sir John, now Lord
Lawrence), when he was sent to Peshawur by Lord Can-
ning, in order, in conjunction with Edwards, to conclude
an alliance offensive and defensive with Dost-Mohammed-Khan, who had just appeared there. The Afghans
were at that time hardly pressed. They needed money
and arms: the hoary Barekzi chief, accompanied by his
sons, made this apparent at every word, and nevertheless his desires were fulfilled in every point without his
complying in the least with the main demands of England. Four thousand pieces of arms (bayonets, sabres,
and cartridge-boxes) and twelve lacs of rupees yearly

were promised to them so long as Great Britain was at war with Persia. .Even after the conclusion of peace in Paris they received a considerable portion of this important sum ; and, nevertheless, the main object of the negotiations in Kabul and Kandahar—namely, to be allowed to have a permanent English representative —was not obtained. Dost-Mohammed-Khan declared, as Kaye tells us in his " History of the last Sepoy Revolution," that he could not take upon himself the responsibility of such a step; that he could not protect English agents against Afghan fanaticism, and that every step would be one of peril, &c. It is inconceivable to me how Sir John Lawrence, who is one of the few men acquainted with the character of the Orientals, could accept the protestations of the Afghan wolf, and how he could believe his false apprehensions. If Dost-Mohammed-Khan himself said that an English mission might remain unattacked in Kandahar, why should this have not been the case also in Kabul ? The British commissioners greatly erred when they doubted for a moment the power of the Afghan chief. It would have required only a little more persistency in order to have procured the English, who had at the time come forward as helpers in the hour of need, not only two, but several diplomatic posts. The Afghans would have soon grown accustomed to their presence, and the diplomatic connections, once formed, could have been permanently maintained.

Sir John Lawrence is now endeavouring in a semi-official article, which appeared in the *Edinburgh Review* (Jan. 1867), to prove how difficult and useless it is to enter into diplomatic relations with such wild and ungovernable neighbours as those with which India is on all sides surrounded. Still I do not understand why the Viceroy does not take example from Russia, who, surrounded by similar elements, nevertheless sends ambassador after ambassador, contrives to procure respect and security for them, and thus advances perpetually forwards towards the desired object. Why does not England pursue the same policy which she once began in China, Japan, and other Asiatic countries? It seems to me that the English are less convinced of the difficult execution of this project than of the amount of good arising from it; or are these gentlemen really ignorant of what a permanent representation in Afghanistan might effect, both for the interests of England and for the benefit of the Afghans themselves.

The diplomatic conduct of Sir Henry Rawlinson in Kandahar, who could successfully maintain himself there for so long a period in the most dangerous position and at the most critical time, is a brilliant proof that even the rudest Asiatics are to be managed. And if this officer could effect so much with the threatening position of a conqueror, what might not be achieved by political acuteness and friendly persuasion?

The manifest results of an uninterrupted diplomatic intercourse would be, if we mistake not—

1. Greater advantage to trade; for as English goods have for a long time enjoyed a high reputation in Central Asia, English productions, if imported direct from England, might certainly drive similar and less-valued Russian products out of the market. This, of course, is not at present the case, for at the present time, in the bazaars of Kabul, Kandahar, Herat, and other places,

far more is sold of many Russian articles — as, for example, iron utensils and tools, coarse cotton and cloths —than of the English, only because the former, at the lower prices at which they are exposed for sale, do not amount to so much as the originally dearer English goods, the cost of which is doubled by the transit. Moreover in Bokhara, occasionally in Khiva, and in Karshi, Russian merchants themselves may be found who, guaranteed by the energy of their Government, are better able to promote their own interests than foreign commercial employés. We should in vain seek for a better apostle or a better pioneer of civilisation than commerce, and we should in vain search for a better converter to our own mode of thought than the mute bales of goods which are imported from Europe. Apart, moreover, from all commercial interests, England should also, for the sake of humanity, facilitate trade in Central Asia.

2. The Afghans, who up to the present day know, under the name of Ingilis or Frengi, only an armed power and a conquest-loving neighbour, will, in the peaceful garb of diplomatic intercourse and well-intended advice, be easily undeceived. In the year 1808, when the Afghans but little feared an English invasion, the ambassador Mountstuart Elphinstone, with a numerous suite, the escort of which amounted to only four hundred Anglo-Indian soldiers, was well received everywhere in Afghanistan, for alarm and mistrust had at that time not taken root. Up to the beginning of the present century, a similar state of things was to be met with in all parts of the Osman empire. Europeans and foes were regarded as identical, and now, after our ambassadors and con-

sulates have, in spite of the resistance of the Porte, insinuated themselves into various places, Osmans and Arabs no longer entertain the same ideas. They have clearer notions with regard to the collective name Frengi, and they know accurately that, for example, Russia is as hostile to the Porte as England is friendly, and that the designs of the one Government are different to those of the other. Without consulates this could never be effected. And thus the Afghans also, so long as they are not brought into closer and peaceful intercourse with Englishmen, will never understand what England or Russia may be able to do for their weal or woe, and which friendship may be more conducive to their good.

3. The Afghans, being the most warlike people of all the races of Central Asia, could, by the vigorous support of English advice, be easily developed into an important military power. All that the *instructeurs militaires* effected in the army of Sultan Mahmud and Mehemmed Ali Pacha, all that the English officers achieved in the troops of Abbas-Mirza, would be nothing in comparison to the success of a similar undertaking among the Afghans, out of whom, so far as we can judge from the military bearing and drill of a few Kabul regiments trained by Sepoy deserters, a regular body of troops might most easily be formed. A similar success might also be obtained with regard to the fortresses of Herat and Kandahar, the fortifications of which, if a second Pottinger were to inspect them, would assuredly present a far less easy prey to the Russian besiegers than if they were left only to Afghan strategy.

4. The principal advantage, however, which we perceive in a permanent representation is, that England,

D

accurately informed of the events in Central Asia, and
of the military and political movements of Russia, will
no longer be exposed to the danger of seeing herself
suddenly surprised out of one hold or another, and of
being unable to take precautionary measures, owing to
her constant uncertainty respecting the true condition of
things. At the present day, the Viceroy maintains, it is
true, some Munchis, without any official character, in
Kabul, Kandahar, and Herat; Munchis, *i.e.*, clerks, and
these Mohammedan, who, sometimes well paid, are
bound to furnish occasional reports. Besides these, on
special occasions, spies or secret emissaries are despatched
in one direction or another, passing through Turkestan
in the incognito of a merchant or pilgrim, in order to
give an account of the political events. Apart from the
fact that I consider both these classes of employés incapable of such an office, for the very reason that, admitted
nowhere, they only register in their note-books bazaar
rumours and caravan politics, I should be inclined, as
one who for years has had intercourse with Orientals, to
give the slightest possible credit to these very people.
Have the authorities in Calcutta ever considered what
Mohammedan fanaticism is? Do they know that by no
amount of gold has it ever been achieved that one Mussulman can be used against another Mussulman to the
advantage of the Frengi? Apparently these emissaries
and spies will exhibit the greatest allegiance, the utmost loyalty, and the most extreme readiness; but in
the interior of Central Asia they will side with those
religious comrades who visit the same mosque and who
prostrate themselves on the same carpet, and will fulfil
the directions of their order. The Anglo-British states-

men will certainly not agree with me in this, yet this is the very reason why they are so badly informed of the events in Central Asia, why the most absurd reports with regard to India are spread over Europe, and why they can see the affairs of the khanates only in the light which Russian diplomacy has kindled.

Far removed from wishing to assume the post of a political counsellor, I consider that these unassuming words of advice alone indicate the means by which Afghanistan can be safely neutralised, and placed as a powerful barrier against the further advance of Russia in Central Asia. In such an important question as to how the possession of East India can tend to the greatness and permanence of English power, it would be dangerous to seek a false protection in palliative measures. Political errors, however unimportant, form in time separate rings of an unbroken chain of misfortunes—a chain which subsequently the utmost efforts and the most acute political judgment endeavour in vain to break.

6. THE GENERAL INTEREST OF THE QUESTION.

We have still to answer the one question, Why we cannot look on with indifference at the danger threatening English interest through Russian ascendancy, and what is the real cause that the decline of the power of England appears to us just as disadvantageous as the too great influence of Russia seems to us a check to the progress of the spirit of the age?

The answer to this question is a very simple one.

Russia was Asiatic, she is Asiatic, and she will long continue Asiatic. We cannot, moreover, for a moment resign ourselves to the consoling prospect that the body of the Russian power, stretching too widely, must, according to the laws of nature, subsequently break asunder into two or several parts, and that a dismemberment of this kind will lessen the threatening danger; we need only look at the character of Russian policy, at her social relations, at the position of the people compared to the higher caste of the Government circle, at the general degree of culture, and at the mental condition of the people, and we shall see how thoroughly everything about them is Asiatic, and indeed barbarously Asiatic, and how, in spite of the long effort after European civilisation, they have, comparatively speaking, appropriated to themselves so little of what we call a European or Western character. Without wishing to apply the hackneyed old saying, "Scrape the Russian and you will discover a Tartar," it is, nevertheless, impossible for us not to perceive—partly from personal experience, and partly from the reports of recent and indeed Russia-loving travellers—that there is still much to be found on the Neva, in holy Moscow, and in other great cities of Russia, of that appearance of civilisation which is employed with advantage by many Asiatic governments for the delusion of short-sighted Europe. Undoubtedly this civilisation fraud in Petersburg is carried on with more success by a Government strongly intermingled with Christian and European elements than it is in Cairo, Constantinople, and Teheran. The Russian nobleman, to all appearance a cultivated European, thoroughly versed in our languages, manners, and modes of thought, will of course cut a far better figure than the half-Europeanised Efendi on the Bosphorus or the Mirza in Persia. The Government which attracts to itself with great expense so much scientific and artistic talent—which has recently eagerly promoted the foundation of schools, universities, and scientific societies—which has its emissaries in Europe to trumpet out the progress of Russian culture, will of course be able to obtain better credit than the Porte or the Persian ministry, who are occupied in maintaining their own languishing existence, and cannot expend so much on the pageantry necessary. It is no wonder, therefore, if Russia seems to the superficial observer more European and more pervaded with the spirit of our civilisation, and thus can easily obtain the sympathies of those who desire to love her with all their might. Nevertheless, let us for once attempt impartially to remove the outer covering, and let us look into the interior of high Russian society, and what shall we see?

It is disappointment, utter disappointment, which meets us at every step when we endeavour to discover among the majority of the Russian people those signs of progress which are said to exist, according to the statements of the Russian contributors to the European press. The Englishman who in 1865 attempted to inform the English public in a similar spirit, in a pamphlet entitled " Russia, Central Asia, and British India," and pointing to the extent of innovations as, for example, the emancipation of the serfs and the introduction of various reforms, held out the prospect of a transformation such as even Russian authors like J. A. Herzen and Dolgorukoff are still inclined to doubt;

this Englishman would probably have himself thought otherwise had he drawn the parallel, not between members of the civilised world, but between the Russian people and the Asiatics.

Everywhere along that gigantic frontier line at which Russia touches Asia, we find that the Russians are at a very low degree of civilisation, and in refinement of habits are far behind those Asiatic races to whom we wish to evidence the advantages of our modern European civilisation compared with their old Asiatic condition.   Alexander Michie, a traveller from Pekin to Petersburg, and so disposed towards Russia that he calls Siberia a second paradise, and speaks of the exiled Poles as enviably happy, cannot, nevertheless, forbear, wherever he finds Chinese holding intercourse with Russians, from proclaiming loudly the superiority of the former.   But this is not the case only in Maimadschin and Kiachta; it is so also among the Mussulmans.   The Russian, as a Northern, will exhibit far more activity than the Asiatic *de pur sang;* still his strikingly dirty exterior, his love of drink, his religion bordering on fetichism, his servility, his coarse ignorance, and his rude unpolished manners, are characteristics which reveal his affinity to the smooth, courteous, and keen-sighted Oriental.   Just as in Bokhara, I heard a cultivated Islam Tadjik speaking with contempt of the ignorance of the Russians, whom he ranked but little above the Kirghiz hordes, the same would probably be done in Transcaucasus by every Chinese and Persian, and in Kasan by every better-cultivated Tartar.   And what, moreover, are these races to learn from them ?

Are the forms of government, perhaps, to awaken

envy among the Asiatic tribes? The bribery of the civil functionaries, their tyrannical and arbitrary conduct under Nicholas, the condition of more than 50,000,000 peasants, who occupy the lowest position, in contrast to the caste of the nobles and officials, cannot truly be particularly attractive to those with whom autocratic institutions, though of the most barbarous character, are combined with patriarchal mildness.

In truth it is difficult, not only as regards the present, but even far into the future, to perceive in Russia's love of conquest any prospect of an advantageous transformation in the social life of the Asiatic tribes ; that is, of a transformation in the European spirit. If we ask ourselves what is become of the Tartars who have been more than two hundred years under Russian guardianship? what of the great number of Siberian tribes, such as the Bashkirs, the Woguls, the Tseremissians, and the Wotjaks, who have been incorporated into the Russian nation, or are on the point of incorporation? must we not regard "Russification" as the greatest result attained?

Russification is of course a step from Asia to Europe. As the government of an Alexander II. has hitherto acted, it may even be called a transition point ; yet who can blame us if we prefer the English system of civilisation to this tedious process, the results of which ever appear doubtful, while, up to the present time, this other system has such brilliant and surprising results to exhibit in India and in every place where it has come in contact with Asiatics.

No one will doubt that the tribes of India, of that land which is the cradle and the birthplace of the

Asiatic civilisation which we pronounce to be incapable
of existence, adhere with great obstinacy to their old
usages and their old modes of thought ; and yet, how
has India been transformed even since the beginning of
the last century ?   I think even the greatest enemies of
Great Britain will not be able to ignore the fact, that
the caste system of the Hindoos and their numerous
inhuman customs have suffered a strong check through
English influence ; no one will be able to deny how
astonishingly these wild Asiatics, in spite of all their
obstinacy, have advanced on the paths of our civilisation.
We find even now in India a vast number of people who
are thoroughly convinced of the beneficial influence of
their conquerors; numerous schools and institutions
spread the light of the European world among all ranks
of the population ; not only are many men well versed
in English, but they even take a lively interest in our
scientific discussions, coming forward as members of
European literary societies, and indeed here and there
taking up the pen with success, and occupying a place
among the authors of the West.   Rajàh Radhakant
Deva Bahadur, Maharadja Kali Krishna Bahadur, Babu
Rajendra Lala Mitra, several Pendits (clergymen) and
other learned private individuals, are to be found on the
list of the French, German, and English Asiatic societies,
and are well known by their works in their respective
circles.   Strengthened in their own national feeling, the
Hindoos have at the present day such a knowledge of
their language, history, and philosophy, as they certainly
never formerly possessed under their native princes.
Societies are formed, as in England, for the extirpation
of certain prejudices, for the abolition of various perni-

cious habits and usages, and for the promotion of social intercourse; and if we take into consideration how much the reading world increases from day to day, and what wide circles the Hindustani papers, such as the *Hirkaru Bengalu* (the *Hirkari Messenger*), the *Suheïli* *Pendschab* (the *Punjaub Morning Star*), the *Oudh Achbar* (the *Oude News*), the *Chairchah Pendschab* (the *Punjaub Well-wisher*), and others, have procured for themselves among the natives, and how much the press is rising from day to day as a powerful Europeanising agent, we shall be obliged to confess that the races conquered by England not only are more advanced in culture than those conquered by Russia, but than many Russians themselves.

How Russia, therefore, under such circumstances, can come forward as the suitable apostle of the doctrines of the European world among the people of Asia, it is difficult to conceive. Only in Central Asia, that old nest of wild fanaticism and rude avarice and tyranny, can the transplantation of Russian civilisation in the place of the native elements be called beneficial; and this not even in all parts and among all the tribes of Asia. The conquest of Turkestan by Russian arms is, as we have already repeatedly remarked, a happy event for the inhabitants. If England could have taken upon herself the same part, it would certainly have been more advantageous. Still, as this was not the case, she may not hinder her rival in the exercise of her duty, and must only be on her guard against further plans of attack.

If we only add to the incapabilities of Russia already mentioned to be the civiliser of Asia, the important circumstance that, by the annexation of half a quarter of the globe, and by the blending of several millions of Asiatics into her own body, she really assumes a threatening position, not only towards Great Britain, but even towards the whole of Europe, we shall see proportionally far more disadvantage arising to our own existence from this gigantic superiority than advantage to be gained by the Tartar tribes of Asia. Russophobia is nonsense, it is said. I wish myself to believe it to be so. Yet it is difficult, when we perceive the mighty influence of the twofold Russian eagle in all parts of Asia ; when we consider how the Court of Petersburg will, by its position on the Hindukush, solve the Oriental question on the Bosphorus to its own advantage, it is difficult, I say, to feel perfectly easy respecting the future fate of our quarter of the globe. The present diplomacy, which often does homage rather to fashion than to *bon sens*, tries to turn into ridicule the Napoleonic prophecy with regard to a Cossack supremacy in Europe. Yet they forget, in so doing, what can be done with our present means of communication by a power extending from Kamtschatka to the Danube, or perhaps to the shores of the Adriatic—from the icy zone of the Northern Ocean to the burning banks of the Irawaddi. Though to many it may appear visionary, it is in no wise impossible that some hundred thousands of the wildest horsemen in Asia may follow the summons of such a power into the very heart of Europe. At the beginning of this century the Don Cossacks on the banks of the Seine have shown the possibility of such a march *à la* Djengis or Timur, and why should it not be repeated in the present day, when there are railroads and steamers at command? Our European tactics would indeed check this rude power : no member of the house of Romanoff could long play amongst us the part of a Djengis or a Timur. Still a contest of this kind, however brief, must be followed by melancholy consequences, and now, while precautionary measures still stand at our disposal, it is urgently necessary to prevent the occurrence of such an event.

Yet setting aside this vast political combination, can any one doubt that the greatness and power of England is of more use to the general interests of Europe than Russian supremacy ? England has many enemies, or perhaps we might better say many enviers. Certain voices, swayed by passion, in the Continental press, will constantly perceive in her proceedings egotism, avarice, and pride ; fanatics will see the blindest materialism in every trait ; but men must be peculiarly blind and prejudiced to desire to ignore those acquisitions which, through English greatness, English capital, and English perseverance, have been of benefit to our civilisation and to our scientific researches. Is it not England alone whose mighty flag has opened Eastern Asia to our commerce ? Is it not English travellers whose bold spirit of inquiry has penetrated to the remotest regions in order to enrich our geographical and ethnographical knowledge ? And what is happening on the Thames, what in all the other cities of this stirring and busy island ? Have those high-flown writers, who are continually finding fault with English materialism, ever taken into consideration that these brokers, in spite of their lively interest in trade and gain, contribute after all most of all to the promotion of science and to the enlightenment of the world ? Where is there a country in which the

Government so readily gives millions for an institution such as the Kensington Museum? Where else are hundreds of thousands of pounds expended only on the catalogue of a library with such liberality as has recently been the case in London? What other Government immediately equips vessels and expeditions in search of an endangered traveller, as has just been done for Livingstone?

Yes, in spite of all her faults, and no country is free from these, we must confess that England, whether it be in consequence of this strongly-blamed materialism or of her often-censured love of power, stands nevertheless at the head of European civilisation; for if Germany and France are indispensable helpers in the dissemination of the light of our high civilisation, England alone is, notwithstanding, the principal agent. With her flag appears the dawn of a better era in every zone and in every quarter of the world. All that the curious detractors of Great Britain relate of her tyrannical proceedings is for the most part only an untruth. Not at the writing-table and in the soft easy-chair, but in the provinces of Asia, these sentimental accusers ought to inform themselves of England's doings; and when they see how the banner of our Western civilisation drives away the vices of the old Asiatic rule, how it seeks to uplift the right of humanity so long trampled in the dust, and leads millions towards a better future, in freeing them from the caprice of a single tyrant, truly they cannot remain indifferent to England's influence in the foreign quarters of the globe.

And would it not be lamentable if Muscovite superiority were to be injurious to such a state? On the

Thames, the mighty will of a free people holds sway; on the Neva, the ambition of an Asiatic dynasty, producing a government system whose capability for future reform remains doubtful, while its great perniciousness in the present is beyond a question.

In fact, it is only in Russia's approach towards India, towards that Achilles-heel of British interests, that the infallible tokens of danger to England are to be discovered. The British lion is now awaiting in the north a harder contest than that which it had to endure in the south with the French when it established its power on the Ganges. The French foe, weaker in numbers and in endurance, had only a small fleet, a sea at that time unnavigable in its rear, and could easily be conquered. The Russian, on the contrary, will be supported by an unbroken chain of fortresses, garrisons, and secure roads; its weapons are boundless ambition, the blind devotion of millions of subjects, and the sympathy of the rude adjacent states. Victory with such a foe will be no easy thing, and the consequences of defeat will be far greater.

On your guard, therefore, Britannia! For should the star of your long good fortune here begin to be eclipsed, the various zones will no longer be able to join in the verse—

> " The nations not so free as thee,
>   Must in their turn to tyrants fall,
> While thou shalt flourish great and free,
>   The dread and envy of them all !"

SUPPLEMENT.

PRINCE GORTSCHAKOFF'S DESPATCH.   (See p. 10.)

"Les journeaux Russes ont rendu compte des dernières opèrations militaires exécutées par un détachement de nos troupes, dans les régions de l'Asie centrale, avec un succès remarquable et des resultats importants.

"Il était à prévoir que ces évènements exciteraient d'autant plus l'attention du public étranger qu'ils se passent dans des contrées à peine connues.

"Notre auguste maître m'a ordonné de vous exposer succinctement, mais avec clarté et précision, la position qui nous est faite dans l'Asie centrale, les intérêts qui servent de mobile à notre action dans ces contrées, et le but final que nous y poursuivons.

"La position de la Russie dans l'Asie centrale est celle de tous les états civilisés qui se trouvent en contact avec des peuplades à demi-sauvages, errantes, sans organisation sociale fixe.

"Il arrive toujours, en pareil cas, que l'intérêt de la securité des frontières et celui des relations de commerce exigent que l'état plus civilisé exerce un certain ascendant sur des voisins que leurs mœurs nomades et turbulentes rendent fort incommodes.

"On a d'abord des incursions et des pillages à réprimer. Pour y mettre un terme, on est forcé de réduire à une soumission plus ou moins directe les peuplades limitrophes.

"Une fois ce resultat atteint, celles-ci prennent des habitudes plus tranquilles. Mais elles se trouvent à leur tour exposées aux aggressions des tribus plus éloignées. L'état est obligé de les défendre contre ces déprédations et de châtier ceux qui les commettent. De là la nécessité d'expéditions lointaines, coûteuses, périodiques, contre un ennemi que son organisation sociale rend insaisissable. Si l'on se borne à châtier les pillards et qu'on se retire, la leçon s'éfface bientôt, la retraite est mise sur le compte de la faiblesse ; les peuples asiatiques en particulier ne respectent que la force visible et palpable ; la force morale de la raison et des intérêts de la civilisation n'a point encore de prise sur eux. La tâche est donc toujours à recommencer.

"Pour couper court à ces désordres permanents, on établit quelques points fortifiés parmi les populations ennemies ; on exerce sur elles un ascendant qui, peu à peu, les réduit à une soumission plus ou moins forcée.

"Mais au-delà de cette seconde ligne, d'autres peuplades plus éloignées encore viennent bientôt provoquer les mêmes dangers et les mêmes répressions.

"L'État se trouve donc dans l'alternative ou d'abandonner ce travail incessant et delivrer ses frontières à des désordres perpétuels qui y rendent toute prosperité, toute sécurité, toute civilisation impossibles, ou bien d'avancer de plus en plus dans les profondeurs de contrées sauvages où, à chaque pas qu'il accomplit, les distances accroissent les difficultés et les charges auxquelles il s'expose.

" Tel a été le sort de tous les pays qui ont été placés dans les mêmes conditions, les États-Unis en Amérique, la France en Algérie, la Hollande dans ses colonies, l'Angleterre aux Indes ; tous ont été inévitablement entraînés à suivre cette marche progressive où l'ambition a moins de part que l'impérieuse nécessité, et où la plus grande difficulté consiste à savoir s'arrêter.

" C'est aussi la raison qui a conduit le gouvernement impérial à s'établir d'abord d'un côté sur la Syr-Daria, de l'autre sur le lac Issyk-Koul, et à consolider ces deux lignes par des forts avancés qui, peu à peu, ont pénétré au cœur de ces régions lointaines, sans cependant parvenir à établir au-delà la tranquillité indispensable à la securité de nos frontières.

" La cause de cette instabilité résida d'abord dans le fait qu'entre les points extrêmes de cette double ligne il y a un immense espace inoccupé où les invasions des tribus pillardes continuent à paralyser toute colonisation et tout commerce par caravanes ; ensuite dans les fluctuations perpétuelles de la situation politique de ces contrées où le Turkestan et le Kokand, tantôt réunis, tantôt séparés, toujours en guerre, soit entre eux, soit avec la Boukharie, n'offraient une possibilité de relations fixes ni de transactions régulières quelconques.

" Le gouvernement impérial s'est donc vu placé malgré lui dans l'alternative que nous avons indiquée, c'est-à-dire ou de laisser se perpétuer un état de désordre permanent qui paralyse toute sécurité et tout progrès, ou de se condamner à des expéditions coûteuses et lointaines sans aucun résultat pratique, et qu'il faut toujours recommencer, ou enfin d'entrer dans la voie indéfinie de conquêtes et d'annexions qui a conduit l'Angleterre à l'empire des Indes, en cherchant à soumettre l'un après l'autre, par la force des armes, les petits États indépendants dont les mœurs pillardes et turbulentes et les perpétuelles révoltes ne laissent à leurs voisins ni trève ni repos.

" Ni l'une ni l'autre de ces alternatives ne répondait au but que s'est tracé la politique de notre auguste maître, et qui est non d'étendre hors de toute proportion raisonnable les contrées soumises à son sceptre, mais d'y asseoir sa domination sur des bases solides, d'en garantir la sécurité et d'y développer l'organisation sociale, le commerce, le bien-être et la civilisation.

" Notre tâche était donc de rechercher un système propre à atteindre ce triple but.

" À cet effet, les principes suivants ont été posés :—

" 1. Il a été jugé indispensable que les deux lignes fortifiées de nos frontières, l'une partant de la Chine jusqu'au lac Issyk-Koul, l'autre partant de la mer d'Aral le long de la Syr-Daria, fussent réunies par des points fortifiés, de manière à ce que tous nos postes fussent à même de se soutenir mutuéllement et ne laissassent aucun intervalle par où pussent s'effectuer impunément les invasions et les déprédations des tribus nomades.

" 2. Il était essentiel que la ligne ainsi complétée de nos forts avancés fut située dans une contrée assez fertile non-seulement pour assurer leurs approvisionnements, mais aussi pour faciliter la colonisation régulière, qui seule peut préparer au pays occupé un avenir de stabilité et de prospérité, en gagnant à la vie civilisée les peuplades avoisinantes.

" 3. Enfin, il était urgent de fixer cette ligne d'une manière définitive, afin d'échapper aux entraînements dangereux et presque inevitables qui, de répressions en représailles, pouvaient aboutir à une extension illimitée.

Dans ce but, il fallait poser les bases d'un système fondé non-seulement sur la raison, qui peut être élastique, mais sur les conditions géographiques et politiques, qui sont fixes et permanentes.

" Ce système nous était indiqué par un fait très-simple résultant d'une longue expèrience, c'est à dire que les tribus nomades qu'on ne peut ni saisir ni châtier, ni contenir efficacement, sont pour nous le voisinage le plus incommode, et que, par contre, les populations agricoles et commerçantes, fixées au sol et dotées d'un organisme social plus développé, nous offrent la chance d'un voisinage tolerable et de rélations perfectibles.

La ligne de nos frontières devait donc englober les premières, elle devait s'arrêter à la limite des secondes.

" Ces trois principes donnent l'explication claire, naturelle et logique, des dernières opérations militaires accomplies dans l'Asie centrale.

" En effet, la ligne primitive de nos frontières le long de la Syr-Daria jusqu'au fort Perovsky d'un côté, et de l'autre jusqué au lac Issyk-Koul avait l'inconvénient d'être presque à la limite du désert. Elle était interrompue sur un immense espace entre les deux points extrêmes ; elle n'offrait pas assez de ressources à nos troupes, et laissait en dehors des tribus sans cohésion avec lesquelles nulle stabilité n'était possible.

Malgré notre répugnance à donner à nos frontières une plus grande étendue, ces motifs ont été assez puissants pour déterminer le gouvernement impérial à établir la continuité de cette ligne entre le lac Issyk-Koul et la Syr-Daria, en fortifiant la ville de Tschamkend, récemment occupée par nous.

" En adoptant cette ligne nous obtenons un double résultat : d'un côté, la contrée qu'elle embrasse est fertile, boisée, arrosée par de nombreux cours d'eau ; elle est habitée en partie par des tribus Kirghises qui ont déjà reconnu notre domination ; elle offre donc des éléments favorables à la colonisation et à l'approvisionnement de nos garnisons. De l'autre, elle nous donne pour voisins immédiats les populations fixes, agricoles et commerçantes de Kokand.

"Nous nous trouvons en face d'un milieu social plus solide, plus compacte, moins mobile, mieux organisé; et cette considération marque avec une precision géographique la limite où l'intérêt et la raison nous prescrivent d'arriver et nous commandent de nous arrêter, parce que, d'une part toute extension ultérieure de notre domination rencontrant désormais non plus des milieux inconstants comme les tribus nomades, mais des États plus regulièrement constitués, exigerait des efforts considérables et nous entraînerait, d'annexion en annexion, dans les complications infinies; et que, d'autre part, ayant désormais pour voisins de pareils États, malgré leur civilisation arriérée et l'instabilité de leur condition politique, nous pouvons néanmoins assurer que des relations régulières pourront un jour se substituer, pour l'avantage commun, aux désordres permanents qui ont paralysé jusqu'ici l'essor de ces contrées.

"Tels sont, monsieur, les intérêts qui servent de mobile à la politique de notre auguste maître dans l'Asie centrale, tel est le but final que les ordres de Sa Majesté Impériale ont tracé à l'action de son cabinet.

"Vous êtes invité à puiser dans ces considérations le sens des explications que vous fournirez au gouvernement auprès duquel vous êtes accrédité, si vous êtes interpellé ou si vous voyez s'accréditer des suppositions erronées quant à notre action dans ces contrées lointaines.

"Je n'ai pas besoin d'insister sur l'intérêt évident que la Russia a ne pas agrandir son territoire, et surtout à ne pas se créer aux extrémités des complications qui ne peuvent que retarder et paralyser son développement intérieur.

"Le programme que je viens de tracer rentre dans cet ordre d'idées.

"Bien souvent, durant les dernières années, on s'est plu à assigner pour mission à la Russie de civiliser les contrées qui l'avoisinent sur le continent Asiatique.

"Les progrès de la civilisation n'ont pas d'agent plus efficace que les relations commerçiales. Celles-ci, pour se développer, exigent partout l'ordre et la stabilité; mais en Asie elles reclament une transformation profonde dans les mœurs. Il faut avant tout, faire comprende aux peuples asiatiques qu'il y a plus d'avantage pour eux à favoriser et assurer le commerce des caravanes qu'à les piller.

"Ces notions élémentaires ne peuvent pénétrer dans la conscience publique que là où il y a un public, c'est à dire un organisme social et un gouvernement qui le dirige et le représente.

"Nous accomplissons la première partie de cette tâche en portant notre frontière à la limite où se rencontrent ces conditions indispensables.

"Nous accomplissons la seconde en nous attachant désormais à prouver

E

aux États voisins, par un système de fermeté quant à la répression de leurs méfaits, mais en même temps de modération et de justice dans l'emploi de la force et de respect pour leur independance, que la Russie n'est pas leur ennemie, qu'elle ne nourrit à leur ègard aucune vue de conquête et que les rélations pacifiques et commerciales avec elle sont plus profitables que le désordre, le pillage, les représailles et la guerre en permanence.

"En se consacrant à cette tâche le cabinet impèrial s'inspire des intérêts de la Russie. Il croit servir en même temps les intérêts de la civilisation et de l'humanité. Il a droit de compter sur une appréciation équitable et loyale de la marche qu'il poursuit et des principes qui le guident.

(Signé)   GORTSCHAKOFF.

SAINT PETERSBOURG, le 21 *Novembre* 1864."

FRESH ADVANCES OF RUSSIA IN CENTRAL ASIA (1868).

I.

WHEN an event of world-wide importance is taking place on the boards of the political stage, an event such as the present rivalship between England and Russia in Asia, it is well worth the trouble for us to give our undivided attention to the separate scenes and acts. The European reader, perhaps too occupied by the petty contests and disputes which fascinate his gaze near at hand, will only follow us with reluctance into the regions of old Asia, and will probably, if he be neither English nor Russian, speedily find an excuse for his indifference; yet I repeat what I have already once said, that the contest going on between these two giant powers is no ordinary drama, no everyday event. Civilised Europe dares not look on with indifference at the spectacle of these two powers wrestling with each other for their superiority in Asia. Both have been nurtured on the common intellectual bounties of our own world; both would exercise a mighty influence on our present destiny, and as victor in old Asia, either of them can come forward in the immediate future in the character of a mighty umpire in Europe. Will it and can it therefore be called obtrusive in us if we turn with curiosity to the East and inquire, what is the position in Asia of England and Russia ?

Why I should venture to speak on this matter, why I should presume to look forth again and again from my peaceful and unpretending sphere of labour upon the battle-field of the contending colossal powers, is a question that can be most simply answered.

What I said in 1865, at the close of my first book on Central Asia, was entirely realised by 1867. The Russians at that time were surrounding Djizzag, and were encamped in the hot valley of the Atalan range. I asserted that they could not remain there, and, in truth, in 1868 Samarkand was already occupied by them, and they were on their way to Bokhara, which has now also sworn allegiance to them. In a word, the Russian outposts will soon have reached the right bank of the Oxus, that very frontier which I at that time pointed out as the object of their march.

After such coincidences I might assume, perhaps, some right to point to the fulfilment of my prophecies. I should do this if the ordinary course of things, the inevitable and easily-recognisable consequences of the Russian policy, deprived my former remarks of even the least pretension to political acuteness. For is it necessary perhaps to be among the prophets, in order to be able to say, at the sight of a mountain torrent rushing down from the height, that it will carry away with it this or that rock lying in the way? Bokhara, Khiva, and Khokand are nothing but rocks of this kind, which the surging waves of the slowly but surely rushing current of Russian occupation are threatening. Their ruin was easy to foresee, though not the details and consequences of the act : with these we will here occupy ourselves.

When in August 1863, on my way from Bokhara to Samarkand, seated in a rattling Tartar cart, I reached that height from whence I saw the old capital of Timur, that city wrapped in the magic veil of Central Asiatic culture, with its gilded and blue-glazed domes, with its fine imposing ruins and fantastically scattered groups of houses close at the foot of the cone - like Tschoban-Ata mountain, I could not really have believed that Samarkand, the proud fort which has done homage to no foreign ruler since the assault of Djengis-Khan, would now be found furnishing a Russianised German with the order of St George ! Probably General Kaufmann at that time had not himself imagined it. That this most eastern point of my wanderings, where even the remembrances of the West and of Christian elements seemed a perfect dread to my brain, should now be frequented by Russian soldiers, and soon most certainly will be haunted by Russian priests, who will sweep along with haughty step where I, pressing down the heavy turban over my brow, only ventured to look round with pious awe, sounds to me really too fabulous, and is too extraordinary for me readily to accustom myself to the reality. Nevertheless it is so !

Samarkand Firdusmanend—Samarkand the Paradise-like—has become a Russian possession !

I am very far from sounding elegiac laments over the Tartars. That this nest of barbarous despotism will be despoiled by Russian bayonets and cast to the ground, may not and cannot grieve me. Just as Mohammed regarded himself as the seal on the ring of divine messengers to earth—*i.e.*, that with himself the succession of prophets was for ever concluded—so may I also regard myself as a humble signet on the ring of Central Asiatic travellers. Samarkand hovered before me in my youth as a magic picture, and although I found a wide cleft of distinction between the image of my excited imagination and the miserable reality of the old Timur capital, yet this city, even after I had been undeceived in it, possessed such great interest for me, that the tidings of its fall agitated me deeply.

With my readers this will certainly not be the case. To them the short narrative of the recent events in Turkestan will of course be welcome, as, although facts belonging to a short period of time, they are of great importance. Russia once having gained a firm footing on the Yaxartes, and now strongly established there, has begun to cast covetous glances in two directions. The right eye is turned to Bokhara, to the territory on the other side of the Oxus and Afghanistan ; the left eye is looking along the Narin, across the Terek Pass to Kashgar. We purpose to speak at length of the two directions, and to describe the *status quo*, and the most recent history of the lands lying in both quarters. We will begin with Bokhara, because it lies nearer to us, it is better known, and also on the Russian side it forms the starting-point of operations.

Let us, in the first place, cast a glance at the Russian army of occupation after the taking of Djizzag. That just this point, the unfavourable climate of which we have already mentioned, should have been chosen as a temporary station, is only to be regarded as a step rendered obligatory by circumstances. The army of occupation in the province of Turkestan, the numerical vastness of which we do not even now accurately know, seems at that time in nowise to have possessed sufficient strength duly to defend, in the first place, the line extending from the north along the Yaxartes as far as Zerefshan, and in the second, the lands watered by the Narin and the Issikköl, and at the same time to pursue plans of further occupation. On the one side there were bands of Bokhariots and Turkomans emerging at different points ; on the other, wild Kirghises and Kiptchak hordes, which caused great trouble ; it was, therefore, indispensably necessary to procure an auxiliary army from the far north, and as this is not so easy to effect, owing to the still defective means of communication in the southern part of Russia, especially the long march through the Orenburg desert of four or five weeks' duration, even under favourable circumstances, the lapse of a greater time and the continuance at an unsuitable halting-place are readily to be explained. In fact, the rumours which at that time reached us from Bombay, the usual channel of all news, with regard to the conclusion of peace between Bokhara and Russia, bear the date of this period. One incident only, namely, the appointment of General Kaufmann in the place of the usually successful General Romanoffsky, is not quite clear ; still a change of persons in Russian plans is of no special signification. Any one remaining always the head would have been obliged to wait till troops, money, and ammunition had arrived to such an extent as to render possible the adoption of a peaceful or warlike tone towards the Emir of Bokhara.

This is the cause why the Russian *Invalide* informs

us that General Kaufmann did not enter into an interchange of diplomatic communications with the Emir of Bokhara respecting peace negotiations until the September of 1867. Whether this pacification was seriously intended on either side is much to be doubted, from the tedious interchange of diplomatic negotiations which was kept up, and which was submitted to on the part of the Russians. Emir Muzaffar-ed-Din sent indeed his Mirachor, Musa-Beg, with a diplomatic mission to Tashkend. The same person had been employed on a similar mission to Orenburg, yet neither from the tenor of the credentials he brought with him, nor from a conference carried on with General Kaufmann, is it possible to conclude what tokens of the peaceableness of the Emir existed. The Russian general (for the reporter of the Russian *Invalide* has an indubitably semi-official character) was justly astonished at the ambiguity, the stupid lies, and the constant change of pretext in this same Bokhara ambassador ; yet, as an honest soldier, he may be pardoned the want of ethnographical acquaintance with the lands of Central Asia. They spoke to the Bokhariot of peace stipulations, ratifications, and other legal expressions, which were utterly unknown to Tartar diplomacy. Cunning was not indeed lacking at Bokhara, yet, like the cunning of all Asiatics, it is often too childish to be of any avail against an armed adversary. Musa-Beg was given repeatedly to understand that they desired to know why he had not long ago brought back a ratified copy of the peace contract sent to Bokhara ? why, now that peace negotiations were going on, it was allowed on the part of Bokhara to make inroads into Russian territory ? In fact, why such an outrage had been committed as to take prisoner a Russian officer and three privates, compelling the former to embrace Islamism and to drill the Bokhariot army. Musa-Beg answered with empty evasions and shameless lies, which subsequently came to light after the emancipation of the above-mentioned Russian prisoners and the arrival of another envoy from Bokhara.

Whoever, therefore, is of opinion that the Russian commander only put a good face on this irritating conduct of the Emir, because he desired to maintain peace at any price (in fact, that, in confirmation of this opinion, he was even on the point of undertaking a journey to Petersburg), I will on no account shake his belief in the peaceableness of the Russians. For my own part, however, I cannot forbear saying plainly, that just as little as the Emir, a man of genuine Islam virtue, wished to enter into a compact with the unbeliever, so the subservience and lamb-like patience of the Russian general, and his desire to instruct the Emir in international law, were nothing else than a pretext for awaiting the favourable moment. During the winter the transmission of troops across the inhospitable steppes of Central Asia, if not quite impossible, was yet tolerably difficult; yet scarcely had the first spring month reached its close than Russian policy cast aside its mantle of peace. Five hundred Cossacks, accompanied by a corresponding number of infantry and artillery, were despatched from Tashkend to strengthen the frontier army encamped around Djizzag. General Kaufmann endeavoured to quiet the Emir with regard to this fact in a Russian document dated March 26, in which he assured him that they only desired to check the inroads which Bokhariot

troops were making on Russian soil. Yet in the very
same document the news was communicated that a division of troops was to be sent for reconnoitring purposes
to the northern declivity of the Nur-Ata mountain, a
proceeding which was, of course, utterly unintelligible,
as this object and the repulse of a few bands required no
such important concentration of forces. Indeed, the fact
that this division, which was commanded by Major
Grippenberg, subsequently fell in with the troops of the
governors of Kette-Kurgan and Tchelek, is a distinct
proof of the assertion we before expressed. Neither a
conclusion of peace nor an accurate definition of frontier
could have been much desired by the Russians. To stop
at the Zerefshan after the advantages obtained was impossible. Russia knows too accurately what moral good
she can derive from the fall of Bokhara. She knows,
however, also no less the weaknesses of the foe opposed
to her; for it is truly astonishing how easily her mere
presence there creates *tabula rasa*, and how easily the
dreaded name of Russian can bring everything there into
confusion.

I have never doubted that the unprecedented obstinacy of Bokharian self-love, and of hypocritical confidence in the sacred character of noble Bokhara, will
never give way even beneath the roar of Russian cannon,
though these might have shattered a part of her clay-
built walls. Any one who has listened to the bombastic
narrations of the tribes on the Zerefshan of the miserable campaigns, or rather predatory excursions, of their
Emir against Khokand, which resulted in his own ruin,
will be able to form some idea of the arrogance of a
people sunk in barbarism. When the Emir asked me

whether the Sultan of Turkey possessed such splendid troops as he? whether he had such long and deep-mouthed cannon as those which I saw lying on the sand of the Rigistan in Bokhara ? and lastly, whether it were such an easy matter for his brother on the Bosphorus as it was to him to summon hundred thousands of soldiers at the stamp of his foot? I had a tolerably sure presentiment of what is happening at the present day in Bokhara. Still I had never imagined that matters would take such a sudden turn, and that the relation between ruler and ruled would assume the form which it has done.

The first blow which shook the loyal feeling of the Bokhariots towards their ruler was the taking of Tash-kend, which, injurious as it was to the interests of Khud-ajar-Khan, a prince much beloved in Bokhara on account of his piety, must have been very displeasing to the inhabitants of the noble city. This conquest, moreover, gave rise to that mistrust which subsequently showed itself more and more decidedly. It must have visibly increased with the fall of Khodjend, and the unfortunate skirmish at Irdjar; yet symptoms of discontent did not show themselves publicly until the Emir, compelled by circumstances, was obliged—in order to replenish his coffers, exhausted as they were by war—to have recourse to means which were most offensive to the Tadjik population of Bokhara ; that is to say, until, besides imposing heavy military contributions, he gathered in the coin most in circulation, called *tenge*, of the value of about one franc, and subsequently issued it again at the value of two francs. If we add to this evil state of things the dulness of trade, and the utter stagnation of all commercial intercourse between Russia,

China, and India, Afghanistan being also for the last
three years the seat of constant war, we shall easily gain
an idea of the melancholy condition into which the commercial and industrial part of the population of Bokhara
had fallen.   The hardest lot was of course that of the
agriculturist or the dwellers in the country.   Apart from
the fact that the constant warfare kept him far from
house and home, as he had to accompany his liege lord
into the field, the members of the family who remained
at home could not sell the produce of the soil at any
price, not even at the lowest.   This was most felt in
cotton, raw silk, dried fruits, and colouring plants, which
generally were exported in great quantities to Russia,
but which were now quite worthless.   And when we
trace the main source of all this misfortune to the constant pressure which the governors exercised on all
classes in the name of the Emir and of the hardly-
pressed Government, the forced change in the public
feeling will become at once obvious to us.

Nevertheless the people had not yet come forward
with the expression of their discontent, and would not
have done so if the Emir had not seized the secularised
property of the influential Ulemas, and if he had not
laid under contribution some mosques and religious
institutions, the flourishing state of whose coffers was a
secret to no one.   Of course, these temporal sacrifices
would not have fallen so heavily on the learned world
of Bokhara if their Islam piety had been really as
true as it assumed to be.   Yet the servants of religion on
the banks of the Zerefshan cling to all that is earthly
just as much as do their brethren on the Tiber and the
Seine.   In vain were they told that their contributions

were designed for the defence of the faith against the Russians—in vain it was explained to them that their refusal was analogous with apostasy; it was all useless. The Emir had scarcely placed his hands on the money of the mosques and colleges than he was himself decried as an unbeliever and a recreant. It is, indeed, inconceivable how such a change could take place in the minds of the Bokhariots. I am seized with indescribable astonishment when I look back to the reverence and the profound respect with which the people spoke of Muzaffar-ed-Din. The Ba-Devlet (the most blessed), the Emir-el-Mumenin (Prince of orthodox believers), this radiant model of Islam virtue three years ago, is at the present day decried as an unbeliever by the Ulemas, who had just been extolling his high virtues to me!

However it may be, the opinion of the capital speedily found a lively echo in the surrounding country. Not only did the governor of Karaköl make common cause with the Turkomans, and incited them not to join the standard of the Emir without exorbitant pay—a pay which the Emir, growing daily poorer, could not give, and the Turkomans in consequence refused their interest; but discontent in the formerly well-ordered state exhibited itself everywhere. The nomad tribes of Khitai-Kiptchak, whom I have mentioned in my "Reisen," p. 163, revolted against the Emir. They were at first accused of secret understanding with the Russians, but this is a calumny; for a genuine Özbeg race, such as the Khitai-Kiptchaks are, would scarcely allow themselves to be guilty of such a crime. In consequence of the great number of horsemen who were recruited from among them, they had always formed the vanguard of

the Bokhara army; and on this occasion, just as at other
times, they only revolted because their services were too
much required.

Lastly, the district of Shehri-Sebz, lying in the south,
and always on a hostile footing with Bokhara, also gave
the Emir much trouble just at this difficult time.
Djura-Beg, who stood at the head of the revolted province, had made, indeed, hitherto no common cause with
the Russians, although emissaries from Tashkend had
of course not omitted to insinuate themselves, if only
morally, in the southern points of the Oxus territory.
For Özbegs are, even in revolt, still honest Özbegs;
and the most essential injury that the Emir of Bokhara
endured was, that, in the first place, 8000 to 10,000 of the
bravest Özbeg horsemen withdrew from him; and that,
secondly, the revolted Shehri-Sebz served as a place of
refuge to his dangerous enemies, amongst whom was one
of his nearest relatives, whom the offended Ulemas in
Bokhara had brought forward as a pretender to his
throne. Much evil had gathered over the head of the
Emir.

Most ridiculous, however, are and will ever be the
demands which the people, goaded by the priests, presented to their ruler; they required of him that he
should proclaim the Djihad or Gaza, the religious war,
and that he should attempt a new engagement with the
Russians, though all former ones had only brought him
misfortune. Whether the Emir, conscious of his weakness and of the superiority of the opposing enemy,
allowed himself to be forced into an open declaration of
war, I am still inclined to doubt. He relied on some
Mohammedan alliance, or on the improvement of his

warlike preparations. Be that as it may, he resisted with much energy during the last winter the demands of the public feeling; indeed, he would not have allowed himself to be forced to the step even in the spring had not every way of escape been cut off to him by the Russians on the one side, and on the other by the priests, who published several *rivajets* (quotations from the Koran) relating to the duty of religious wars. He saw that he must yield, and must decide on war. Before setting out, he was on the point of visiting the tomb of the sacred Beha-ed-Din, after the usual Mohammedan fashion, when his enemies in the city spread the report that, from fear of the war, he was going to flee. Great multitudes assembled at the Mezar gate in order to prevent his exit, but meanwhile he was already in the village Beha-ed-Din, and, in fact, was returning from his pilgrimage. Seeing the impatient masses, entrance into the city seemed impossible to him, and so, accompanied by their imprecations and curses, he took his way to the second saint of the kingdom, Khodja-Abdul-Khalik, whose native place is at Gidjdovan, a small town in the north of the Khanate. Here also he was threatened by the mob and exposed to invectives, and it was only with the promise that he would drive away the Russians as soon as possible from the sacred soil of Turkestan that he was allowed to repair to the army at Samarkand, along the usual route through Kermineh.

The Djihad was declared in the closest sense of the word; yet as Bokhara did not venture to take the defensive, and proposed planning a surprise after the fashion of true Tartar tactics, the Emir was obliged for a time to watch the movements of the enemy. He had already

occupied the heights of Nur-Ata, Daul, and Kette-Kurgan, when the Russians, on the 14th May, after having
spent some time in small attacks and skirmishes, set out
from Tasch Köprück, a stone bridge between Jengi Kur-
gan and Samarkand, to take the latter place. So far as
I can remember the country, the Russians had no specially favourable ground compared with their enemies
on the heights; they had, in the first place, to cross the
Karasu, a small tributary of the Zerefshan, and then
to wade through the latter river itself, which is not particularly high at this season of the year, but from its
marshy banks it presents considerable difficulties to an
army advancing to attack. Still a regular troop of
Russians was not to be deterred by impediments
of this nature; they had, besides, a well-concentrated
force at their disposal; for 21 companies of infantry,
450 Cossacks, 16 cannons, were drawn up in battle
array. We may from this satisfactorily conclude how
great was the number of the centre and the reserve.
It is easily comprehensible, therefore, that they successfully overcame the difficulties of the ground, drove away
the Bokhariots at their mere appearance, and soon after
took possession of the city of Samarkand in consequence
of the invitation of its nobles. Neither Colonel Abramoff,
nor Major-General Golowascheff, nor even the general
commanding, had any occasion to employ any special
strategical skill in accomplishing this victory. The result
was easily to be foreseen, and in the whole catastrophe
there are only a few details which may be brought forward.

In the first place, the Samarkandians, after the unsuccessful issue of the engagement, closed their gates to their

fleeing countrymen, and even to their ruler himself, in order, as may be readily imagined, to prevent the hardship of a possible siege by Russian artillery. How this act of infidelity could take place in Samarkand, the summer residence and favourite resort of Muzaffar-ed-Din, is truly astonishing, and speaks plainly for the baseness of the character of the Tadjiks, who, here as in Bokhara, form the majority of the population, and who, in spite of all the Islam fanaticism upon which they pride themselves more than even the Özbegs do, undoubtedly form that fraction of the population which is most inclined to undermine the power of the Emir and to destroy their own faith and independence.

The second and still more remarkable circumstance is that on this march to Samarkand, those Afghan soldiers fought under the Russian standard who had only a month previously gone over to the Russians in consequence of a dispute with the Emir of Bokhara, to whom Afzal-Khan had sent them from Belkh as auxiliary troops. These Afghans whom, as model troops, Afzal-Khan had sent to the Emir to train his army, had quarrelled with the Emir on account of the irregularity with which their pay was remitted to them. Naturally the vindictive Afghans had never stood on a footing of special friendship with the inhabitants of Bokhara; still that Mohammedan fanatics, such as the Afghans are, should combine with the unbelieving Russian against the noble Bokhara, the seat of all Islam knowledge, and that Iskender-Khan, a son of Azim-Khan and grandson of Dost Mohammed-Khan, should be found at the head of these deserters, is a fact

F

which may in nowise be overlooked by the Anglo-Indian Government.

Samarkand was taken. The tidings of victory surprised Europe, the Court of Petersburg, and even the Russian general; for I will impute it alone to this surprise, that, dissatisfied with the splendid booty of his contest, he marched on the next day but one through the gate of Shah Zinde, for the sake of continuing his conquests on the very road to Bokhara which the fugitive army of the Emir had taken. In order not to leave the smallest number of foes in the rear, two different divisions of troops were despatched, one to the citadel of Tchilek situated towards the north, and the other to that of Orkud on the south-west. The former place surrendered itself readily; the latter only yielded after a desperate engagement, in which, as the Russians tell us, more than 15,000 Bokhariots took part, 1000 of whom were left on the field of battle. General Kaufmann himself, during this flank movement, had continued his way to Kette-Kurgan, a place strongly fortified. It surrendered, however, without resistance, and the march against the capital would certainly have been continued, if a strong force of Bokhariots had not meanwhile assembled and begun to dispute with the Russians the ground lying between Kette-Kurgan and Samarkand. It is clearly manifest that, under such circumstances, it was urgently necessary to thin the close ranks in order not to lose the chain of communication with the Russian possessions. The Russian general, therefore, attacked the enemy at Sere Bulak on the 14th June, with eighteen companies of infantry, six bodies of cavalry, and four cannons, as the well-informed *Saturday Review* tells us, defeated it utterly, as may easily be imagined, and not only thus rescued himself from a dangerous position, but again liberated Samarkand from the insurgent populace who had meanwhile cruelly distressed it.

The Özbegs, supported by a numerous army from Shehri - Sebz, commanded in person by Djura - Beg, had secretly entertained the design of reconquering their second capital. While the Russians had withdrawn from the citadel in order to pursue their victory, and had left behind only a feeble garrison together with the sick and wounded, several troops of Özbegs had surprised the citadel, which, so far as I remember, though well situated, was only weakly fortified. The contest, as we have learned from Russian sources, must have been a very obstinate one, for even the sick and wounded left their beds ; indeed, all who could discharge a pistol or handle a sword came forward to repulse the besieging enemy. The Tartar startegy of occupying the attention of the general commanding by an apparent attack on Kette-Kurgan, and of preventing immediate assistance, would have certainly succeeded in a remarkable manner, if the well-known cowardice of all Orientals and the absence of true heroic spirit had not here also been clearly manifested. That a band of several thousand warriors, heated by wild religious fanaticism, could not scale a wall at the most twelve feet high, defended by a few hundred Russians, and these to a great extent incapable of fighting, and could not take the citadel, sounds truly almost like irony ; and yet so it was! The Muscovite garrison, whose valour stands out brilliantly compared with the cowardly conduct of the Tartars, had endurance enough to continue the contest, until General Kaufmann, informed of their condition by spies, hastened to assist the besieged, scattered the enemy like chaff, and took possession of the threatened Samarkand.

Whether the Emir or one of his generals led the Bokhariots in these operations against the mighty adversary, is a question which constantly forms a subject of curiosity to our European journalists, and which cannot with certainty be stated. The Emir was indeed the ruling head, but his power consisted principally, in the first place, in the troops directly subordinate to him, which were paid by him from the public treasury, and which, for the most part, were commanded by Persian soldiers, who had come to Bokhara either as deserters or as Turkoman prisoners; and in the second place, in the contingents furnished by the different governors, Hakim-Begs, who indeed, according to the rules of the constitution, were to be unconditionally subject to the orders of their ruler; but at this time, as we may conclude from the events, were fighting more on their own account, and were not so anxious about their common fatherland as *pro aris et focis.* We see, therefore, only the Hakim-Begs of Kette-Kurgan, Kermineh, and the Khitai-Kiptchak districts actively engaged at this time. A united opposition, such as the dangerous position of things demanded, we have never yet met with, although a general summons, and, indeed, an urgent appeal from the Emir was certainly not lacking. The contrary even was the case, for while the Emir was fighting hotly with the Russians, the Beg of the northern district of Nur-Ata had risen in rebellion against his lord.

Yet even if united co-operation had been possible, what forces could the extremest effort on the part of the Bokhariots produce? I need only recall to mind the picture of the solemn victorious entry of the Emir of Samarkand; I need only remember the Karaköl and Karshier troops with their miserable broad-swords, guns, and daggers, to declare all the utmost efforts of the Tartars, however united, as unavailing. Twenty, ay, even thirty Tartars may oppose a single Russian, yet victory will remain with the latter.

The Bokhariots, although so fabulously superior in numbers, lack, in the first place, all idea of strategy; their military authorities, such as Sharuch-Mirza, a cousin of the present King of Persia, Zeinel-Beg, and other Persians, who have fled thither as a refuge and have been brought thither as captives, have too slight a knowledge of our military science to be able to act as teachers; there are none of those Afghan-Hindoo instructors who have fled from the ranks of the Anglo-Indian army across the Indus, leaving behind them perceptible traces of the system of English drill. In addition to all this, they are deficient, as we have frequently said, in valour and endurance, so that, as we have before pointed out, the victory of the Russian arms in Central Asia is certain, and can in nowise be prevented. But we will return to the course of events.

After Samarkand had been again taken, and probably for ever, and the victorious Russians had advanced as far as Kermineh, along the valley of the Zerefshan, on a good road that had been used by the greatest armies of the Middle Ages, it was suddenly declared that the now completely humbled Khan of Bokhara, submitting to the wish of the White Czar on the Neva, had entered into negotiations for peace. The treaty in question stated, in the first place, that the Emir would pay the Czar yearly one and a half laks *tillah* in gold ; secondly, that he would allow fortresses to be built in Karshi, Ishikardjin, and Kermineh ; thirdly, that the Emir, if he faithfully fulfilled his promises, was to receive Samarkand back again; fourthly, that he would permit the Russians to erect fortresses, at their pleasure, on the Zerefshan, or in the north of Samarkand, and construct a road to Bokhara at the Emir's expense, &c.—points in which the Anglo-Indian press perceived a dangerous move against her interest in India on the chessboard of the present contest, and against which, as may be readily conceived, she raised an outcry. Whilst in Europe the authenticity of this document was much discussed, General Kaufmann, the proud conqueror, accompanied by a numerous staff, travelled through Orenburg to Petersburg. His journey to the Muscovite capital furnished in the first place the best proof of the temporary pause in Russian warfare in Turkestan ; and in the second place, he wished to introduce a new race of Asiatics to the great ruler of half Asia—namely, the Afghan prince, Iskender-Khan, the new mercenary of the Russian Imperial force, who accompanied General Kaufmann on his journey both to see and to be seen. There is no doubt that this scion of the Bareksi house—this grandson of Dost Mohammed—the first Afghan at a Christian European court, will be ardently admired by the ladies in Zarskoe-Selo. The Afghans, although not such Adonises as English authors allege them to be, are, nevertheless, very stately-looking personages. I envy him the pleasure which many a young Russian will exhibit, as, at the sight of the fantastic and romantic-looking Afghan turban, he dreams of the Czar's dominion on the Hilmend and in the valleys of the Hindukush. But Iskender-Khan will have also much to see. The splendour of Indian viceroys, of which the grandees in Kabul have heard, can be easily eclipsed on the Neva. He will see fine military reviews; he will visit arsenals, &c.; he will bring back with him rich presents—in a word, on his return to his cousins at home, he will have much to tell of the White Czar, of his power, his greatness, and his goodness, and he will thus contribute in making the name of Russia beloved among the Afghans. Whether, therefore a cessation of arms or a peace occurs, we see that Russia never ceases to struggle morally—just as in the last year, so also in this, the pause is very necessary; and just as in this year, so in the spring of the next, the contest will be continued.

In Bokhara, meanwhile, to make the misfortune complete, the flame of discord had burst forth between Muzaffar-ed-Din and his son Abdul Melik Mirza. This son, the unworthy child of a father distinguished for gentleness of character, pursued by misfortune, and plunged into calamity through his erroneous views, had been three years before governor of Samarkand, a post which, according to the custom of the country, belongs to the successor to the throne, just as Tebris belongs to the Veliahd of Persia, or Dauphiné to the eldest prince in France. It was murmured even at the time of my journey that he was not living on the best terms with his father, who was well known to be a pious Mussulman, and who wished to preserve his son also on the path of strict belief. Though I am far from wishing to cast the least suspicion upon him with regard to the catastrophe at Samarkand, where this very son was at the head of his troops, and first took to flight, still it is certain that this Törekelan (the word signifies elder, greater prince, and is not to be regarded as a proper name, as it is used in the journals), supported by his uncle, who was among the insurgent Shehri-Sebzans, would not have made the least scruple, even without the consent of his people, in entering into a peace with the Russians, or coming to a mutual understanding with them, if the court of Petersburg had manifested the slightest wish for transactions of the kind.

Yet the Russians cherished no such intentions; they cannot and dare not desire peace; for whilst in the last year the reaching of the right bank of the Oxus was regarded, according to the Russian plan, as the *non plus ultra* of a successful issue, late events in the lands lying between the Oxus and the Yaxartes have raised their hopes and wishes far higher. What need is there now of a garrison in Tchardjui, Kerki, or by the ferry of Khodja-Salih? Many other things are now rendered possible; the Russian Cossacks may now longingly stretch out their hands towards the cream-pots for which old Herat is famed. In fact, the present aim of the Muscovites is directed towards Meimene Belkh and Herat—to that Herat, the ancient title of which, "the chief gateway of Central Asia," has been recently contested *à tout prix* by the great English diplomatists, and which now, nevertheless, will serve as the gateway through which the Russian eagle, in its bold flight towards the south, will probably take them by surprise.

All that has rendered the execution of this plan feasible, and has made it a necessity in the arrangements of Russian policy, must form the subject of our present considerations. During the victorious campaign of twelve months in Turkestan, especially during the march from Khodjend to the gates of Bokhara, events of great importance have taken place not only in the neighbouring khanates, but on the other side of the Oxus, in Afghanistan. Russia has tolerably smoothed the difficulties apparently insurmountable in the eye of her rival ; she is now not only mistress of the interior country and of the territory on the Zerefshan, but she holds equal sway over the adjacent khanates, and, moreover, she has entered into relations with Afghanistan from which she must speedily obtain a certain and not insignificant reward.

That Khokand has lost for the present its actual independence, and not its nominal at once also, is to be ascribed not so much to the moderation of Russian policy, as perhaps to the circumstance that the complete annexation of the khanate would require a garrison of three times the number of troops, even though no Russian institutions were at first introduced in its interior organisation. To take Khokand, Namengan, Mergolan, and other eastern places of importance, would have been a very easy matter for the governor of Turkestan, but not so the watch over an enemy always on the lookout for an opportunity. This inhabited part of the khanate was, moreover, situated beyond the marching route of the Russian plan. In order to arrive at Kash-

gar, Fort Vernoe and the territory of the Narin river
had been secured; the fortified communication from
Tashkend and Khodjend led to Bokhara; and as it
was known with tolerable certainty that Khokand, so
lovingly surrounded on all sides, would not subsequently
be able to resist the somewhat ungentle embrace of the
Russian bear, it was desirable, in order to give a new
colouring to the long-expressed desire for a peaceful
policy, to leave Khokand for a time in its present condition, and in order to show the Khan of Khokand that
he was treated as a reigning prince, or more justly, to
remove all fear of possible danger, General Kaufmann
had not delayed, even before the outbreak of formal
hostilities against Bokhara, to conclude a treaty of peace
with Khudajar-Khan, the ruler of Khokand, of which the
following is the purport :—1. All the towns and villages
of the Khanate of Khokand, without exception, are open
to Russian merchants, and all Russian markets are
accessible to traders from Khokand. 2. The Russian
merchants are at liberty to have their caravanseries, in
which they alone can store their goods, in any towns of
Khokand that they may please. 3. For the control of
regular commercial intercourse and the lawful levying
of duty, the Russian merchants are allowed the right of
having commercial agents in all the towns of the khanate if they wish. The merchants from Khokand have
the same right in the towns in the Turkestan territory.
4. All goods brought from Russia to Khokand, or passing from Khokand into European and Asiatic Russia,
are subject to the same duty as in the Turkestan territory—*i.e.*, 2½ per cent. of their value, in each case no
higher duty than that demanded from the Mussulmans

who are Khokand subjects. 5. The Russian merchants with their caravans have free and safe passage through the Khokand territory into the adjacent countries, and the caravans from Khokand are in like manner to pass freely into Russian territory. These engagements were confirmed, and on the 29th January 1868 were signed and sealed in Tashkend by the Governor-General of Turkestan, and by the commander of the troops in the Turkestan military district, the adjutant-general of Kaufmann. As a token of the acceptance of these engagements by the Government of Khokand, Seid-Mohammed-Khudajar-Khan ratified them at Khokand on the 13th February 1868 with his seal.

These precautionary measures were, however, not at all necessary. Surrounded on all sides, humbled by the defeats suffered, enfeebled by internal discord and want of money, and recently especially threatened by the ruler of the "Six Cities," a former vassal, the Khan of Khokand, even without this treaty, would not have felt the slightest desire to rise against the Russians, from whom he was now only awaiting his deathblow. Indeed, his views on the matter are best expressed in the answer which he gave to the powerful ruler of the "Six Cities," when the latter invited him to make common cause with him against the Russians. "Yakub Kushbegi must first give the Russians an essential blow, and then I will join myself to him; in the contrary case, I should be the first upon whom the retaliation would fall."

A similar opinion prevails also in Khiva, which, from fear of the approaching storm on the lower stream of the Oxus, remains as quiet as a mouse. It is, indeed, possible that this striking repose in the warlike elements of Khiva, which has the bravest Özbegs in its army, besides having more than 60,000 Turkoman horsemen at its disposal, is influenced by the fleet on the Sea of Aral. The gentlemen in Petersburg will probably be of this opinion; still, I believe that the fearful tidings of the catastrophe in Bokhara and Khokand are far more serious to Khiva than the threatening position at the mouth of the Oxus. Moreover, Khiva has never allowed the guilt of self-admiration to amount to such an extent as Bokhara; the people are more homely but more earnest; they are quieter, but steadier, than on the banks of the Zerefshan. No one in Khiva ignores the fact that the independence of the Özbegs is threatened with immediate danger, yet it is not for a moment doubted that the Russian soldiers will not find victory here very easy; for although the Turkoman races of the khanates — I mean the Tchaudors and the Yomuts — will desert their countrymen for the smallest trifle, and will march arm-in-arm with the Russians, the taking of Khiva alone will cost nearly as much time and sacrifice as the conquest of the whole of Bokhara and Khokand.

Moreover, the absolute and immediate possession of the khanate on the lower Oxus is all the less an urgent necessity, as a temporary intimidation, supported by the before-mentioned outposts on the Sea of Aral, may procure them a position in Old Khahrezm analogous with that at Khokand—*i.e.*, they may here also obtain neutrality for a time without any actual conquest, and without thus frustrating the means of subsequently overcoming their prospective and much-surrounded prize.

And why, when we are speaking of the easy practicability of Russian plans, should we not take into consideration those political powers which have been an important assistance to every conqueror on the left bank of the Oxus, and must be so also to the Russians? I refer to the petty Khanates of Kunduz, Aktche, Shiborgan, Andchoi, and Meimene, which altogether can furnish scarcely more than 40,000 horse, but which separately can be of great use to the advancing power, by the constant and unrelenting feuds that prevail among them. Through these Tartar Lilliputian princes, who now acknowledge Afghan sovereignty, though not Afghan commands, both Yar Mohammed Khan and Dost Mohammed Khan have recently succeeded in rendering themselves masters of the Paropamisus in the north, and in becoming dangerous rivals of the Emir of Bokhara; in fact, we could almost admit that even the rulers on the Zerefshan were only powerful when their policy was able to procure them authority on the other side of the Oxus—that is, in the places we have before mentioned. It is to me as if I saw already the Özbeg princes who have been driven away by Afghan power, and possessing a nationality which, strongly mingled with Sartish and Tadjik elements, has been far from preserving that genuine and pure Özbeg character which distinguishes their brethren on the lower stream of the Oxus,—it is to me as if I saw these princes, suddenly emerging from their corners of concealment, join the columns of the Russian army, and march delightedly towards the mountains of Afghanistan, in order to avenge themselves on their old adversaries, if the Afghans do not get the start of them and sooner solicit the Russian alliance, the probability of which we have also already pointed out.

Or is it perhaps the Turkomans who will stand in the way of the Muscovites? I have already expressed myself distinctly as to their untrustworthy character, and only for the sure convincing of my political adversaries I will observe, that the Turkomans, although an important power, are very different at the present day in the eyes of all Asiatics from that epoch when they appeared as mighty agents in history; as, for example, under the Timurides, the Sefevides, and Nadir. It is indeed true that the Ersaris, and especially the numerous Tekes, the brave Salors, and the rash Sariks, could occasion any Asiatic power, even at the present day, much trouble; yet what can a body of troops effect, however courageous the horsemen and fleet the horses, against the iron wall of a square of Russian bayonets? The Asiatic is well acquainted with warfare as regards impetuous attack or feigned flight; but to stand firm, awaiting the fatal bullet, to trust his personal courage to the strategic guidance of another, this is unknown to him; and although the Turkomans are far more brave and resolute than the Özbegs, all their efforts against the Russians have ever been vain and fruitless.

Apart from this deficiency in physical superiority, the condemnatory testimony of every traveller as to the morality of the Turkomans is sufficient pledge that this people, among whom neither religion nor nationality, nor even principle takes root, will be the first to enter the Russian service. They are not only to be employed against the khanates or against the Afghans, as is best proved by their recent depredations upon Tchardjui and Karaköl, places which they laid utterly waste, but they will act against their own races; and difficult as it will be to the Court of Petersburg to subdue these wild sons of the west, and to treat them like the Kirghises, it will be easy to make their services available to its own ends.

However much I may endeavour to avoid falling into repetition, it is almost impossible to me here, when speaking of the most recent movements and the Russian projects in Central Asia, not to make mention again of Persia, whose conduct is of such great importance in the question now under discussion. In my paper, " Persia and Turkey," * I have already pointed out the condition of Russia's influence in Teheran, and the errors of the British diplomacy in the same place. I should have remained satisfied with this glance, if during the course of this year events had not occurred which cast a distinct light upon my former insinuations. I mean, in the first place, Persia's quarrel with the Porte, which has not indeed yet given occasion to an open feud, but which, like a spark hidden under the ashes, is only waiting the moment to burst into a flame: Ottoman and English interests are regarded as completely identical in Persia ; the English ambassador is designated in derision the Frengi Sunnite, and the Ottoman the Sunnite Frengi ; even the daily intercourse between the two palaces of the Embassy is far more close, firm, and brotherly in the capital at the foot of the Demavend than it is elsewhere, so much so, that I cannot imagine an attack on Khanikein (Ejalet Bagdad) without a secondary design upon Herat or *vice versâ*. Whatever the Sultan likes, that is decidedly hated by the Shah ; wherever the latter goes, the former keeps

* Cf. " Unsere Zeit," new series, iv, 1. 767–780.

away; hence the disappointment of Napoleon III. not to be able to receive the successor of the Darians in his capital at the time of the great "Exposition;" for although the Shah had accepted the invitation earlier, he despatched a letter of excuse to the banks of the Seine as soon as the definitive journey of the Sultan was made known.

In the second place, I cannot conceal my astonishment when the visit occurs to me, which Nasreddin Shah, this shadow of God upon earth, this radiant climax of humanity, paid to the Russian Grand Duke, when the latter on his tour visited the Caspian fleet and the Russian Caspian coast-lands. I will not here discuss what the sovereign of Persia thought as he traversed the blue waves of the sea once belonging to him, on which he now cannot even send out from the shore a fishing-boat for his amusement; for we cannot doubt for a moment that he had his special thoughts in the conference, the hearty friendly character of which we learn from the newspapers of the time. Herat, the rich and golden Herat, where the best cream in Central Asia flows, where the most beautiful women are to be found, where the fields, according to the statement of the aborigines, need only to be tilled by children in order to bear rich fruit—this Herat is a place after which Persian rulers in every age have longed, and with only a slight promise on the part of the Grand Duke to cede Herat with the adjacent annexed lands—I mean Ferrah, Sebzevar, and Gurian — to the Persians, the Shah would at once pledge himself not only to allow the Russian army to pass, if it desires to repair to Herat along a good road, through Astrabad, Kabushan, and

Meshed, but to support most vigorously the Court of Petersburg in all its plans on the territory on the other side of the Oxus. If the politicians in the council of the Persian king would take into consideration the subsequent consequences of a Russian alliance, if they would cast a glance at the map, and attentively consider the precarious position of their country from the Russian line of frontier enclosing it on the north-west and north, and now also on the north-east, they would certainly lose all desire to increase the vicinity of Russia; for with the extension of Russian influence in Armenia and Kurdistan on the one side, and in Turkestan and Afghanistan on the other, the future of Iran is already endangered; the bond may eventually pass into the sweetest feeling of friendship, but Iran cannot escape being absorbed by the gigantic body of the Northern Colossus. Unfortunately, however, the Persians, those clever children of the East, are far enough from pondering upon future plans of the kind; they care alone for the accomplishment of plans which afford present advantage. A Russian alliance gives a better prospect of wars, of diplomatic disorders, and therefore, also, of a certain influx of bribes and peculations for ministers; and as, besides, the youthful Nasreddin Shah wishes at any rate to adorn the old Keiwan crown with the laurels of fresh victories, it is resolved, once for all, that Iran under any circumstances must take the same path as Russia, and support this empire in her plans upon the adjacent territory of Afghanistan.

If I have not deceived myself in these conjectures, the Court of Petersburg has furnished the surest and clearest evidence that, in its advance to the south of Central Asia,

G

it has in view not only to gain a firm footing on both banks of the Oxus and Yaxartes, but that the aim of its endeavours is at present to smooth and prepare the way for a future plan which has long been traced out. If Khokand and Khiva are maintained as sovereign states, the whole tract of land from Tashkend to Kerki is nothing but the highway on which the advance will be made, from Andchoi and Meimene to Herat, and from thence to Afghanistan ; and the gentlemen in Peshawur will scarcely have time to inspect with their telescopes, on the summits of the Hindukush, the movements of the Russians, before the latter will have taken possession of Herat, and will, perhaps, have reached with their outposts the banks of the Hilmend.

If the optimists and adversaries of my views in England or India doubt the possibility, or at any rate the speedy possibility, of an unexpected move on the part of the Russians, I will point to the fraternisation which the above-mentioned Iskender-Khan so easily entered into with the Russian general at Tashkend, and I will draw attention to the fact that in all engagements which took place near Samarkand, there were regiments of Afghan cavalry and infantry taking part in the contest against the Emir. At the present moment, Azim-Khan's star in Kabul as well as in the whole of Afghanistan is as rapidly sinking as the fortune of the once-oppressed Shir-Ali-Khan is on the ascendant. The latter has not only marched into Kabul as a victorious prince, and has not only obliged his brother to fly to Belkh, but he has converted a great part of the troops of his enemy into friends, and is on the point—so says a vague report which speaks of important Russian subsidies, with the help of which he is thus vigorously carrying on operations—of consolidating his throne by Muscovite support, in the same way as his father did so by the help of English arms. I only ask the wise gentlemen in the Indian Council, will Iskender-Khan, who has already given such splendid proofs of his vengeance, be able to forbear taking revenge on the arch-enemy of his father, when he enters Afghanistan supported by a great power? Or will he, forming probably a part of the Russian advanced guard, not at once come forward as the bitterest enemy of Shir-Ali-Khan and of England? I believe none will doubt such an event. There is no need to be a Mountstuart Elphinstone or an Alexander Burnes; the slightest knowledge of the Afghan character is sufficient to render apparent that the fraternal contest which has been going on among the descendants of Dost-Mohammed-Khan is just as advantageous to the success of the Russian plans, as it is critical, and perhaps dangerous, to the interests of England. If some thousand Afghans who have been despatched for the protection of a threatened neighbouring sovereign, a relative, moreover (for the readers of my "Reisen" will probably remember that the two eldest daughters of the Emir are married to Afghan princes, former governors of Serepul and Aktche), and for the defence of an endangered faith, can so revolt, on account of the faulty receipt of their pay, that they pass over to the enemy, and indeed soon after join him in attacking their brethren in religion,— why should it sound so fabulous when we say that the fallen party of Mohammed-Azim-Khan, who was never on very good terms with England, will now, in order to take twofold revenge, with open arms give place to

Russian intrigues and Russian auxiliaries? And is it not striking that England, in this open hostility to one Afghan party, cannot stand on the best footing also with the other? The fugitive Mohammed-Azim will turn his glance towards Peshawur with threatening gesture from his summer residence in Mezar, and will say— "You may wait, Inglis Kafir; you have not helped me !" But Shir-Ali-Khan also, this pretended protégé and partisan of England, cherishes deep resentment in his heart. Not only did England, at a time when he was pursued by misfortune and was in the utmost necessity, not only not give him a farthing, nor lavish on him a word of comfort, but the Viceroy wrote the following lines, in a letter dated from Simla, the 11th June 1866, addressed to Afzal-Khan, who had implored his friendship:—"My friend,—England associates herself only with the real sovereigns of Afghanistan. If your Highness is in a position to consolidate your power in Kabul, and you are deeply animated with feelings of friendship for England, I will gladly receive your Highness as a friend and ally."

Are these words of friendship, or would the Anglo-Indian politicians persuade themselves that, amid Afghan court intrigues, the contents of the letter in question would remain unknown to Shir-Ali? Of course, no one would think of this; in fact, I go further, and assert that the rumours of the understanding between Shir-Ali and Petersburg, if they have any foundation, are only to be ascribed to the reasons we have mentioned.

It would really be too naïve if the English diplomatists in India or London endeavoured to ignore that the Afghans, this warlike race, averse to all culture and civilisation, and consequently still strongly biassed by the childish ideas of the Orientals, would trouble themselves particularly with the consideration of vast political plans. Every Afghan knows that they can endanger English interests by manifest inclination towards Russia; yet whether Afghan interests would thrive in consequence of an alliance with the north or with the south is a matter about which there is as little concern in the mountains of the Hindukush as in Teheran. In the time of Dost-Mohammed-Khan a demonstrable and successful attempt at unity existed; but at the present day the pay-loving soldiers are anxious only for battle and feud, and whoever promises them the nearest opportunity for either is most welcome to them—they are ready to fight under his standard, and so long as his star of fortune is true to him., *i.e.,* so long as he can pay, they will remain faithful to him. In this lies the cause of the changeful fortune of the leaders in the present fraternal contest—in this also lies the possibility that the advancing Russian general may be able to purchase a large number of ready Afghan blades for ready imperials; for in such a service there is, moreover, an old feeling of revenge—a feeling which every Afghan, whether Durani or Yusufzi, whether Gilzi or Kakeri, blindly obeys. At the time that the twilight of Islam sanctity still surrounded me, more than one Afghan has with pious pride introduced himself to me as a former warrior against the unbelievers, *i.e.,* as a slayer of Englishmen—of course, in order to gain the favour of the supposed saint. This contest, although five years have now passed since it occurred, still lives with incredible freshness in the memory of every Afghan. Every family is distinguished by some proud remembrance — every spot in the neighbourhood of Kandahar, Kabul, and Djelahabad is marked by some memorable heroic deed ; and Akbar-Khan, the treacherous murderer of MacNaughten, has been so glorified even after his death, that his son, Djelal-ed-Din-Khan, is more highly considered among the Ulemas than any other Afghan prince. Djelal-ed-Din knew this long ago; but in order to ingratiate himself still more with the people, he made a pilgrimage to Mecca; indeed, this Hadshi-Djelal-ed-Din-Khan will, it seems to me, yet play a conspicuous part, if the civil war raging in Afghanistan should bring about Russian influence, for no one will think of asserting that the Cossacks will have to be dragged by force to the banks of the Hilmend.

I can never agree, therefore, that the Persians, the English, or the Russian Christians would be simply indifferent to the Afghans, as Sir Charles Trevelyan endeavours to show in his letter published in the *Times*, and dated 20th January 1868. This has been proved sufficiently by the above-mentioned Iskender-Khan; it has been proved by the propaganda of the recent adventurer, Firuz-Shah, who, with his anti-Anglican tendencies, is sufficiently well known to the pious Mohammedans of Peshawur and Yarkend ; and it will probably be proved most clearly in the immediate future. Sir Charles Trevelyan, whom the *Times*, ill-informed as it is in Oriental matters, proclaims to be a great authority, is much mistaken if he thinks that the Indian Government will gain the sympathy of the Afghan nation by peaceful intercourse and by the promotion of commerce. He cites Rohilcund as a once flourishing Afghan colony. He points to the extensive trade which Kabul and Kandahar merchants carry on with India; yet he seems to me to know very little of the true character of the Afghans, when he imagines that the position of tea, spice, and indigo merchants exercises the slightest influence on the war-loving chiefs who, *par excellence*, constitute the nation !

I need not draw the attention of the English Secretary of War to the thorough description of the Afghan character by Mountstuart Elphinstone, nor to the constant wars which will draw many a peaceful caravan-knight, and, indeed, many a shepherd, beneath the military banner, as soon as war holds out to him the prospect of gain ; he need only see an Afghan hidalgo walking about the bazaars of Herat, Kandahar, or Kabul, armed with shield, spear, pistols, gun, sword, and yatagan, which he never lays aside if he goes ten paces from his dwelling; or Sir Charles Trevelyan need only linger in the neighbourhood of many an idyllic Lohani, bearing at night, in his romantic valley, a gun bound round his neck with an iron chain, that it may not be cut off, and he will perceive that the furtherance of trade and agriculture is not particularly dear to the Afghans, and he will see why the policy of Lord William Bentinck met with encouragement from the Emir of Sint and from Rendjid-Singh, and why the commercial and peaceful mission of Sir Alexander Burnes to Kabul was followed by the calamitous Afghan war.

Yet why this continual controversy? The Afghans are a mountain race, devoted to warfare, and as, if there is a lack of foreign enemies, they make war upon each other, as history and the present time prove, we can easily imagine with what haste and eagerness each Pashtu will seize the straight, two-edged sabre, when such a fortunate occurrence as the prospect of a Russian-Afghan alliance offers itself to him for the execution of his favourite idea. At the time of the Sepoy revolution in India, the iron hand of Dost-Mohammed-Khan, who was bound by the golden fetter of English rupees, restrained the war-loving Afghans from invading India and joining the rebels; but now the iron hand of Russian ambition impels them forwards, and will they be forbearing?

It is curious to observe how the English Government has recently behaved with regard to these events Whilst, during the year 1867, the whole press, or at any rate the greater part of the press in England, and the official papers in India, indulged in somewhat violent expressions against my political views, and the *Pall Mall Gazette* honoured me even with the title of chief alarmist; now, after the lapse of a year, since my paper upon the Anglo-Russian rivalry in Central Asia has appeared in the columns of *Unsere Zeit*, a strange turn has taken place in political views—a turn which surprised me as much as it will do many of my readers. While the *Times* of January 1867 applauded the Indian Viceroy's policy of "masterly inactivity," and ridiculed the plan then entertained of occupying Herat, we read in the same paper of 10th July the opinion: "It would be difficult for any one to prove that the Russians had no designs on British India;" it is as if I were hearing the echo of the words expressed by myself in 1864, and at that time ridiculed by this very *Times*, which spoke of me as an Hungarian, and therefore a foe to Russia—

as a traveller, and therefore a man of exaggerated ideas ; and expressed its satisfaction that the English of 1864 were no longer those of 1840, who, alarmed at the phantom of Russia's advance towards India, at once prepared for arms. Not only the *Times* of London and Calcutta, but others, some English, some Indian daily, weekly, and monthly papers, did not join in the chorus of the song, " Fürchte dich nicht, mein knäblein," and the helpless infant of English diplomacy slumbered truly, though it was plain to perceive that sleep did not so easily weigh down its eyelids.

It slumbered till the cannon roar sounded in its ears from the Yaxartes, the noise of which was made still more threatening by the chatter in the Kabul bazaars. It was the beginning of April 1868 that the slumbering lion began to show signs of waking. To send a diplomatic inquiry to Petersburg they neither could nor would ; for the English papers, and indeed the Government organs, had before screamed themselves hoarse in asserting that Russia was most welcome as a neighbour on our north-west frontier in India—of course, far more welcome than the hordes of fanatical Afghans, Beludje, and others ; that she was forced by circumstances into an aggressive policy in the south of Central Asia, just as we had ourselves once been to the incorporation of a dozen Indian kings. They could not, therefore, make much ado ; yet, as the report of the advance of Russian Cossacks and of their brilliant victories drew nearer and nearer, and a feeling of uneasiness, as we may well imagine, was aroused in Calcutta, they were compelled to deviate from their boasted path of indifference and strict neutrality, in order, as we now see, to adopt an entirely opposite course, namely, one of defensive, and, if appearances do not deceive us, of even offensive policy.

Of course, the public feeling in India itself, besides the events on the Oxus, have greatly contributed to bring about this change of conduct. The Anglo-Indians are, as my readers know, almost entirely Russophobists. They live among the Indian people; they know their modes of thought; they are also tolerably well acquainted with the neighbouring races; and we cannot therefore be surprised if they are rather more alarmed at the approach of the Russians to India than the official world on the Hooghly, who join in the refrain of the Viceroy, or than the politicians on the Thames, who understand but little of Asiatic policy. These Anglo-Indians have been reproached with desiring the policy of intervention, not from patriotism or political conviction, but from love of adventure and of military excitement—in fact, there was a regular dispute beween both parties; and when we take into consideration the passion with which this war with the pen was fought out, we shall then first perceive how great the danger must have been which obliged the gentlemen on the Hooghly to surrender to their irritated adversaries..

Yet, what are the symptoms, I shall be asked, from which I perceive this change in the policy of England towards Russia? The answer to the question is very simple.

The first is the withdrawal of the Viceroy, Sir John Lawrence, from the supreme direction of affairs, and the appointment of the Earl of Mayo, the Irish Minister, as his successor. The papers tell us, indeed, that Sir

John Lawrence was compelled to leave the injurious Indian climate on account of his health, and that he required physical refreshment. Natural as this may sound, it is scarcely intelligible to me, that a thorough Anglo-Indian, who had for years lived in India, must suddenly and at such a conjuncture retire from the harmful influences of the climate, which, as is well known, after the first few years of trial, agrees well with every Briton for the rest of his life.

Sir John Lawrence, up to the present time, has not only been beloved in London, but he has been even petted, so that I regard his withdrawal from affairs as identical with the withdrawal of the policy alluded to. We will speak presently of the mistake in the appointment of his successor, that is, in the choice of a man who has hitherto had nothing to do with Indian affairs.

In the second place, the change of policy is also recognisable from the tone of the press. The *Times*, the *Spectator*, and their whole genus from within and without the boundaries of Great Britain, have latterly remarkably forborne to inveigh against the so-called "Alarmists"—in fact, without intending it, they have become alarmists themselves ; and if they have not directly advised intervention, they have entered upon dangerous questions, such as, Would it be better to attack Russia on this side or on that side of the Indus ? How could Afghanistan be neutralised ? How could Persia be made an ally ? &c.

In the third place, some steps have been already taken which confirm our assertion. The order has been given for the rapid completion of the railway from Delhi to Peshawur, and also for the completion of the railway in the valley of the Indus, in order thus to expedite the communication from Calcutta and Bombay. A corps of engineers has been despatched to survey the Bolan and Kheiber passes, and to construct there, at suitable places, fortresses, arsenals, and provision magazines. Lord Napier of Magdala has to turn aside from the apotheosis of the English, and to undertake the command of the Bombay army in India, whither he goes accompanied by the best hopes of the British people. In fact, they go still further, and intend to renew the old fortifications in Quetta and Beludjistan, and to fill them with English garrisons. These are, without doubt, important steps, indicating no indifferent political views. But what most essentially confirms us in our opinion is the already adopted initiative of an offensive war, intimated by the recent tidings which have come to us of the revolt in Agror. Ever since the campaign of Sittana and Bhotan, it has been universally known that the line of English military posts is not in the securest state in this north-east frontier of India, which swarms with such easily inflammable elements. Here, moreover, are to be found those colonies of wild, fanatical Mohammedans, who, from their inexorable hostility to the régime of the Kafir, are securely banished to these mountainous districts, and who, under the direction of chiefs such as the Achond of Swat, the temporary saint, and the adventurer Firuz-Shah, who asserts himself to be the last scion of the royal house of Delhi, endeavour to create constant disturbances, in order to turn them to their own material advantage under the pretext of intellectual efforts, and thus frequently to perplex the governor of Peshawur.

Every one will understand that, under such circumstances, there is rarely a lack of skirmishes and depredations; and the tidings that on the 10th August a troop of the Tchigerzai race had attacked the guard of Agror in this very Hezareh district, and had been put to flight by Colonel Rothney, would certainly not have excited our attention to the same extent, if the Indian papers had not given extraordinary importance to the circumstance, and depicted the threatening danger in the most glaring colours. After the band had been repulsed as quickly as it had advanced, it was suddenly reported that the Tchigerzai and Hassanzai were mighty descendants of those Pathanes who form the dreaded Swat confederation, and that the Government would do well to concentrate a strong force in this quarter. Of course, the statement of the threatening reports is exaggerated in England, and it is even asserted that not only in the north of Peshawur, but also in the south—for instance, among the Bezutis—symptoms of disorder are showing themselves; and no one is astonished suddenly to see in Peshawur an army of observation, consisting of 10,000 men, under the command of General Wilde, in order to extinguish the flame as speedily as possible. It is also stated that a great part of the troops who had served in Abyssinia are ordered to the north-west corner of India not far from Peshawur.

Whether these Tchigerzais in Hezareh are in any way allied with the Afghans is much to be doubted, yet no one will deny that this concentration of English troops is not directed against the bands of booty-loving adventurers, however much Mohammedan fanaticism may lie at the background of their plans. The English army of observation, which is to be still more strongly reinforced, stands on the frontier of India, to watch the events of Central Asia and Afghanistan. It has been observed that the show of peaceful inclinations and neutrality is useless in reconnoitring ; a telescope of cannons has therefore been adopted, for of late John Bull prefers to cast his amorous glances upon his Russian rival through the mouths of several thousand gun-barrels.

I do not, therefore, think I am mistaken, when, from the tokens I have mentioned, I infer a decided political change in the English Ministry ; and when I inform my readers that the Conservative Ministry on the Thames, through their representative on the Hooghly, are noting down a new air in place of the old and variously played " Etudes sur laisser aller,"—an air which can very easily be played with the thunder of cannons and other sensational accessories, to the accompaniment of a Turkish Banda.

If this be really the case, only a few questions are left for us to make. In the first place, what are the steps which England has to take against her powerful adversary ? In the second place, what are the results which may be expected from the future measures of Great Britain on the other side of the Indus and in the villages of the Hindukush ?

No one will or can condemn a return to the path of necessary activity and a renunciation of this long inaction, although a change of policy three months ago would have been far more beneficial to the interests of India and far less dangerous to England. To be able to assert that Russia will mistake the true object of the concentration of troops round Peshawur, and will not see in it an act of hostile opposition, one must either be an extreme optimist or but little acquainted with the Oriental cunning and suspicious policy of the Petersburg Court. Whilst these measures could have been taken before the occupation of Samarkand without exciting the slightest suspicion among the Russians, it is hardly possible in the present day to avoid a diplomatic correspondence between Petersburg and London on Central Asiatic questions. For Russia, circumspect Russia, cannot help seeing at the first glance, in this movement of the Britons, an hostility to her own designs on the Oxus territory.

To the Afghans, also, a decided step on the part of England, instead of her constant tardiness, would have been far more helpful than it is now. Whilst the English Government, as the Mohammedans say, halted prayer-less between two mosques, Shir-Ali, at least so report informs us, when no subsidies came from Calcutta for the recovery of his throne, procured them in Petersburg. I repeat, this rests only on report. Yet would it not have been better if England, when she saw Azim-Khan's star declining—and a watchful state should observe everything—had half-secretly, half-openly offered her hand to the courageous, ambitious, and ardent Shir-Ali-Khan, who is no Shah Shedsha, and, as the support of the house of Dost-Mohammed-Khan is almost traditional on the part of England, had helped him with arms and money on his way to Kabul? For that Shir-Ali-Khan, who was trying all possible means to bring the gentlemen of Calcutta to his side, would have accepted money, ay, gladly accepted it, every one in India knows well, and Sir John Lawrence best of all. Would it not have been better to be now seeing the supplanted son of

Dost-Mohammed-Khan arriving before Kabul with the help of English money? Would not the prospects be far more satisfactory if he had placed the royal Afghan mesned (throne) under English protection, and his son, Serdar-Yakub, had gained English defence for the citadels of Bala-Hissar, and if he had been able to maintain his conquest only by looking to the further support of the Frengi? No one will certainly answer this in the negative; and in order, therefore, not again to fall into further errors, in order to step onwards with success upon the beaten path, England has most speedily laid aside the suicidal weapon of irresolution. The favourite maxim, "What do the adjacent, wild, barbarous hordes concern us? We wish to have no new entanglements, we wish for no new Abyssinia," must be given up. England must act, must act speedily, and she must act with united powers.

Above all, the errors committed must be compensated for, and Shir-Ali-Khan must be made the friend of England.

If the friendly union begun after the death of his father is relied upon, and no third party interferes, the renewal of an offensive and defensive alliance between Afghanistan, who needs money and arms, and England, who possesses both, is no particularly difficult task. A diplomatist well acquainted with the locality and full of practical and theoretic knowledge would now be especially valuable. Shir-Ali-Khan's attention should be drawn to the critical position of his future—*i.e.*, to the possible alliance of his rival with Russia; in fact, he ought to be convinced of this, and the English alliance should be proposed as a suitable counter-balance. No one will for a moment doubt that, if such an initiative were successfully carried out, he would gladly comply with the desire of England, namely, that he would commence diplomatic relations, and would erect a few forts destined for his own protection and occupied for his comfort by a mixed garrison; in a word, that he would be far less opposed than his father to an open and sure approximation to British India. If this, however, is not the case, if Shir-Ali, as report tells us, owes his present success really to Russian and Persian influence, and shows himself hostile to all English insinuations, then nothing is left but by force to give advice to this child of Afghan diplomacy, since he will not see the threatening danger from which he cannot save himself alone. The armed intervention, which would have been avoidable in the year 1867, is no longer so under the present circumstances; the English must make themselves masters of the two chief stations on the easy way to India (I mean Herat and Kandahar); they must regard these as the advanced works of their frontier fortifications, and must as such defend them. I, for my part, lay great weight on this road, for the far shorter way from Herat to Kabul across the Hezareh Mountains, which the English have so often sent to explore, and with which the Russians also wish to acquaint themselves, yet which the scientific traveller Nicholaus von Khanikow was not allowed to visit, is very impracticable; in fact, it is almost inaccessible to an army, and this has been plainly shown during the recent campaign of Shir-Ali-Khan against his brother. The former had the Hezarehs on his side, and yet in his contest with his rival, he chose the circuitous route through Kandahar and

H

Gizne. Unfortunately this armed intervention, the results of the errors of English diplomacy, is now the lesser evil to choose from. England has no other expedient. It is all the same whether the English flag waves on the battlements of Herat and Kandahar, and whether English influence predominates in Kabul; something must be done to show the Court of Petersburg that the approach of the Cossacks to India is in nowise regarded with indifference, but rather with the utmost mistrust.

Had this taken place sooner, Russia would certainly have advanced more cautiously and slowly in her hostile move, although she would not have wholly given up her plan, than she has advanced under the shelter of English indifference. The Russians, although unprecedented in the tenacity with which they carry out their plans, are never wont, as history teaches us, to step forward with surprising movements. Like the mole under ground, whose movements are manifested on the surface of the clod, often standing still to gather up its strength for further advance, so the Russians—as, for example, now with regard to Bokhara, whose capture would be only the work of a few hours—are wont to give themselves up to a temporary repose, in order to arrive at their aim with surer success. They do not indeed turn back when they are attacked, but they are more cautious; and it is this caution which leaves the enemy time to prepare for the encounter which will and must ensue. We have spoken of the forcible entry into Afghanistan— a proceeding which at once brings to the mind of every Englishman ghastly and terrible images — to every Englishman who remembers Lord Auckland's rash policy and its melancholy results. Still I think, with the gifted and clever English writer who has published the best papers on this question in the *Friend of India* and *The Englishman,* that it is time no longer to regard this catastrophe, which was rather a consequence of the incapability of the general commanding, or the English inexperience of the country, with the feeling of panic-fear, but with the eye of testing criticism. So much has been already said of the unexampled valour and heroic behaviour of the Afghans, that the world looks upon each individual one as a knight *sans peur*, though not *sans reproche.* Yet much, very much is exaggerated. The Afghans are, like the Sikhs, braver than the Özbegs, the Persians, the Turks, and the Arabs. They are mountain races, accustomed to murder and rapine, trained in labour and privation, averse to luxury and effeminacy; still they are ever Asiatics, who talk of the butchery of days, of Niagara-like cataracts of blood, of heaps of corpses high as Mount Elbrus, of the battle roar, compared with which the thunder is a soft whisper, when, after a fierce contest of days, after an engagement on both sides, no more than a hundred or two hundred bodies cover the field. Königratz and Magenta, even under Timur and Djengis, whatever Oriental historians may say, would never have been conceivable in the East, and could never have occurred. The Emir of Bokhara was in Khokand in 1863 with almost 8000 soldiers. The campaign lasted four or five months, and the number of the slain, of those smothered in the tumult, and of those who perished by immoderate tea-drinking, amounted to no more than sixty! Or is it credible that the Bokhariots who fell in the recent contests were all killed by the Russian guns? I would wager that the half perished by flight. Indeed when we ourselves talk of these famous Afghans, who amongst us has seen the battle-fields of the fierce fraternal contest on the Hilmend, where they tell us of a hundred and often of a thousand slain? The British soldiers who perhaps make so much of Afghan and Sikh valour, in order to cast a halo on themselves, will pardon me if I whisper confidentially in their ear that much in this respect is *bosch* (nonsense); and that if the English policy were compelled to inter-pose by force in Hindostan, Snider rifles and Armstrong cannons would do their duty satisfactorily, if managed by English and not Sepoy hands; weapons which, in the Afghan campaign of 1839, overcame with astonish-ing ease apparently gigantic difficulties. Afghans are certainly not much better than the Marabuts under Abd-el-Kader, or the Absache and Tchetchenzes under Shamil; and yet the former were conquered by Frenchmen, and the latter by unskilful Russians. It would therefore now not only be unsuitable, but highly dangerous to exhibit fear. The Northern Colossus, which is gigantic even in its plans, is threatening British India in two directions; the first, that on the north-west, has formed the subject of our preceding remarks; the second, that on the north-east, a route comparatively still vaguely dim, passing to India through East Tur-kestan through the Karakorum Pass, we will discuss in the next paper.

II.

From Bokhara and Khokand, from this comparatively better known and more discussed part of Central Asia, owing to the crowd of recent events, I will now take my readers to a region only scantily mentioned by the ablest geographers—to a region which, even since the visits of the enterprising Venetian Marco Polo and the zealous Catholic brother Goes, has been brought so little nearer the eyes of the West, that a thicker obscurity envelops it as regards ourselves, than prevails over any of the remote parts of Africa or Australia.

As the name indicates, this is the eastern part of that region of Asia which was formerly known under the name of Tartary or High Tartary, and which now bears the name of Central Asia or Turkestan. East Turkestan is also called Tartary by many Chinese, because Chinese rule extends over the Tartars there. Formerly it was also named Little Bucharia. In Central Asiatic documents it is often called Alti-Shekr, Alti-Tchakan, the " Six Cities," or Yiti-Shekr, the " Seven Cities." The oddest thing, however, is that the natives themselves have no special name by which to designate their home. I, at least, have only heard of Kashkarlik, Kashkarians, Yarkendlik, Yarkendians, and others ; and, if I do not mistake, there is no especial denomination in the ordinary popular tongue : the before-mentioned European and Asiatic names are at any rate unknown there.

Although nameless in itself, this part of Asia, which we will designate by the most suitable name of East Turkestan, is nevertheless of great interest. Surrounded on three sides by lofty, and for the most part snow-covered mountains, it has in the centre a fathomless plain of sand—namely, the western point of the vast and fearful Gobi Desert. On the north, Turkestan is separated from Khokand, Russia, and the Chinese province Ili or Dsungaria by the southern branches of the Thien-Shan, or, according to the native dialect, Tengri-Ula (the Celestial Mountain). This boundary is in many parts like a steep rocky wall, rising higher and higher until it reaches the Muzart, which is covered with perpetual snow and ice, at about 42° 28′ north lat. and 80° 38′ east long. On the east, it is separated from the wild and unappropriated district of Bedachshan by the Bolurtag (Crystal Mountain), also called Boluttag (Cloud Mountain), and the tableland of Pamir, which is designated in Central Asia as Bamidünja (the Roof of the World). On this high plateau is the lake Sariköl (Yellow Lake), in which the bold English traveller Wood discovered the source of the Oxus ; and at the southeastward runs the lofty mountain range of Pushti-Khar, according to recent English measurement 19,000 feet above the level of the sea. To the south stretches the mountain chain of Kün-Lün or Kuen-Lun, some of the peaks of which are known, as Dsing-Lin, Mustak, and Karakorum, and which, according to W. H. Johnson's statement, contains vaster plains, at a height of 17,300 and 16,700 feet, than the less lofty mountain range of the Himalayas. Lastly, on the east, the Gobi Desert, also called the Belikava Desert, forms a barrier, if we may so designate it ; a desert which, in some parts—as, for example, from Karashehr to Turfan and Komul, or from Kultcha to Khoten—is only a field for the most fearful stories of hobgoblins and phantoms, a region to which just as little attention is given by the natives as the Deshtikuvir in Persia, or similar tracts of land in Turkestan and Arabia. There is a remarkable fabulous story told of three great cities which are said to have stood in the place of the present Khoten, but which subsequently were so completely buried by a tremendous sand-storm that at the present day it is only in extraordinary storms that some of the buildings appear above the sand. I call this a fabulous story, but that places have been buried under the sand is proved by the successful excavations which have brought a number of objects to light, a fact frequently mentioned by Mr Johnson.

In the nature of its soil East Turkestan is, on a smaller scale, somewhat similar to the present Iran, which likewise is surrounded on three sides by mountains, and has a large desert in its centre. On the other hand, it is comparatively more watered and fertile, although not so industriously cultivated as the lands of the King of Persia. From the high mountains, both those on the north as well as on the west and south, flow many brooks, streams, and rivers, frequently wildly swollen by the melting snow from the heights, but rarely, in fact never, dried up. We will not weary our readers with the names of these streams and rivers, because those at present geographically established are in my humble opinion as faulty as possible. The Yarkendian calls the brook flowing through his district the Yarkend-Deryah; so also the Kashkarian, the Aksuan, and the Khotenian all name the stream after their own town, as is the case in many places in the East, where the same river has a different name in almost every district; we shall therefore be more distinct and intelligible if we state that the masses of water flowing from the three sides mentioned into the lower basin of the central part of East Turkestan unite into one important river. This river is called the Tarim, which means fertility in the language of the country. It falls into the Lopnur—*i.e.*, the Dragon Lake—after having passed through a large tract of barren land.

Besides this important river-system, East Turkestan is traversed by a still greater number of artificial and natural canals, called Oestek and Yap in the language of the country, which give extraordinary fertility to the vigorous soil along their banks. Added to this we must mention the favourable climate of the country, which renders it possible for more manifold and more various productions to thrive in a small district than can be cultivated in other tracts of land five or six times larger in extent. Whilst in Aksu the winter is rude and severe, and the ground is for three months covered with snow, we find near Yarkend and Khoten a perfectly southern temperature, and rice, cotton, and silk flourish in luxuriant abundance. Vegetation, therefore, although the heights are less woody than in Khokand, is, so far as I can speak from acquired information, more rich and beautiful, as the recent Russian traveller there, Captain Welichanoff, described it to be: the wheat and barley are finer than in Bokhara and Khiva. There is a great abundance of fruit and kitchen produce; and although there is no trade carried on in these articles with the adjacent countries, the fact that the population can recover in an unusually short time from the sore wounds of constant civil war and discord, furnishes the surest testimony to the wealth and fertility of the soil.

Equally little has Turkestan to complain of its animal kingdom, both as regards quality and quantity. Horned cattle are indeed but rare here as elsewhere in Central Asia, but the sheep are the best of their kind; indeed, the fine Cashmere wool, which we assign to the valleys of the Himalaya, comes from Khoten, Yarkend, and Aksu, from whence — as we learn from a pamphlet recently published by T. D. Forsyth, who, for the sake of making some commercial observations, spent some time on the borders of Cashmere—it is yearly brought, especially from Yarkend, over the Karakorum Pass, to Cashmere, and is there prepared. The horses, although not so beautiful as those of the Turkomans, are strongly built, and are very cheap in the country. They are as much in request for the transport of goods as the camels, which, according to the statement of my former travelling companions, surpass even the famous breeds of Andchoi and Belkh. Lastly, we must also mention the goats, which are larger and stronger here than elsewhere, and about Yarkend are employed as beasts of burden.

As regards the mineral kingdom, we have only scanty or vague information; nevertheless, almost all travellers speak of the abundance of gold, which is obtained not from mines, but from the sandy shores of the rivers. There is reference to this also in Herodotus' fabulous statement of the gold-dust of these regions, which the old Father of History tells us is dug up by ants as large as dogs. There is, besides, much silver, iron, tin, copper, saltpetre, and brimstone; especially famous, however, is a kind of stone, which is highly valued in China, called by the English yade—*i.e.*, Ya-stone, and by the natives

Yadatashi; it is considered an antidote to dangerous snakes and scorpions, and is held in high esteem throughout Central Asia, and especially in China.

Space fails us here for a more accurate description of the nature of the soil and the products of Turkestan ; yet I had sufficient opportunity, from the prosperity of my travelling companions—all, comparatively speaking, belonging to the lowest class—to infer the wealth of the land. Enthusiastic as these men were as to the excellences of one district or another through which I travelled with them, they allowed, nevertheless, that no tract of land, either in Turkey or in Persia and Central Asia, could dispute the palm with their native country, and both Khokandians and Bokhariots agreed with them.

That Turkestan is not more flourishing, under such favourable circumstances, may simply be ascribed to her constant civil wars and unceasing contests with the Chinese sovereign. The places of importance at the present day are Kashgar, the most considerable of the six cities or districts, the presumptive capital of the whole of East Turkestan, containing more than 15,000 houses built of coarse clay, seventeen medresses, several kervan-serails, which in time of peace swarm with Bokhariots, Khokandians, Afghans, Jews, and people of Cashmere, who carry on an important trade, but not till after they have, at great expense, gained the necessary privileges for so doing from the Chinese magistrates. Kashgar is less famous for its schools and mosques than for the burial-place of Apak-Khodja, about a mile from the town, over whose remains stands a high dome, covered with blue glazed tiles, in form and size rather like the tomb of Hazreti-Shah-Zinde in Samarkand.* It is also famous for its citadel—a structure more dreaded than beloved—which formerly lodged a Chinese garrison 5000 men strong, and in which can be had, as my gastronomical friends assured me, not only the strongest lashes, but the best mantuis, a kind of minced meat. The latter is certainly more highly esteemed than the former by the good people of East Turkestan. All round Kashgar there are a great number of villages and small isolated farms, the most important of which are Feizabad and Khanarik. The entire district is uninterruptedly well cultivated, and the journey to Yarkend can be made through an unlimited succession of fields and gardens. On the way to Yarkend lies the Yengi-Hisar, called also Yengi-Sheher district, with a capital of the same name, and about 8000 houses (according to Welichanoff). The territory of this province is comparatively small, but, nevertheless, it is tolerably well cultivated. The town has gained a reputation from the fact that here the best lac is prepared for embellishing saddles; still the inhabitants, owing to their limited mental capacity, hold a very doubtful reputation even among the races of East Turkestan. And this is, indeed, an extraordinary *testimonium paupertatis!*

From here the way lies to Yarkend, the most populous city in East Turkestan, situated on both banks of a river which rushes by with the speed of an arrow. The town is said to contain about 32,000 houses; it is the residence of the Chinese and Mohammedan governors. It carries on considerable trade; among others, a despicable slave-trade, which here lies in the hands of the

* See my "Reise in Mittelasien," p. 165.

Bedachshans. These import their goods from the mountainous district of the Kafirs, or Siah-Pushs (the black-dressed), and also from the ranks of the Wachanis; * but, nevertheless, they have acquired an odour of sanctity among the native races. As this place is a main emporium for the trade going on between East Turkestan and Southern Siberia on the one side, and between Cashmere and India on the other, Yarkend may in time, if political affairs should become settled there, grow into a place of commercial importance, as Tashkend has recently done; for it has enjoyed at all times a reputation of great wealth, just as Kashgar has been known by its intelligence and piety.

The important places of the district are Maral-Bashi in the north; Yularik and Kargalik in the south.

Khoten, or Iltchi, as it has recently been called, may be reckoned as the fourth district. It is situated in the extreme south, and in old times was famous throughout the whole Islam East for its excellent musk. At the present day, it is, however, remarkable for the manufacture of various silk materials, which are even to be met with in the bazaars at Constantinople; it is no less distinguished for the Ya-stone before mentioned.

The capital contains about 40,000 houses. There is a good bazaar, and on Thursdays a weekly market is held. By the name "bazaar," my readers must not imagine anything but an ordinary row of low, clay huts, the roofs of which are fastened with cane-mats; and they must not imagine streets arched over, only scanty remains of which are to be found in the East of the present day. Equally poor are the fortifications of

* *Cf.* my " Skizzen aus Mittelasien," p. 266.

Khoten, as well as of the other towns of East Turkestan. In Bucharia they are proud if a wall is built twelve or fifteen feet high, of clods of earth three feet broad, intermingled with chaff. Walls of this kind are regarded as iron fortresses; for, in Chinese Tartary, as I have been repeatedly told, no single wall is more than eight feet high and two feet broad.

Other places of importance are Kargalik, Baza, Kilian, Bish-Arik, and Melik Shah, all situated on the road leading over the Karakorum Pass to Cashmere.

If my readers, whom I have wearied against my will with Tartar nomenclature, will now accompany me through the desert of Gobi, across the Tarim to the north, they will arrive at the north-west frontier of Turkestan in the Usch district. The capital is Turfan, more frequently called Usch Turfan. This capital is no better than a poor village of 4000 or 5000 houses; famous for its excellent tobacco, for its extensive pastures, and perhaps also for the historical fact that in 1765, during a revolt, all the inhabitants were massacred by the Chinese. The eastern boundary is formed by the rich, large, and important province of Aksu, with its capital of the same name, in which a lively trade is carried on with southern Russia over the Thien-Shan Mountains. Here the caravans yearly meet on their way to Kizil-Djar (Petropawloffsk) and Pulad (Semipalatinsk). They are far larger, especially the spring caravans, than those of Tashkend, as this road is used for all the demand for Russian productions not only in East Turkestan, but even in Cashmere and Thibet. Aksu also prides itself not a little on its learning and piety. My great friend, Hadji-Bilal, who is not

unknown to the readers of my " Reise in Mittelasien,"
estimated the number of the eager students of the
Koran by thousands, and often boasted that in the sixteen mosques of his native city there were more prayers
offered, than in the two hundred mosques of Constantinople, which is already becoming half apostate.   Like
every other place, Aksu also has its speciality ; here it is
excellent grease, good bread, and the strikingly low
value in which women are held.   This does not astonish
me, for the industrious and busy inhabitants of this
province are famous for the fact that two-thirds of their
offspring are always female, and only one-third male ;
and, moreover, the women are strikingly deficient in
physical charms.

Many people, as, for example, the above-mentioned
Welichanoff, are accustomed to reckon the provinces
Bai, Sairam, and Kutche as belonging to Aksu, thus
rounding off the territory of the Six Cities; yet this
seems to me rather a geographical idea than an actually
existing distribution.   The present inhabitants of East
Turkestan will no longer recognise the expression Alti-
Shehr, for, according to their statement, the three last-
mentioned places, as well as the more easterly districts of Karashehr, Turfan, and Komul—in a word, the
whole of the Celestial Empire which the Chinese designate as one province by the name of Thien-Shan-Nan-
Lu—belong to their native land ; and were it not that
the communication eastwards is impeded by strict
political measures, we should annually meet with as
many Komulians, Karashehrians, and Turfanians on the
pilgrims' route to Mecca, as is the case among the
inhabitants of the first-mentioned six provinces, who are

firmly attached to the great Islam body in West Turkestan. So, as matters now are, or rather, to speak more correctly, as they were at the time of my travels in Central Asia, only a few East Turkestanians had ventured, or even can venture, to penetrate to Komul; still my ever-restless friend, Hadji-Bilal was there, and he told me that the whole tract of land of forty days' journey was thickly peopled and cultivated, so that in a journey of more than a month, few days elapsed on which the traveller could not offer prayer in a regularly-built mosque, or in one raised on terraces on the highway. It is a remarkable fact, communicated to me on good authority, that the Komulians, on their pilgrimages to the Mussulman west, either travel through the provinces of Shen-Si and Hu-Peh to Canton, therefore without touching Peking, or through Thibet and India —so strictly is all intercourse with the Western brethren of the faith forbidden.

This little sketch of East Turkestan would certainly be still more incomplete than it already is if we did not mention the routes by which this part of Central Asia communicates with the adjacent lands.

These routes run in four different directions to all the four quarters of the heavens. The route leading to Bokhara or to the west generally, passes through Kashgar, across the Terek Pass to Osch, and thence to Khokand. This is a very old, almost the oldest road, by which the inhabitants of the Celestial Empire had intercourse with Western Asia and with Europe by land. Here those silk goods and articles of luxury were transported which were sent to Rome, and which excited to such a great extent the indignation of the philosophers on the banks of the Tiber. This highway also, comparatively speaking, is the safest and the easiest. It is usually traversed in sixteen days, and the time would certainly have been considerably shorter if some narrow and slippery mountain roads on the steep declivities of the Terek Pass did not impede communication; for although the predatory Karakirghises abound in these districts, it is very rarely that we hear of acts of violence committed on caravans.

Southward from this Terek highway there is a road leading from Samarkand to Kashgar, which, passing through Wachan, Bedachshan, and Khulm, to the northern point of the Pamir plateau, is half as short again as the road from Samarkand through Khokand to East Turkestan. As I am informed by eye-witnesses, nothing but the before-mentioned predatory nomads prevent this shorter way from being used; yet this seems to me to be a mistake. The road through Bedachshan to the Oxus was never a frequented one; not in consequence of the predatory nomadic tribes, but far rather on account of the lofty, steep, and inaccessible heights of the Bolur mountain.*

There are two great highways in the north—one passes through Aksu eastward from the lake Issikköl to Kizil-Djar (Petropawloffsk) and is taken chiefly by caravans proceeding to Russia; it is, moreover, the favourite route of all those pilgrims who intend to halt among the Nogai-Tartars on their way to Constantinople.

* My opinion on this point has recently been refuted by the personal experiences of the Yarkend traveller, Mr Shaw. Mr Shaw asserts that the road through Tchitral to Yarkend may be indeed a circuitous one, but it is far more practicable than any other route whatever across the Kuen-Lun.

From Aksu, besides this road, there is another towards the right to the province of Ili, and to its capital, Kultsha; but this is chiefly used by Chinese and by the Tarandjis. settled there. From one point to the other it measures about 417 English miles; it passes, however, through the most mountainous part of the Thien-Shan mountain, across the ridge Muzart, famous for its high glaciers. This is one highway in the north; the other, likewise frequented by Chinese and Mongols, leads from Komul through Turfan and Urumtchi to Dsungaria.

In the Middle Ages this Urumtchi, at that time called Bischbalik, was a place of great importance, and the eastern capital of the Khanate of Tchagatai. At the present day it is famous only for its strong Chinese garrison, its great tea emporium, and the great horse-market. If we turn towards the south, Cashmere and India can be reached from two different points; namely, from Yarkend, as well as from Khoten, across the Kuen-Lun mountain through the Karakorum Pass. The former road, namely, the Yarkend, is the most frequented, although the cold is often insufferable on the heights of the pass mentioned. In fact, an Englishman, Mr Johnson, never ventured to sleep on his way to Khoten in November; and he tells us that he rode for a long time in the morning sun with his head covered with icicles. The other, namely, the Khoten road, joins the former only on the banks of the Karakash, and so far it is also tolerably safe. From thence to the foot of the mountain, the traveller is much exposed to the predatory nomads. These, if I mistake not, are the Karakirghises, who in a remarkable manner extend their excursions as far as

I

the south-easterly point of Turkestan.   The inhabitants of East Turkestan, especially the pilgrims and
merchants, for the most part take the road past Yarkend
to Leh, the chief place in Ladak or Central Thibet;
and although the accounts of moving plains and hills,
which have hurled whole caravans into deep mountain
abysses, of benumbing cold, and other things, alarm
travellers, still the Yarkend-Kilan and Karakorum route
is the most frequented, and is traversed in twenty-five
or thirty days, while that leading to Khoten, although
much shorter, is comparatively less used.

Recently, however, the way through the Tchang-
Tchenmo Pass has taken the place of all former ones,
although this is also not practicable at all seasons of the
year.   It begins at Leh in Ladak, passes through the
Masimik Pass (18,784 ft.), the Tchang-Tchenmo Pass
(17,501 ft.), and the Tchang-Lang Pass (18,839 ft.),
across the lofty plain of Lingsi Teng (17,164 ft.), with its
chilly winds; it then takes a north-westerly direction to
Tchong-Tasch, from whence the traveller can proceed
in a straight line across the Dipsikul to Shadulla, the
southern boundary of East Turkestan, arriving there far
more rapidly than by any of the ways known hitherto.
From Shadulla (11,951 ft.) there is of course still a very
difficult road to the plain of East Turkestan, yet this
route is increasingly taken in consequence of the favour
with which the English regard it.

The eastern road, that to Peking, has been already
mentioned in my " Reise in Mittelasien," p. 318.   The
traffic on it was never very lively, if we except the tea-
caravans, which repair from the middle of the Celestial
Empire to East Turkestan, and the transmission of

troops; but at the present time, since the outbreak of the revolution in these districts, it has wholly ceased.

As regards the present inhabitants of East Turkestan or Chinese Tartary, we must preface their characterisation with the remark, that they are undoubtedly the descendants of that part of the great Turkish race which distinguished itself earliest above the other races by a political life and by pure Turkish social relations; in short, that they are the remains of the oldest Turkish race in the world.

This East Turkestan—that part which stretches from the Chinese province of Kansu, that is, from Yu-Tchou, the most western portion of the Chinese wall, to the eastern edge of the Pamir plateau—has been inhabited by Turks from time immemorial, at any rate as far back as historical records take us. Western Europe was first acquainted with them through the Nestorian missionaries, who repaired hither in the second century after Christ. Subsequently, that is, in the time of the French traveller Rubruquis, they were first called Uigurs; but this is not their correct denomination. They were Uigurs, because they belonged to the Uigurian race of the Turks, which is still in existence; yet they called themselves Turks; their language was the Turkish dialect, and the name Uigur is as little to be found in their documents as the special denomination of the nation, as any other branch or family designation of the Özbegs is to be met with when the entire Özbeg or Turkish race is in question. It does not belong to my present task to examine the statements of my learned predecessor on this subject, the gifted author of " Western China" (*Edinburgh Review*, April 1868), who considers the

Uigurs to speak the Chinese language. It is sufficient to mention that the Uigurs have played a very remarkable part in the history of the civilisation of Central Asia, and perhaps for this reason are not wholly unworthy of the attention which I have bestowed on them in my work, "Uigurische Sprachmonumente und das Kudatku Bilik." The influence of their culture has asserted itself from the beginning of our era to the appearance of Djengis Khan—on the one side, in the north, far into the Mongolian steppes; and on the other side, to the east, to the banks of the Zerefshan. The first Christian missionaries found them zealous followers of the doctrine of Buddha, which, from their vicinity to Thibet, that old seat of the Buddhist religion, they had received unalloyed. Subsequently, Christianity also made considerable advances among them; for, as the learned Colonel Yule informs us, there was in Kashimgar, probably the Kashgar of the present day, even in the fourteenth century a bishopric of the Nestorian Church, which sounds all the more strangely, as the Arabs made no small merit of having converted this region only by the flash of Kuteibe's sword.

The most important traces of the civilising influence of the Uigurs were to be perceived among the Mongols. After Djengis Khan united their separated *olosse* (races) into one nation, they adopted the written characters of the Uigurs. Uigurian writers and accountants were placed in all parts of the gigantic empire; indeed, even in the fourteenth and fifteenth centuries, when the Uigurs had ceased to exist as a nation, their language and written characters remained as eloquent monuments of past culture, not only in their old home, Turkestan, but as far as the shores of the Sea of Azov and the Crimea; indeed, among all the Turkish races acquainted with the art of writing, except the Osmanlis and Azabeidshanians.

They never seem to have formed a great independent power, so far as we can give credence to historical tradition. Even before the time of Djengis, it was only the prestige of their past that preserved their importance, and subsequently this also vanished. The original inhabitants of East Turkestan became so intermingled in language and physiognomy, owing to new-comers from West Turkestan and from kindred nomadic races, such as the Kirghises and the Kasaks, and, on the other side, by affinity with their Persian Mohammedan neighbours, the Sarts, that, in the place of the old original Turkish or Uigurian characteristics, we find those general Turkestan marks which belong to all the inhabitants of present Turkestan.

At the present day, therefore, the difference between the inhabitants of the Six Cities and those of the rest of Turkestan may be traced to the following points. For want of special physiognomical characteristics, we shall divide the inhabitants of East Turkestan into north and south. The northern races, those of the Aksu and Usch-Turfan provinces, are smaller but broader of stature, and have strikingly Kirghese features, especially exhibited in their small, fiery eyes; while the southern races, those of Yarkend and Khoten, although plainly betraying the Mongol type, yet in their slender stature and black complexion and hair exhibit unmistakably the influence of a southern climate, or perhaps more justly that Cashmere-Mohammedan influence which has existed there at all times.

Their attire is in the fashion, but in the old fashion of Bokhara, with strikingly clumsy over-garments, somewhat like wadded smockfrocks, which are made of linen and cotton. They wear large, awkward boots, and the only mark of their East Turkestan costume is a fur cap with a turned-up brim, rather like that which now forms a part of the Hungarian gala dress, and which we see on the petrified heads of Huns still found in Switzerland. Blue is hated by them as a colour which is worn by the Kafirs (the unbelievers), that is, by the Mandju Chinese magistrates and garrisons. Their food is the same as in the other parts of Central Asia, with a slight addition of Chinese dishes. Their drink consists exclusively of green and black tea; spirituous liquors, although imported from Khokand, are only consumed there by Khokandians and Cashmerians.

With regard to character, the East Turkestan people —I mean that part of the population speaking Turkish —are strikingly simple, and it would be difficult, looking at a Turfanian, Kashgarian, or Aksuan, to imagine that these are the descendants of the most civilised Turkish race in antiquity. In fact, from the heavy rule of the Chinese, which has burdened them for centuries, they are intellectually more crippled than the wild nomad races on the steppes.

Their religious feeling is far stronger, and certainly deeper, than in other parts of Central Asia. Khodjas (descendants of the Prophet), even if they have committed the most disgraceful crimes, are honoured as holy, and are half deified, as we shall subsequently have occasion to see; and touching was the description which my Aksu friend gave of the reception of the first Muymubarek (sacred hair from Mahomet's beard) which arrived at Aksu. The poor believers, without taking food or drink, remained praying for hours, and even days, before the receptacle of the relic, although it may easily have fared with them as with other Turkestanians, and they have been made game of by some swindler returning from the West, who passed off a hair from some grey ass as a hair of the Prophet.*

This religious fanaticism evidences itself in every part of their social and domestic life ; and my readers will be able to understand something of the Mohammedan zeal of the East Turkestanians when I tell them, that not only Constantinople, Mecca, Damascus, &c., but even Bokhara and Khokand are no longer regarded by the present devotees of Kashgar as the pure fountain of Islamism. Besides the religious zeal and the before-mentioned simplicity of the East Turkestanians, we must mention their remarkable cowardice—a cowardice which is always a consequence of long-suffered tyranny, but which appears nowhere in such glaring colours as among the inhabitants of the Six Cities.

Next to the natives of Turkestan, the Töngens or Tunganis, as they are erroneously called, occupy the most conspicuous place. These Töngens, in their origin, their language, and their physiognomy, are Chinese, but in religion they are Mohammedans ; and having had much to endure from the Chinese magistrates in consequence of their apostasy from the

---

* The true tokens of the genuine hairs of the Prophet are, that they cast no shadow if held in the light, and that as soon as the words "Allah Ekber" are thrice repeated before them, they make of their own accord a most humble reverence.

doctrines of Kon-Fut-Tse, they cherish the bitterest hatred both against their Chinese brethren and the Mandju population of their province. Their home is in the province of Kansu and in a few parts of Dsungaria. The former they inhabit in masses; in the latter they appear sporadically, although considerable colonies of them are to be found in the Six Cities. According to the statement of my Kashgar friends, these Töngens * were converted in the time of Timur; others assign their conversion to an earlier period; others, again, think that the introduction of Islamism proceeded from the southern province of Yünnan and Setchuen towards the north.

Be that as it may, the Töngens remain a remarkable member of the great Islam body; they profess themselves mostly as belonging to the sect of the Shafeis, which has only a few adherents among the Western Islamites; and though they are only distinguished from the Chinese by the growth of the mustache and the generally scanty beard, still they feel themselves greatly offended if they are ever regarded as true sons of the Celestial Empire; for they assert that the Nul-ul-Islam (correctly Nur-ul-Islam, the light of Islam) should be at once discovered on their countenances, and their Arabian descent † should be

---

* Hence the name Töngen (the converted), from Töng-mek (to convert). So also in the Osmanli dialect, Dönme—a renegade according to our notions. The word Tungani, used recently in Europe, is a corruption of the original word, caused both by the Russians and the Tadjiks, who have no " ö " in their language.

† Similar claims to Arabian origin are also advanced by the Chinese Mohammedans in the provinces of Yünnan and Setchuen, by the Tadjiks in Central Asia, and by some of the Circassian races.

at once guessed in spite of their snub noses and slanting eyes.

That, with the remarkable indolence of the religious feelings of the Chinese, their apostate brethren the Töngens should be prosecuted by the usually tolerant Government, is only to be explained by the fact that these members, separated from the great body of the Chinese nation, adhere firmly together, and, from their industry and sobriety, enjoy a far better state of prosperity than the opium-eating Chinese and the lazy Mandjus. The Töngens have given considerable sums to pious institutions, not only in the Six Cities and in some places in the provinces of Shen-Si and Kansu, but also in Mecca and Medina, without the local authorities in these towns having been informed of the Chinese origin of the dispensers ; for most curiously all Töngens are regarded in Turkey as Cashmerians, while the Mohammedans of Yünnan and Setchuen parade at the tomb of the Prophet as true Chinese without pigtails, though with long hair. Nevertheless it is a curious fact that they do not stand on the most intimate footing with the East Turkestanians; indeed, intermarriages rarely take place between them. The reason of this, however, rests with the Töngens themselves ; for as the hired soldiers of the Chinese governors, they have made themselves hated by their brethren both in creed and race.

Beside their strict adherence to Mohammedanism, the Töngens are known by their honesty in trading with the Russians, who are glad to make use of them in their transactions with the native Mandjus or Chinese.

Small in number, but of importance in the commercial,

social, and religious affairs of East Turkestan, are the
Sarts—a race with which the readers of my "Reise" and
of my "Skizzen aus Mittelasien" are already acquainted.
The word Sart, as I lately discovered from a manu-
script, signified "merchant" even in the time of the
Uigurs; this denomination, therefore, was applied to
Persians of Central Asia who were engaged in trade.
Just as in ancient times Persian thirst for gain drove
the inhabitants of East Iran among the warlike and
predatory Turks, so is it still at the present day. The
Tadjik or Sart thinks of no danger, no distance. He
is to be met with everywhere where trade promises him
gain; from Salar (the chief city of the province of
Kansu) to the remotest north among the Mongols and
Kalmucks in East Turkestan.

The Cashmere race furnish a considerable contingent
to the population of Yarkend, and are to be found in no
small number in Kashgar and Khoten. The people of
Kabul, only a few of whom live in the kervan-serails
at Kashgar, Yarkend, and Khoten, are no longer so
enterprising as they were, and rarely come in contact
with Aksu and Turfan.

A retrospective glance at the past history of the Six
Cities, of the Uigurs, and the adjacent Dsungaria,
presents a lamentable succession of internal confusion,
disputes, and attacks on the part of the Chinese, the
Mandjus, the Kalmucks, and occasionally also of the
Kirghises and the Khokandians. We will give a hasty
sketch of these historical reminiscences of East Turkestan, because it is indispensable to the understanding of
the state of things at the present day.

In the time of the Uigurs—and by this we mean the

period about 600 years after our era—the western part of East Turkestan, *i.e.*, the Six Cities, stood chiefly under national rule, acknowledging as temporary suzerain either the Chinese Emperor or the princes of the Dsungarians; they professed partly Buddhism and partly the Christian religion, which had been introduced there by the Nestorians. In the ninth century Mohammedan emissaries made their way into East Turkestan, amongst whom Sheik-Hassan-Basri and Eban-Nassar-Samain are the most famous, and they contrived to procure a firm footing for their doctrines even at that time in Kashgar. These were carried by force in 1051 by Bokra-Khan into the eastern districts of Turfan and Komul; and although Togluk-Timur-Khan, a Djengiside, embraced Islamism in 1376, and compelled several Mongolians as well as Uigurs to follow his example, it was not till the sixteenth century that Islamism obtained a complete victory over Buddhism. From that time East Turkestan became ever more and more the seat of that extravagant Mohammedan religious zeal which spread itself from Bokhara over the whole of Asia. As is the case everywhere, the saints had here also only worldly interests in view. Apak-Khodja, however, by his disputes, soon drew Galdan, the chief of the Dsungarian Kalmucks, into the quarrel. In the year 1678 the latter conquered East Turkestan, and placed Apak, with sovereign power, upon the throne. Yet the way was thus opened to foreign interference. The contest between Kalmucks, Mongolians, and Kashgarians lasted long, until at length the powerful Chinese interfered, and took both Dsungaria and East Turkestan into their possession.

It is readily conceivable that, after the Chinese conquest, those princely saints, the Khodjas, were obliged, as chief causers of the constant disputes of the Six Cities, to flee to Khokand; still they considered their sojourn there only as temporary, and they were always endeavouring to recover their lost power by making attacks on the Chinese territory, supported partly by the Khokand people and partly by the rulers of Khokand and Bokhara. It would be unnecessary to describe the series of contests which these intruders carried on against the Chinese, at the head of the war-and-plunder-loving races of Central Asia. Scarcely did the barometer of Chinese influence begin to fall, than the Khodjas appeared; and scarcely had it risen again, than the Khodjas, hardly allowing themselves time to collect their treasures, took to flight. The last inroad of importance took place in 1825, under the direction of a certain Djihangir-Khodja, who attacked the Chinese with much success, made the whole of East Turkestan independent, and is said to have commanded an army of more than 200,000 men. In spite of this he was overcome by the Chinese, who attacked him with a considerable force; he was taken prisoner, and put to death with great cruelty at Peking as a traitor. After him, Welichan-Töre revolted. His rule, which did not last long, is held to us in sad remembrance from the fact that the brave German traveller Adolf Schlagintweit fell a victim to his barbarity, and his head was placed as an ornament on a hill of skulls.

This bloodthirsty libertine soon made himself so hated by his unprecedented cruelty, that the freed inhabitants of East Turkestan longed for their former masters, the

Chinese. In the year 1858 everything was again in its former order; and although a small part of the inhabitants of the Six Cities preferred the Chinese yoke to the Khodja disputes, the great mass were nevertheless eager for perfect freedom. Stimulated by Bokhara and Khokand, negotiations were constantly going on with the predatory adventurers of Khokand, in spite of the strict severity of the Chinese police. In the beginning of the year 1861, two high Chinese Mohammedan officers, and a great number of the people of East Turkestan, fell victims to the political intrigues. In Kashgar, several members of the Apak family were thrown into prison, which of course led to still greater exasperation, and increased the longing looks directed to Mergolan and Namengan.

. This was the state of political matters in East Turkestan when the smothered fire of revenge, fired by events in the neighbouring provinces and countries, burst anew into a flame. In the west, the restless Khodja elements had found opportunity enough in the disputes of Khudajar-Khan with the Kiptchaks in Khokand on the one side, and in the war of Khokand with Bokhara and Russia on the other, to arm themselves secretly, and to gather together a considerable number of freebooters, adventurers, and booty-loving fanatics, partly from the warlike Kiptchaks, and partly from the cities of Namengan, Mergolan, and Osch. With these adherents not only Buzurg-Khan, the son of that Djihangir-Khan executed in Persia, but also many other Seïds thirsting for Djihads (religious wars), waited for some time on the frontier, watching the first opportunity for surprising Kashgar, and for beginning the often-attempted task of expelling the Chinese, and of establishing a dominion of a few months' duration.

It is remarkable that these plans, which were forbidden even in Khokand, in consequence of a treaty with the Chinese authorities, and were therefore kept secret, penetrated, notwithstanding, borne by the telegraphic current of voluble Hadji tongues, as far as Samarkand, where my travelling companions from East Turkestan related them to each other with perceptible consternation. Indeed Hadji-Bilal was of opinion that affairs in his home had assumed such a form that he would not long remain watching the impending disputes in his native city, but that in the following spring he would start on a second pilgrimage through Yarkend and India. I recall this accurately to mind.

The fears of my friend were not groundless; they were realised, not in the course of the same winter, but in the following spring, and this not through Khokand and the Khodjas, but from a totally unexpected direction.

That the Taïping revolution in China would penetrate into all the veins of the gigantic and feeble body of the Celestial Empire, and leave behind in many places traces of dangerous excitement, was to be foreseen from the first; and it was still more confirmed when the bold navigators of the Yang-tse-Kiang—I mean Lieutenant-Colonel H.A. Sarel, Dr Alfred Barton, and Captain Thomas Blakiston —after having advanced with indescribable difficulty as far as Ping-Shan, were obliged to give up their proposed plan of travelling through the province of Yünnan, through Burmah to China, because both Setchuen and Yünnan, being full of revolutionary unrestraint, forbid all passage through them. Just as the raging storm in the midst of the ocean is only evidenced on the shore by a succession of billows, so the revolutions which are taking place in the interior of China are only manifested by the outbreaks which meet our eye in the frontier lands. The spies of the Viceroy of India have probably long heard in the bazaars in the towns of Nepaul and Burmah of the revolt of the Mohammedan Chinese in Yünnan, yet they could know nothing for certain until a proclamation of the newly-elected Sultan, which was circulated in Lhassa, fell into their hands. In this document, drawn up in Arabic, the same style prevails in which the tidings of the victories of a Sultan Selim, of a Mohammed II., and of a Shah Thamasp, were proclaimed. As the author of the article " Western China" informs us, it is written in excellent Arabic ; the Sultan calls himself as just as Abu-Bekr and as brave as Ali, and announces the immediate overthrow of the idolatrous Chinese power.

How much reality there may be in this bombast, any one can readily guess who is even slightly acquainted with the Eastern mode of expression. It is, moreover, not our task to speak of the power and character, and of the accomplishment of the plans of the Mohammedan ruler in Tali-fu who calls himself Soliman, but who is called Tuventsen by the Chinese. How long he will carry them on it is difficult to foresee ; but one fact speaks in his favour, namely, that he has now survived the twelfth year of his independence of Peking. This independence has on the one side greatly injured the English, as it has almost entirely impeded the trade which was carried on with China through Mandelay and

Bamu, and along the Irawaddi through Yünnan; it has injured Russia also, who, by a roundabout way through Siberia and Peking, exported Russian cloth to Mandelay. It has been, however, most injurious to China herself, as the flames of rebellion not only spread over a number of provinces, but the dangerous spark being scattered in the extreme west of the Celestial Empire, caused a conflagration, by which the weakened but still selfish Chinese were to lose the province of East Turkestan and Ili, not for a short period, as had formerly been the case, but for ever.

The tidings of the victory of the insurrectionary Mohammedan inhabitants in Yünnan and Setchuen could not remain a secret to the Töngens in the north. As they had never been contented with the Mandju Government, but had always been a thorn in the eye of the Chinese, the victories of the Taïpings were likely to fill them with malicious delight at the losses of the ruling dynasty.   The heart of the fanatical Töngens beat quickly, therefore, when they got a sight of the before-mentioned proclamation of the Sultan of Yünnan, for that they did get a sight of it cannot be doubted; reports find their way everywhere—in Europe, by railroads and telegraphs—in China, after Chinese fashion. I am, therefore, in nowise inclined to ascribe the first outbreak in Singán-fu, the capital of the Shen-si province, in the year 1862, altogether to a dispute which took place between a Töngen and a Mandju merchant.   The germ, the strong germ, of discontent was there; the Government, severely weakened on the one side by Taïping, Yünnan, and Nien-fu rebellions, and on the other by the Anglo-French invasion, was not to be dreaded. The revolt of the Töngens increased to an astonishing extent; it advanced towards Kansu, where a certain Sochum-Djan, in Salar, placed himself at its head, proclaimed a religious war, and, with the utmost severity towards his own people, began the bitterest contest against the hated and idolatrous Chinese. A communism, such as certainly had not existed at the time of the first beginning of Islamism, was introduced: all goods and chattels, all gain and booty, were held in common; strict laws against rapine, theft, and other crimes were instituted; Buddhist temples were laid even with the ground; Buddha worshippers were compelled to profess Islamism, and to efface every trace of their Chinese origin; even the Chinese costume was exchanged for the Bokhariot.

It is therefore not surprising that in this state of things Chinese troops, even those which were 40,000 men strong, could effect nothing against the insurgents. Holding the town of Salar or Sutchau in possession, the stream of revolt surged over Komul, Urumtchi, and as far as Dsungaria. In these places the garrison was fortunately formed by almost 60,000 Töngens, whose valour was never doubted by the Mandju authorities. In Urumtchi the mercenaries soon made common cause with their brethren in the faith, compelled the Sarts there to join their party, killed the whole Mandju population, and after the unhappy town had been utterly reduced to ashes, owing to an accidental fire, they advanced forwards in two columns, one of which marched to the north-west, and the other to the south-west.

The Töngen insurgents proceeding to the north-west, made a rich capture of artillery guns on their

K

way through Kirkara-su; and their success in the province of Ili, in taking from the Chinese the two chief towns of Kuldja and Tchugutchak, of which Kuldja especially, according to the statements of Radloff, was inhabited principally by merchants, simple artisans, and a great number of Imams and Mollas, must be ascribed chiefly to those 6000 Tartar families who, separated from their race in the Six Cities, and living here under Buddhist elements, among Kalmucks and Chinese, did not, of course, idly look on at the invasion of their brethren in the faith; but, indeed, as we are told, joined them with every man capable of bearing arms. The contest also drew into its vortex the neighbouring nomad races, such as the Kalmucks and Kirghises, who had always entertained hostile feelings to each other; and as the former are considerably the superior in number in those districts, their appearance produced a most fearful slaughter among the Kirghises. All the cattle and the entire booty were moved to Tchugutchak, and nothing was left behind on the steppes but 1500 dogs, which, feeding on the corpses of their own masters, were subsequently, in their want of food, so dangerous to travellers in these districts, that a mountain-way there, according to the statement of the Russian district overseer, was not safe for a solitary horseman.

After the changeful fortunes of battle, both citadels, with their garrisons, fell at length into the hands of the Töngens; and although they suffered some defeats in the East from the Chinese troops sent from Peking, and lost the town of Komul, the whole of Dsungaria is nevertheless at the present day under their dominion. Whether they can long hold out against the warlike inclinations of the nomads of that district, and still more against the Russian authorities, who in their present position in Fort Wernoe, and indeed along the whole chain of the Ala-Tau Mountains, are watching opportunity for intervention, the future will decide. The revolt has produced a transformation of things in East Turkestan, and by it the Six Cities have probably been lost for ever to the Chinese.

The division of Töngen insurgents proceeding from Urumtchi to the south-west, had scarcely reached Kuldja, when the Mohammedan population joined them, and slaughtered the small minority of Chinese living there. A Khodja, enveloped in the odour of sanctity, was placed at the head of affairs—a matter of course among the Chinese Tartars, as in their eyes the Khodjas were workers of miracles, and indeed demi-gods whose superhuman powers could be doubted by none. The name of the Kuldja prince is Rashid-ed-Din. Under his direction the towns of Aksu, Osh-Turfan, and Lai-Mesdjid were taken ; and although the Chinese in the capitals of Yarkend and Kashgar, informed of the approaching storm, did not delay to take the necessary measures for defence, they could not defend themselves against the ever-increasing flames of revolt. The misfortune for the Chinese commandants of these places was, as usual, that their soldiers consisted exclusively of Töngens, from whom, instead of succour, they feared their own destruction ; and even when here and there, as in Khoten and Kashgar, the attempt was made to remove them by treachery, the Tartar inhabitants, usually so pacific, encouraged by the distant cry of victory from their brethren in the faith, had nevertheless energy enough to fall upon their foreign rulers and to annihilate them.

It is true the author of " Western China," whom we have often quoted, tells us that Rashid-ed-Din-Khodja, with 7000 horse and 250 guns, hastened to the assistance of the oppressed Yarkendians; yet I am of opinion that the catastrophe occurred in all these places without any succour of the kind, for the confusion of the Chinese magistrates at every outbreak of the repeated contests in East Turkestan was only equalled by the exasperated fury of the Mohammedans, which, like a lighted straw, flamed up high at first, but was as speedily extinguished.

Will this be the case even now? Will the Chinese once again become masters of the Terek Pass? That is the question which is of interest to us, and which we must discuss for a few moments.

Intentionally avoiding the details of the contest in Kashgar, Yarkend, and Khoten, we cannot forbear recalling the name Buzurg-Khan-Khodja to the remembrance of our readers. This debauchee, with whose servants I travelled for several months, needed only to show himself in Kashgar in the spring of the year 1864, with five hundred horse, for the most part Kirghises and Kiptchaks, in order to induce the population to besiege, under his direction, the strongly-fortified citadel.

The siege lasted a year. Buzurg-Khan meanwhile occupied himself more with the conquest of yielding female hearts, than with the taking of the citadel. Aware of the great consequence to the people of East Turkestan to ally themselves with a Khodja, and, yet desirous to withdraw from the slightest semblance of the cares of government, he surrendered the reins of power entirely into the hands of his Kushbegi (vizier)—a Kushbegi whom he had received at the beginning of his undertaking as an available servant from the Kiptchak chief Alem-Kul, and as such he really proved himself.

The Kushbegi, by name Yakub-Beg, now of course Yakub-Padishah, is of Persian descent — *i.e.*, in the Turkish language a Sart, as is customary throughout Central Asia in appointments in which the knowledge of writing is a *conditio sine qua non.* His birthplace was Pishad, in the Kurama district, in Khokand; and as he possesses the cunning, the mental activity, the energy, and the perseverance of his race in a high degree, it was an easy matter for him, under the rule of Mehemed-Ali, to raise himself in a short time from the position of an ordinary secretary, or rather accountant, to that of a Divandji (head receiver of customs). In the year 1847 he was governor in Ak-Mesdjid, the Fort Peroffsky of the present day, where he entered into forbidden transactions with the Russians, and ceded to the Russians a lake situated near this fort, named Balik-Köl (Fish Lake), for the sum of 12,000 tillah, = £7800 sterling. He was subsequently appointed Ponsad by Alem-Kul—a military rank, combined with the supreme command of five hundred men. In this capacity he was sent to Buzurg-Khan. Buzurg-Khan made him his vizier. So long as the field was uncertain, and the means for obtaining dominion were scanty, he contented himself with this rank; yet scarcely had he learned the extent of the devotion felt by the East Turkestan people for the affairs of Buzurg-Khan, than, gaining over to his side the chief of the Apakian family, he speedily convinced the whole Molla world of Kashgar of the sinful conduct of their favourite, and saying, like Nadir Shah, "What, then, becomes of me?" he plotted in the face of his master with such success that the people of Kashgar, perhaps also compelled by the threatening position of the cunning Sart, deified the new leader, completely let fall Buzurg-Khan, and placed the Kushbegi in his stead at the head of affairs. Yakub-Padishah, who at the very first would suffer no rival far or near, after he had felt himself tolerably established in Kashgar and the separate rebel divisions had gained successes over Chinese supremacy, had nothing to do but to attack in order to place himself at the head of everything. He first attacked Yarkend. The inhabitants of the city were divided into three different parties. One, the most powerful, consisted of Töngens, who, after the extirpation of the Chinese, had retained for themselves the Chinese citadel, which they had before occupied as the garrison of the Emperor of Peking, and by their military superiority they stood rather in the way of the others. The second party consisted of Mohammedans from Cashmere, who had come hither to settle themselves from the territory of Maharadja - Golab - Sing (Prince of Kashgar), and who constituted a considerable portion of the Yarkend population. Lastly, there was a third party—namely, Khokand fugitives and Khodjas, who had come hither from Kashgar. This was the one which was joined by Yakub-Padishah. The contest was long; but in 1866 Yakub took Yarkend from the Töngens, and added this important town to his possessions.

Of course these constant advances in power and greatness were not made without recourse to some dishonourable means. Wearied, probably, of despatching military forces and money subsidies, Yakub-Padishah proposed to bring over to his side, by cunning, the southern town of Khoten, which was comparatively weak. At that time, in 1865, a certain Habib-Ulah was ruling there—a man who, under the Chinese, had held the post of Kazi-Kelan (head Kadi), and who after their expulsion had exchanged the highest hierarchical dignity for the highest political position. When Johnson, an officer of the Indian Trigonometrical Survey, visited him, he was an old man of eighty years of age, of a tall and noble figure, fine complexion, and of a somewhat imposing appearance, with his silk upper garment and Asiatic turban. Having in his earlier years visited the sacred places of Islam, and therefore become a Hadji, he had had opportunity on his journeys to become acquainted with English government and English order. He expressly remarked to the above-mentioned English officer, that the inhabitants of India were far happier than the other subjects of any kingdom whatever, and were not to be compared with those of Russia, who were tortured by cruel functionaries, and were compelled to perform military service in the remote distance. That the good old man placed at that time great hopes upon an alliance with England, and wished ardently to bring it about, is a plain proof that he early perceived the danger approaching in the person of Yakub-Padishah.

Yakub-Padishah began, after the taking of Yarkend, by immediately imprisoning the political agents of the

Khoten prince, in order to extort from him, by violence, information as to the condition of the army, the exchequer, and the political feelings of the people. After these successful attempts, he set out on the way to Khoten ; and when two days' journey distant, he despatched assurances of friendship to the old Khan of Khoten, who at first refused to give a hearing to them, but subsequently, nevertheless, allowed himself to be deluded by them. The Khan entered the Yarkend camp, and there was compelled to call upon his subjects to capitulate. The town was taken, with everything that it contained. The former Kushbegi found a large treasure of gold and silver, and speedily returned to Yarkend, whither he took with him the captive Habib-Ulah and his son, and where he soon after ordered both to be put to death for a remarkable reason, and one which seems to us by no means cogent. This reason, a matter which rarely occurs in the history of the East, arose from a catastrophe produced by the numerous harem of the old Habib-Ulah. The women of this harem, after the taking of the town, were distributed among Yakub's principal officers. But scarcely had these ex-maitresses found their new masters in a defenceless condition, than they fell upon them and murdered them. If this be true, it furnishes a striking evidence of the resolution of the women of East Turkestan, who have won by it certainly a higher reputation for valour than their own husbands.

Immediately after the complete subjugation of Khoten, Yakub-Padishah set forth with a troop of 15,000 men to incorporate the northern part of East Turkestan, where at that time the reins of power were in the hands of the

Töngens in union with a few Khodjas. Aksu surrendered itself without difficulty. He advanced soon afterwards upon Kuldja, defeated the enemy in three engagements, and routed them in an easterly direction as far as Kune-Turfan. He pursued them, and after having taken Sairum, Shah-Yar, and Ish-Turfan, he returned to Kashgar. Of course great watchfulness and energy were required to hold together these rude elements; thus, for example, the conspiracy in Kuldja, where one of the governors left behind, named Mirza-Ahmed, revolted against his master, and the Kushbegi effected the restoration of his authority by the slaughter of several thousand rebels; yet at the present day he possesses in an unlimited manner the whole of East Turkestan, with a population amounting in number to more than one and a half millions, who, in spite of the detestation felt there, as throughout Central Asia, against people of Sartish origin, recognise him as the only support of the Mussulman rule in East Turkestan, or perhaps fear and honour him in consequence of the great power he has obtained. He has gained large resources, partly by levying contributions, partly by booty taken; for, as we are told, not only Chinese and Töngens, but even the rich merchants of Cashmere in the bazaars of Yarkend and Kashgar, have been laid under contribution: indeed, even the simple natives have not been spared: and in addition to the fact that many have voluntarily given up their possessions for a cause that was declared sacred, the former Kushbegi has seized upon the religious institutions of the towns, and is undoubtedly far better equipped and prepared for every chance than were his predecessors in East Turkestan.

The circumstance, however, that has been of most advantage to him, is the late Russian occupation in Khokand. However much we may extol the extension of Russian conquest in these regions as a means of advancing civilisation—however much a few Sarts and peaceful merchants may have ardently desired the settlement of affairs, still a considerable number of the Khokand people, especially fanatical Mohammedans, Seïds, and other religious heroes, are to be found, who flee from the shadow of the Russian standard. Western Bokhara was long ago pointed out as a quarter where the Russian wind blew; and although no one would resolve to utter the impious prophecy of impending ruin, still the zealous people of Khokand preferred moving to the east rather than to the west, and they have escaped to Chinese territory rather than to Bokhara.

It is easy to imagine that it is of great importance to these people to maintain their new home, and to keep it secure. It is these people—and they form a considerable and influential portion of the half-conquered khanates—who rendered essential help to the ambitious Yakub-Padishah, and compelled him to assume such a position with regard to the Chinese as hitherto has been assumed by no rebel in the valleys of the Thien-Shan range. It is not political combinations nor vast plans—these I have always denied among Orientals, and shall ever deny—which compel this Nadir of modern times to resolute resistance. He cannot return to Khokand, as the once successful period of the Khodja invasion is long past, and Russia would certainly prevent the appearance of a foreign power on the banks of the Yaxartes. In the south, east, and north there is no possibility of escape; nothing, therefore, is left for him but to strengthen himself in the Six Cities, to consolidate his dominion, and to frustrate, once for all, any future pretensions of the Chinese to these territories. All this Yakub - Padishah, the former Kushbegi, is doing.

From China, therefore, there is little or nothing to fear. There is but one thing that can disturb the crafty conqueror in his possessions, and that is Russia; and that he already perceives the danger in the distance is evident from his laborious efforts at self-defence, and from the iron force by which he is endeavouring to grasp the bond of unity. Russia, as we have before pointed out in the course of these pages, stands with watchful eye at the western frontier of the Chinese Empire, at that part which stretches from the sources of the Irtish to the south-eastern point of the tableland of Pamir. Long ago master of all the passes and roads in the province of Semipalatinsk which led across the Ala-Tau range to Dsungaria, he is yet forbidden, by Chinese mistrust, to send his merchants to Kuldja and Tshugutshak. Indeed, as the learned German philologist Radloff, who travelled through these districts as a Russian officer, informs us, he was not allowed to remain in Kuldja more than three days, in spite of all the difficulties of the long journey. Not venturing any open step in the north against the feeble, but nevertheless important power of China, those parts of the frontier must be approached where Chinese authority is weaker and interior anarchy greater—namely, the banks of the Issikköl, in the north of which Fort Wernoe was built, and in the west Fort Tokmak—in order here, on a comparatively surer basis, to await the events of the future. In the strategic plans communicated to the world, it is universally said that the advance · in this neighbourhood is a flank attack on Khokand, and that the two different armies of occupation will subsequently meet on the Yaxartes. This, moreover, is not quite a fabrication. The force on the Issikköl has rendered good service, but its essential success rests in the fact that Russia has approached very close to her feeble neighbour in this region also. Indeed she stands ready to take possession of the heritage she has appointed for herself even before the actual death of the future testator.

Yet the question will be asked, What are the Russians to do with the Chinese Tartars ? Have they not enough of the Tartar element among themselves ?

Russia herself would not be able to give a decided answer to this question ! Still it must not be forgotten that the matter in question here is not the possession of a thousand square miles and some millions of inhabitants, but rather the revival of the great old commercial highway from the interior of China to the west, which was in a flourishing condition up to the end of the middle ages ; and the formation of it into a powerful and fruitful channel, carrying blessing and fertility through the great body of the Russian Empire. This is no chimera. If for centuries in succession Chinese products were conveyed into Europe through Komul, Kashgar, Samarkand, Belkh, Tebris, and Constantinople ; or through Bokhara, Astrakan, and Nishni Novgorod, why should not this be the case now ? Are not facilitated communication and the security of dry land to be preferred to the treacherous waves of the sea ? It is indeed true that Russia has already completely appropriated to herself a path of communication from Peking to Petersburg; yet this is never a frequented one, owing to the rude Siberian winter and the inhospitable steppes of Gobi, and is valueless compared with the road from east to west, which leads along a highway from Peking, used centuries ago, from the banks of the Yang-tse-Kiang, through the provinces of Shensi, Kansu, and East Turkestan.

As everything indicates, the accomplishment of this design is of great consequence to the Court of Petersburg. Russia wishes to get the start of England, who likewise has perceived the importance of a commercial highway by land to the interior of the Celestial Empire, and in spite of the sleepiness of the present Indian Government, has sent out a surveying party for the construction of a road through Burmah from Assam to the province of Yünnan. Of course, in this instance also, the English have been, as usual, beaten by the Russians. The expedition was obliged to return without having effected its object; and the English semi-official report of the Viceroy states that it was not at all a pity that this step, though undertaken with authority, has failed.

If they were as languid on the Neva as they are on the banks of the Hooghly, Russia would have paused after the taking of Fort Wernoe; but the men of the icy zone are more vigorous than Britons, exhausted by the heat of the Indian sun, for they will not remain in Fort Wernoe, and it will probably not be long before we hear that Russian Cossacks are on the point of crossing the Terek Pass on a visit to Yakub-Padishah. It is therefore for the present a matter of conjecture at what point the attack will be made on the part of Russia, whether in Dsungaria — that is, near Kuldja — or whether through the Terek Pass, in the Kashgar territory. That serious plans, however, are entertained, is proved by the ten sotnias of Cossacks—each numbers one hundred men—by the eight battalions of infantry, and the twenty cannons which are stationed at the eastern parts of the Issikköl, and which, nevertheless, are probably not intended to be used against the wandering tribes of the Karakirghises to be found there; also by the doubly-strong army of observation occupying the same territory, only to the west of the Issikköl. We may therefore certainly expect some advance, and it will, if I mistake not, first be made in the southeastern part of the frontier mentioned—that is, on the present territory of Yakub-Padishah.

This new ruler of the Six Cities is, as we perceive from Russian statements, not on the most friendly footing with the Khan of Khokand, his neighbour and former suzerain; for no one will probably have forgotten that Buzurg-Khan received, though secretly, the most important subsidies for his attack from Alem-Kul, and therefore indirectly from Khudajar-Khan. What the cause of this breach of friendship is, it is easy to explain. Yakub-Padishah, who has the disposal of a better filled exchequer than the Khan of Khokand, has recently taken all the war-loving Kirghises into his service, men who in the first place had renounced obedience to the ruler of Khokand, their lawful master, and in the second place had plundered his own frontier, and in fact—and this is more fatal to all parties—had endangered Russian subjects and Russian caravans. Moreover, Yakub - Padishah plainly refused to pay Khokand the yearly tribute for the Six Cities, a duty which his proudest Chinese neighbours had discharged; and as he knows only too well the weakness of the neighbouring Khokand, we cannot feel surprised if he now, as the stronger power, threatens Khokand with conquest and annexation. He has little to fear from Khudajar-Khan, the present prince of Khokand—he can intimidate him so long as he will. This is not the case with the Russians; and the attacks which his Kirghiz mercenaries are making on the Narin, or on the banks of the Issikköl, will probably cost him dear, if they do not lose him his entire independence. How the usually cunning Kushbegi can go so far as to provoke the Russians, whose power he so well knows, is inconceivable to me, yet undoubtedly it was he who gave cause for quarrel.

In the beginning of this year two Russian caravans were proceeding from Tashkend to East Turkestan: one belonged to Mons. Michæel Chludoff, and was visiting the eastern bank of the Issikköl; it intended reaching Aksu through the Zauker Pass. The first arrived happily at Kashgar, where it was at once seized by Yakub-Padishah; all the goods were paid back in silver,[*] and any further appearance of Russian subjects on his territory was forbidden with the severest threats. The second caravan, proceeding to Aksu, had of course heard nothing of this threat; and scarcely had Chludoff arrived at his place of destination than he and his com-

* *Cf.* my "Skizzen aus Mittelasien," p. 317.

panions were blindfolded, robbed of their goods, and thrown into prison, where they were obliged to remain until an advancing Russian force liberated them.

While this alone affords a sufficient reason for the march of the Russians to the Six Cities, the step must certainly have been accelerated by the fact that the present ruler of East Turkestan strongly fraternises with the Kirghises on the Issikköl, who are under Russian sway, and that he gives plenty of work in consequence to the Cossack garrisons stationed there. General Kalpakoffski, the commander of Tokmak, has been disquieted several times by the appearance of Kashgar troops ; and as Yakub-Beg stands on friendly terms with the Emir of Bokhara, the Russian conjecture that a diversion in favour of the hardly-pressed prince on the Zerefshan is to take place here, is not unfounded, or at any rate it is a cogent reason for the approach of the Russian bayonets to the Terek Pass.

Thus we again see how completely the Russians will be compelled to plant their standard on the citadels of Kashgar, Yarkend, and Khoten; for it will never occur to any one that the people of East Turkestan can place more hindrances in the way than the other inhabitants of Central Asia. In fact, if a single battle were to take place to Yakub-Padishah's loss, the East Turkestanians would be at once compelled to lay down their arms and submit. The yoke of the unbelievers is, as is well known, no utterly foreign matter here — whether Buddhist or Christian, both bear the title of "Kafir;" and Europe, perhaps even Russia herself, will be amazed at the small cost and sacrifice with which this important and rich part of Central Asia has fallen into her hands. We need hardly say that after the taking of the Six Cities, Dsungaria, which is in the possession of the Töngens, will not long be able to maintain its freedom. Russia, who has long observed with keen eye this north-western part of the Chinese Empire, and has glanced longingly at the commercial towns of Tchugutchak and Kuldja, has in her possession all the roads and passes in the province of Semi-palatinsk leading to these very towns. Moreover, the Kalmucks, as declared enemies of the Kirghises, and as powerful opponents of the Töngen revolt, are favourable to the Russian plans. Russia, besides, will find these districts indispensable as a second highway of communication with the Six Cities ; so that if East Turkestan falls into her possession, the Trans-Ili district, stretching to the north of the Thien-Shan Mountains, may be regarded as included in the conquest.

Apart from the utility, already pointed out, of a great commercial highway from the interior of China, we must not overlook the advantage which the Court of Petersburg obtains by the possession of a soil so fertile and so rich in metals as that of East Turkestan. The idea of an extension in this direction is as little new as all the other plans on Central Asia ; in fact, the encouragement which was given on the part of the Russian Government to the Kirghiz-Russian traveller Welichanoff in 1852, on his incognito tour to Kashgar and Aksu, was not wholly free from political designs, although the journey was taken under the banner of the Russian Geographical Society, and thus for scientific purposes. The Anglo-Indian Government has recently begun, by the advice of Captain T. G.

L

Montgomery, to send highly - cultivated natives to foreign regions inaccessible to Europeans. Russia has long ago made use of this strategy ; and the experiences of the Russianised Kirghises, only a harmless abstract of which is imparted to the world, have been lying for many years in the archives of the Russian military staff as a safe guide to Turkestan.

If we now take into consideration both the distance and the importance of the interests which stimulate Russia in her relations to East Turkestan, and measure also the distance and the interest which arises to England from her possessions on the Himalaya, and from her political position in Cashmere, Nepaul, and Thibet, with regard to the Six Cities, the thoughtful reader will at once ask why the Viceroy at Calcutta has not got the start of the Russians ? why, when mighty commercial interests call him also to East Turkestan, he has not placed himself in communication with these outposts of Indian power before the Russians have done so, who come forward as avengers of offences, while he apparently receives friendly invitation, and would be received both by the people and the courts with open arms ?

Apart from my personal experiences, according to which the Indian Government is regarded by the people of East Turkestan as a model of justice and order, ranking even high above the Chinese, and the Moham-medan-Bokhara rule—an opinion evidenced by the fact that two-thirds of the Turkestan pilgrims to Mecca, instead of taking the convenient road through Bokhara, prefer to cross the dangerous and difficult Karakorum Pass, and to traverse the long circuitous road through India and across the Persian Gulf to Arabia,—apart from this, I say, we cannot ignore the indisputable proofs in favour of our assertion. Not only does the old Habib-Ulah most courteously invite Johnson to Khoten, entertain him hospitably, and send him back to the Viceroy with messages and presents, but invitations of the same kind have been made to him even by Yarkend; the possession of the town was indeed proposed to him. The bold traveller was ridiculed in Calcutta; Sir John Lawrence's semi-official papers declared plainly that any one who led British attention in this direction was "an enemy to his country." Yet I cannot understand how an assertion of this kind can be combined with the true mission of the Ministry in Calcutta, to whom the extension of English commercial interests should be the object desired. Or did Sir John Lawrence perhaps not know how much Turfan wool is yearly sent to India—that is, to Umritsir, for the manufacture of Cashmere shawls, and that within the last ten years £500,000 sterling have been annually realised in the sale of this article? Or ought he not to endeavour to procure a certain and easy market in Turkestan for the tea-plantations on the Himalaya, which since Robert Fortune's mission to China have cost the Anglo-Indian Government so much, and are still a heavy expense to it? Long ago this article of food, so indispensable to the people of East Turkestan, found its way through Komul to Aksu and Kashgar, and fetched of course a high price, so much so that I remember paying fourteen *tenge* in Samarkand for the green tea imported from China—tea for which I afterwards paid only six *tenge* at Meshed to a Kabul merchant who was importing green Indian tea of the same quality to Persia. If the difference of price in times of peace is so considerable, why should the English Government not try to procure introduction for their teas, universally in favour, as they are, in the Six Cities, now that the commercial highway through Komul is completely closed ? This could very easily have been done if the system of Aksakals (commercial consuls), which had existed for centuries, had been adopted, and if, following the example of Cashmere, Khokand, Thibet, and Kabul, an English Aksakal, either a native or an Englishman, had been placed in the commercial towns of the first rank ! Was this, perhaps, a matter not worth the trouble ?

Or did Sir John Lawrence ignore the entire statement of Dr Henry Cayley ? This officer was despatched by Sir Richard Temple to inquire into the commercial affairs of these districts, and he communicated to us the following opinion respecting the Kushbegi : "The Kushbegi, he says, is, without doubt, a brave, energetic, and clever soldier ; an able, although not very conscientious, ruler. It is said that he maintains strict discipline in his army, that he punishes the smallest fault ; but, on the other side, he treats the soldiers well, and rewards them generously. He is friendly, also, in his conduct to merchants ; the taxes imposed by him are not particularly oppressive, and he is certainly feared and honoured by his subjects. The fact that he unites all the provinces of Turkestan under his sway, is of great advantage both to this country and to the adjacent lands, and is very beneficial to himself ; and I think it would produce the best results if we were to send an accredited envoy to the Kushbegi at Yarkend, in order to give him a true statement of our wishes and intentions. There is no doubt that he is very anxious to remain on a friendly footing with us; still we are a little suspicious to him as to our motives, and since he receives only false and distorted intelligence upon political matters, he can never feel true confidence until we have taken the steps necessary for mutual explanation." *

Unfortunately Sir John Lawrence is wont to discover the germs of subsequent complications in every attempt at a mutual understanding with the adjacent lands. He desires as far as he can to remain in the favour of the tax-paying English public, still he seems to forget that it is better to spend a penny at the right time than to be obliged afterwards to spend a pound. That by disregarding the commercial interests so strongly defended by the English in all times, and obstinately refusing to exert the necessary political influence, he has neglected to turn his attention to East Turkestan, he may for a time justify by that principle of inactivity which is asserted as the essence of wisdom. But what will he do when the Russian bear, resting comfortably on its paws, begins to blink at Ladak from the summit of the Karakorum Pass? or if he is allowed to exchange friendly glances with the ruler of Cashmere, whose fidelity towards the English Government is still very questionable? For at the present day, so long as Yakub-Padishah stands in his way, and the Russian

---

* For further details with regard to Yakub-Kushbegi, see the paper, "Ein Mohammedanischer Eroberer in Asien," which was written five years later, and the dates of which are more reliable in consequence of the travels of Shaw, Hayward, and Forsyth.

merchant cannot proceed to Cashmere, the approximation is certainly difficult; but observing other political combinations going on in East Turkestan, it seems scarcely conceivable that a Russian-Cashmere alliance will not ultimately be effected. No one will, however, persuade me that the gentlemen on the Hooghly will regard it with friendly eyes, or will shout applause, when the ruler of Cashmere, now forced into a loving union with India, extricates himself from British embraces to rush into the open arms of the Muscovite power!

PERSIA AND TURKEY (1868).

NOTHING manifests so much the decline of Islamism, nothing proves so thoroughly its slight prospect of a lasting future, as the sensible want of all unity of idea, the want of an instinctive feeling, which could lead to common defence against the foe, growing, as he is, into a threatening phantom. Whether tendencies of this kind have ever existed in the complex states of the Islam world, no one can assert with absolute certainty. It is long ago that the followers of the doctrine of the Arabian Prophet, gathering under a common standard, were led along one path by the bright torch of their common faith. This torch burned only under the first Caliphs, during the Crusades, and in a few places, at the time that the unrestrained Mongol hordes from the *officina gentium* of Central Asia were making towards the West, bringing with them destruction and desolation. In fact, we should be almost inclined to assert that with the awakening of the spark of life in the Western world, the light of unity kindled by the Koran declined in the same measure as the other light increased in power in the far horizon of its present sphere of brightness.

If we look at the gigantic empire of Islam, from the interior of China over the whole of Asia and Africa, as far as the western shores of the Atlantic Ocean, this lack of unity of idea will nowhere astonish us so much as in Turkey and Persia. These countries, justly called the Great Islam States, contain a compact mass of about thirty millions of orthodox believers—thirty millions of beings who regard Mohammed as the God-sent Prophet, and his doctrines as the one path to blessedness—thirty millions who must look with horror upon Europe as the primeval nest of infidelity, the first duty imposed upon them being to make war with all holding a different creed. We Europeans, in the intoxication of our certain victory over the East, never think of entering into combinations against the forces proceeding from a possible alliance; our Cabinets, in their diplomatic transactions, have never taken into consideration the result of a step of the kind. Nevertheless, the last effort of the Mohammedan nations struggling in death, were they but once united, might disappoint them mightily. Although weakened, the prostrate foe could convulsively collect its strength, and could be no inconsiderable adversary. Of course, as recent affairs have taught us, all precautionary measures of this kind were unnecessary. I ascribe this not so much to the great wisdom of our statesmen, as to their false sense of security, which is supported by the foolish conduct of the great states above mentioned. Deeply penetrated with the idea that Western civilisation is far more elevated and far more beneficial than that of the East, we have no desire to render the task of Europe in Asia more difficult by giving proof of the erroneous policy -

by which Turkey and Persia have long, and especially recently, distinguished themselves. That which is to happen will happen! Our influence will ever be directed against these two lands with increasing force; yet it is in the interest of that all-important balance of power that we wish to see one strong united barrier, instead of separate and isolated forces, opposed to the ambitious and greedy efforts of one over-large European power. A good understanding between the Courts of Constantinople and Teheran would in nowise disturb the advance in the new era. It might, indeed, aid the design of well - meaning Europe just as much as it might impede the intrigues and grasping plans of the Court of Petersburg.

It may seem surprising to many that we can believe in the unity of such heterogeneous elements as Turks and Persians. It is true the national, social, and religious differences are great—far greater, indeed, than any to be found in social and political conditions in the West. The present population of Iran—a motley mixture of the original inhabitants of the country, of Turks, Arabians, Beludjans, and Kurds, and various ingredients of Asiatic tribes—have preserved, nevertheless, in spite of their chameleon-like origin, the stamp of old Persian civilisation in their exterior. They are supple, quick both in mind and body, courteous, and full of imagination; at times submissive, at others arrogant and proud; remarkably active, without meriting the epithet "industrious,"—in a word, a great mixture of vice and virtue, and neither in detail nor as a whole showing any affinity with the characteristics of the Turks. The Turks, who are nothing else than an amalgamation of

Seldjukish adventurers, Greeks, Armenians, Slavoni-
ans, Kurds, Arabians, &c., being a powerfully ruling
race, have been able to disseminate the qualities of their
national character : this is everywhere sharply stamped ;
their indolence, heaviness, want of wit, and external
grace stand out in such strong contrast to the qualities
of their neighbour, that on closer consideration Turks
and Persians must really appear as elements which not
only have no affinity, but have never come into any
contact with each other.   That in consequence of these
original qualities the two states must have been differently formed is indeed obvious.   The Persian, whether
belonging to migrated races or to the original inhabitants, has always regarded himself as the model of
Islam civilisation.   He has considered himself a master
in poetry, music, philosophy, and other sciences ; and
he has looked upon the Turks as the representatives of
rude power, and as barbarians.   This is an old-established
custom, which is justified by history, since the destroyers
and devastators of Iran were mostly Turks; and although the old state of things no longer exists, still the
Persians, like true Orientals who cling tenaciously to
old opinions, are not inclined to alter their ideas on
this point.   Their Western neighbour never could inspire them with respect ; nor could they inspire it in
return, for the Turks look upon them as cunning and
cowardly, as devoid of truth and without principle.
The constant change of dynasty in Iran, and the civil
wars in consequence, have produced wild tyranny, and
this again has called forth cunning and deceit.   Not
only have all the provinces rarely formed a compact
whole, but party disputes have separated single races

and families, each having in view his own immediate
interest, and being little, or not at all, intent on the
welfare of the country generally. In Turkey, where
tyranny is weaker and the fear of Christian elements
stronger, the Osmanlis, whether *de pur sang* or descendants of proselytes, have always firmly united against
internal or external foes. The adherence also to the
ruling house, which has never changed since the empire
was founded, has been far stronger than in the adjacent
country; and this difference is to be found even at the
present day in all the institutions, and in all the customs
and habits of the two nations.

It was religion, however, which mostly sowed the seed
of discord, and prevented every possibility of unity of
feeling. It must not be imagined that the schism
occasioned by the disputed succession of the first
Caliphs, or by the justice or injustice of Ali's pretensions, produced such a cleft as that which we now
find between the two sections of believers; this was
only widened in course of time by the ambition and
egotism of hierarchical or temporal princes. Shiism
was declared to be identical with Iranism. In every
approximation to Sunnite elements the independence
of Iran was considered endangered even in the time of
the Dilemites; we cannot therefore be surprised if the
two sects, after more than a hundred years of effort in
this direction, have brought matters so far that they
scarcely consider each other any longer as fellow-
believers, and this is especially the case as regards the
Persians. Trifles, such as the form of ablutions, prayers,
dress, and externals of this kind, have an almost incredible weight with Orientals. That the Persian uses

at prayer the pentagonal tile instead, of carpet; that in his pious ablutions he washes the arm not from the elbow to the hands, as the Sunnites do, but from the hand to the elbow;* that he regards every one who does not follow the Koran as impure and polluted, and not, as the Sunnite, simply as an unbeliever; that in prayer, instead of turning towards the south-east, to Mecca, he prefers turning towards Kerbela and Nedjef;—these are not only simple religious usages, but mighty vital questions producing a religious schism marked by wilder animosity than was the case in Europe even in the earliest beginnings of Protestantism.

No one can deny the existence of this difference of faith and the mighty breach it has produced. We cannot be astonished that, in order to effect the latter, every possible lever was placed in motion during the past century. At that period Islamism had no dangerous adversary, Russia and Europe existed only in name, Islamism was itself the aggressor, and had no need to think of defensive measures. All the more does it now surprise us, especially since the beginning of the nine-

---

* This custom reminds me of a droll incident which occurred to myself during my incognito in Bokhara. As is well known, the difference in the washing of the arm produces apparent consequences. On this part of the body among the Sunnites, in consequence of ablutions five times a day from earliest youth, the points of the hairs incline towards the palm of the hand. Among the Shiites, on the contrary, they incline towards the elbow; and hence from the appearance of the hairs the religious sect of the individual may be inferred. The astonishment of some Bokhariots may be imagined when they discovered that my hairs neither inclined upwards nor downwards, but grew all round my arm. "A remarkable Mussulman that!" they said; "an unknown race!" And I am certainly regarded by many, even at the present day, as an abortion in the Islam growth of hair.

teenth century, that Turks and Persians, fully convinced as they are that Russian plans are hanging over their head like some fatal Damocles' sword, persist in maintaining their former position of brooding discord and disunion. That they, having learned with the clearest perception in their early years the "divide et impera" of Lokman's fable of the lion and the two fighting oxen, should nevertheless not perceive that all the tendencies of the Court of Petersburg aim at their common ruin, is all the more striking, as in Teheran and in Constantinople, using the boastful tone of European civilisation, there is much said of diplomacy, of diplomatic intrigues, and political combinations. That this behaviour of the respective courts, especially of the Court of Teheran, is not the way for safety, and that the policy of the Sefevides must be now given up, has been sufficiently proved to us by Nadir Shah in his otherwise vain attempt to heal the breach between the Sunnites and the Shiites. It was the expedition of Peter the Great to the Caucasian shores which suggested to him the advantage of the alliance of the two great powers. At his death the idea was again totally relinquished, and the dynasty of the Kadjars have since their accession to the throne, in spite of their Turkish origin, and in spite of all the hatred to which they have been exposed on the part of their genuinely Persian subjects, not only neglected to approach the house of the Ottoman prince, their old relative, but it is the Kadjars exclusively who not only have neglected every possible opportunity of extirpating the hatred of the people, but who, even since the beginning of the nineteenth century, have most contributed to fan the flame of discord, unmindful of the fact that this flame will light the victorious march of their common foe just as much as it threatens Iran itself with the most fatal injury.

From the time when General Olivier was sent by Napoleon to Turkestan, in order to effect an alliance between Persia and Turkey against Russia—attempts which were frustrated in spite of the strong efforts of Aga Mohammed Khan, founder of the Kadjar dynasty, against the aggressive power of Russia—up to the present day, when Russia has gained a footing on the Araxes, and has raised fortresses on the eastern shore of the Black Sea and in the Circassian Mountains, many opportunities have presented themselves to Turkey and Persia for placing considerable hindrances in the way of their common foe.

It is remarkable that this important question of a federation not only has not occurred to either of the two countries, but that all conceivable occasion for dispute is sought for. It was chiefly the frontier question which, both under Feth-Ali-Shah and Mohammed Shah, as well as subsequently under Sultan Mahmoud and Sultan Abdul-Medjid, disturbed all idea of union. As is well known, from the Oriental mode of government, that province lying furthest from the central point of administration is the worst ruled and is the most exposed to anarchy and unrestraint, so that the want of communication not only impedes the transport of goods, but even the transmission of the orders of the Government. In fact, just as in ordinary life the courtier and civil functionary trembles in the presence of his lord, while at a comparative distance from the threshold of the splendid palace he loses his exaggerated reverence and slavish submission; so the civil functionaries, removed from the controlling hand of their superior, not only soon lose all respect, but behave themselves as arrogant and sovereign vassals. This state of things is chiefly the case on the frontier provinces of Turkey and Persia, in that portion of land which stretches from Bayazid to the Sea of Basra. The Eyalets of Kurdistan and Arabistan were thirty years ago regarded rather as fiefs by the Turks; and the Pashas who were sent there as governors, acted always independently, and occupied themselves very little with political combinations. This is the case at the present day with the Walis, who were sent from Teheran to the west frontier of the kingdom. Since appointments fall here, as in old times, to the highest bidder, the respective Khans, who only desire their own enrichment and not the administration of the provinces, trouble themselves but little about peaceful agreement, or about the unity of Islamism. At the present day the Shah is of far less importance here than the Sultan was thirty years ago. It is no wonder, therefore, if, at all points where these great states come into contact as frontier neighbours, constant disputes arise. It is no wonder if at every moment, from the continual friction of the civil functionaries, sparks arise, which, from unskilful or capricious management, speedily burst forth into the bright flames of dissension.

Passing over all petty disputes and disturbances, we will only speak of the wars which took place in the first half of this century. In the year 1821 (1236 from the Hegira) the governors of Erzeroum and Azerbaydshan entangled the two Islam states in a quarrel. Just as in the present day the Kurdish nomad tribes were the cause of it. Abbas-Mirza overstepped the frontiers of Iran, and took Toprakkale, Diadin, Bidlis, and other frontier towns of Turkestan. The Turks meanwhile were attacking Kirman-Shah in Persia, but were repulsed and beaten by the Persians; and if the Persian general in command had not died of his wounds, Bagdad would certainly have fallen. In the north, also, the Persian arms were successful. Abbas-Mirza, the brave son of Feth-Ali-Shah, utterly defeated the governor of Erzeroum, until at last peace was concluded after much bloodshedding on both sides; and with the exception of the great booty which the avaricious sons of Iran took into possession, everything remained as before. Peace for some time reigned between the two parties, a peace which was not caused by any pacific disposition, but by the hard struggle which Persia was carrying on with Russia; for scarcely had Feth-Ali-Shah died, after a reign of thirty-seven years, and had been placed in the splendid mausoleum at Kum, than Mohammed Shah, or more truly, his vizier, who had been advanced from the post of private tutor to that of Prime Minister, conceived the strange idea of desiring to test in open battle the productions of his cannon-foundries, in which the former pedagogue and scholar was eagerly interested.

In the year 1843, when the bombardment and massacre of Kerbela was deeply wounding the hearts of the Shiite Persians, and was exciting a strong feeling of hatred and revenge against the Sunnites and their representative, the Sultan of Constantinople, the war-

loving Cabinet of Teheran would have actually soon
entered into a war with Turkey had not the ambitious
zeal of the strange vizier been somewhat damped by the
unfortunate issue of the war with Afghanistan. As is
well known, the city of Kerbela, situated only a few
days' journey from Bagdad, early became the shrine of
Shiite zealots, from the fact that it contains within its
precincts the remains of Imam-Hussein, the beloved
national martyr of Iran. A hundred thousand Shiites
annually make their pilgrimage to his tomb in this city.
Even the dead like to be brought here for their long
sleep ; and this is in nowise annoying to the Turks,
since living and dead are only admitted on payment of
a considerable tribute. The people of Iran had long
thirsted for the possession of this Kerbela and Nedshef ;
they felt that it belonged to the tragic character of the
history of the house of Ali, that the resting-place of
the martyr, so severely persecuted in life, should remain
even after his death in the hands of their arch-enemy.
This is laid especial stress on in numerous elegiac
poems ; and if we take into consideration the constantly
precarious position of Turkey in this part of its dominion, it seems indeed as if the Persians had not
wrested Kerbela and Nedshef from the Osmanlis just
for the sake of imparting an intenser colouring to the
tragic and romantic epopees, in which their national
and religious humbug is so rich. The Persians have
only once had this place in their possession, and then
only for a short time. Nevertheless, both people and
Government are for ever striving in this direction.

There are always crowds of Persians in Kerbela.
Freely and openly revolutionary plans are devised

against the Turkish Government, and in spite of the fact that the latter may be regarded as a model of endurance, it nevertheless now and then agrees to an act of chastisement. The immense massacres and heavy taxations inflicted on the refractory Persians may be regarded, therefore, as the natural consequence of such a state of things.

In the year above mentioned, nearly 18,000 Persians forfeited their lives in a few hours. It must have been a fearful carnage, the remembrance of which, even at the present day, awakens the wildest feeling of revenge in the breast of every Persian.

In addition to this, disputes were still going on, which had existed for some time, but had subsequently increased with unrestrained vehemence, relative to the frontier of Kurdistan, a province which, divided between Turkey and Persia, has produced unspeakable mischief. The Kurds under Ottoman rule are Sunnites, those under Persian sway are Shiites. Still, as both parties really own no rule, and religious differences are only employed as a justifiable pretext for rapine, murder, and plunder, anarchy has at all times produced so much misery in the romantic valleys of lovely Kurdistan, and especially at this period, that the loud cry and lamentation of the sufferers, which remained unheard at Constantinople, penetrated even to the banks of the Seine, the Thames, and the Neva. Whether impelled by peaceful motives, or in pursuance of certain political tendencies, France, England, and Russia have no longer been able to look on calmly at this state of things, especially since the infamous Bedr-Khan-Beg has made himself conspicuous by his war of extermination against the Nestorian Christians. In a conference at Erzeroum it was decreed that delegates furnished by these states, in conjunction with Persian and Turkish functionaries, should settle the frontier disputes, and should reconcile the great Islam states engaged in them. The preliminaries alone for peace lasted five years, and it was not till the year 1848 that the respective delegates—namely, Dervish Pasha for Turkey, Mirza-Djafar-Khan for Persia, Colonel Williams for England, and Colonel Ktchirikoff for Russia—began to discuss a more accurate line of frontier, which was to stretch from Basra to Mount Ararat. This difficult task was completed in the year 1852.

This was followed by an apparent peace between the Courts of Teheran and Constantinople, a peace which was not brought about by any sincere understanding on both sides, but rather by foreign wars and by the internal disorders of the respective states. Persia was occupied with the wars in Chorassan and Afghanistan, and with the repression of the Babis; Turkey was employed by the Crimean war; and although on the part of both states causes for quarrel were not lacking, the outbreak of war has been prevented up to the present time.

On the accession of the youthful Nasreddin Shah, it was universally believed that the Court of Teheran would adopt the path of reasonable policy, and introduce the era of peaceful relations with Turkey. But it was not so. Nasreddin, who may be justly regarded as the true reformer of Iran, since the introduction of European institutions and the entrance into the European confederacy of states has really begun under his rule, was nevertheless unfortunately so blinded, partly by the vehemence of his youthful character, and partly by the traditional policy of all Persian rulers, and especially those of the house of Kadjar, that he too has disdained on principle this only means of self-preservation, and has preferred turning to Petersburg instead of to Constantinople. That by so doing he went himself into the very den of the lurking lion never occurred to him. Although religiously educated, he preferred to give a hearing to the Persian Achondes (clergy), who were thriving from the Shiite and Sunnite disputes, and were constantly whispering to him that a league with the blackest unbeliever would be more advantageous to Iran than that with a Sunnite power, acknowledging in truth one and the same Koran, and one and the same Prophet. Russia, cunning and watchful Russia, did not of course delay skilfully to turn this great error to her own advantage. The Court of Teheran was thoroughly ensnared; the representatives of the Court of Petersburg, Prince von Dolgoruki and Mons. von Anitschkoff, who since the assassination of the Russian ambassador Gribayedeff have resided in the royal palace, were treated as members of the royal family, and were held by the Regent in high regard as the sincerest friends of the Kadjar interests; in fact, it is a matter of wonder how Anglo-French insinuations contrived during the Crimean war to prevent a collision between the Persian forces and the Turkish, since the Court of Teheran, even at that time, was meditating an alliance with the Russians against Sultan Abdul-Medjid. Of course in the Shah's Cabinet there were a few sober ministers who dissuaded from a proceeding of this kind, and in whom the ambassadors of France and England found an essential support. After the fall of Sevastopol, this party for peace exulted at their discretion; and much as might have been learned from the great danger which had threatened Islamism in the West, no sooner had the sound of the cannon-shots of Alma and Inkerman died away than the foolish work of dispute went on as before.

In the last ten years Persia has done her utmost on the one side to stir up the hatred to Turkey at home, and on the other to intrigue against the Turks by new European diplomatic intercourse, and to show that the Persians, an old, civilised people, are far more in affinity with the spirit of the nineteenth century than the Turks with their janizaries.

In spite of these assertions, the Shiite ecclesiastics, with the Regent at their head, desire to increase the rude worship of Ali, which already borders on fetichism. This Caliph has been, as is well known, elevated by one sect, not only above Mohammed, but even above God. This sect is called Ali-Ullahs, and I mention them only to show that there was no necessity existing to give the worship of Ali an official expression; yet the worship of Ali is identical with painful regrets at the misfortunes of the Fatimites; this regret is identical with hatred of the Sunnites; and this, again, with revenge against the Turks, and against the Turkish Government. Such is the chain of reasoning in Teheran; and in order to carry out this principle consistently, the Shah had a miraculous discovery made in a remote part of India for the edification of his subjects. This was the portrait of Ali painted on canvas with oil colours. Hitherto this Caliph had only been known, or rather had not been known, by a portrait which represented him thickly veiled. A picture was desired, portraying his sacred features. If only to prove that painting had not been forbidden by Islamism, in spite of all the counter-assertions of the Sunnites, a picture of this kind must have appeared as a direct evidence. The picture was solemnly conveyed to Teheran; an order (Timsal) set with diamonds was instituted in its honour, and this is only bestowed on the highest dignitaries, and never on an unbeliever. Indeed, the idea was entertained of sending the grand cordon of this order as a mark of distinction to the Sultan of Constantinople.

No less offensive to the representatives of the Porte at the Court of Teheran are the constant efforts of the Persian Government to invest their festivals with a certain splendour, involving the glorification of Shiite grandees, and public insult and childish derision of the Sunnites. Of these festivals we will first mention that of Omer Suzani (the burning of Omer), in which this brave Caliph and founder of Islamism, whom the Shiites especially hate, is carried round the towns by day in the form of a figure stuffed with straw, which by night is filled with powder, and is blown up into the air by a rocket inserted at the back. So far as I remember, Haydar Efendi, the Turkish ambassador, protested against this in Teheran during the time of my residence there. It was therefore publicly abstained from, but the boisterous noise outside the town was all the more wild ; and how thoroughly demonstrations of this kind bear upon them the character of hostility to the Turks is plainly proved by the act of Count Gobineau, at that time the ambassador of Napoleon, who, in order to give expression to his anti-Turkish feelings, blew up an Omer into the air himself, as representative of most Christian France. It must be obvious to every one that the gaping wound produced by the fanaticism of old Islam tendencies, instead of healing, would be more and more cruelly laid open. In the same manner, in the dramatic Passion plays, in which the tragic end of Hussein and Ali Egber is represented, an unbelieving Frank envoy, indignant at the barbarousness of the Sunnite Yezid, becomes a partisan of the Shiites ; and thus in daily life such a bias is given to popular feeling, that the masses in Persia are more friendly in their sentiments towards Europe, or rather to the Christian element, than to Turkey, their fellow-believer and neighbour for more than a hundred years. The word Efendi ($a\dot{v}\delta\epsilon v\tau\eta s$), the absolute, in the language of the Osmanlis, borrowed from the Greek only after the taking of Constantinople, and given to the usurping Caliphs as a title of derision, is identical with Antichrist ; Osmanlis and Britons, whose alliance is not unknown here even among the people, are set down as wild followers of Beelzebub, compared with whom Russians and French have even the preference ; and as the Persians in former times had really much to suffer from Turkish anarchy in their pilgrimages to Mecca, Jerusalem, and Bagdad, which is now no longer the case, the remembrance of past sufferings, combined with the wilfully-cherished hatred of the present, excites feelings of animosity which admit of no reconciliation.

As regards their diplomatic intrigues and plans of rivalry, the Persians, though without any special advantage, have adopted the deceptive conduct and dissimulation of our own diplomatists.

In order to imitate Turkey, which ever since the time of Sultan Mahmoud had carried on uninterrupted diplomatic intercourse with Europe, the Persians also desired to enter into an exchange of envoys with the West. Ferruch-Khan, an ambassador gifted with refined Persian manners and stately appearance, was just the man suited to deceive many a shallow European minister with Persian dissimulation of desire for civilisation and of longing for European customs. Morier's Hadji-Baba was already forgotten; the ostentatious bragging was accepted as pure coin, and it was French superficiality especially that was deceived. Not only did the above-mentioned Persian succeed in forming diplomatic alliances with most of the European states, but he even obtained from Napoleon the title of Emperor for his master in Teheran, a title which Napoleon at once granted him, and the King of Persia occasionally styles himself as actually Empereur de Perse.

The importance of our diplomatic posts on the Bosphorus has always been obvious to me, yet I have all the less been able to understand the ridiculous behaviour of these officials at Teheran. These *petits rois* in the East, both at the Court of the Shah and at that of the Sultan, as soon as there is any lack of soirées, receptions, congratulations, and representations, make a *question politique* out of the smallest disputes that occur in their household, in order to assume the most important political appearance just when there is least to do. What England, Russia, and Turkey seek in Teheran is no longer a matter of doubt to any

one, in consequence of direct and indirect neighbourly
relations; but what France desires in Teheran is and
ever will be a riddle to me. That Napoleon III.
can make constant and important mistakes has been
proved by recent history; yet it is almost inconceivable
what advantage the imperial policy can derive from
the fact that its representative signalises himself by
constant intrigues in a capital where France has no
political or commercial objects to advocate. Not even
as an inactive spectator can I find the French minister
in his place at Teheran. As the bearer of the policy
of his Cabinet, he ought, as in Teheran the matter at
stake can be only the Oriental question and Central
Asia, to draw the Shah to one side or to another,
according as circumstances require. He ought either
to support Russia against Turkey and England, or
both of these against Russia; he cannot carry on
purely French policy, and he has none, moreover, to
carry on. That a mediating position of this kind does
not become a great nation, I will not deny; it is, moreover, an utterly useless one, for the Persians know well
how far they need side with France in this respect.
They place, besides, not the slightest importance on the
fact whether they stand on a good or bad footing with
the French ambassador; for however much the latter
may consider himself an influential adviser, as was the
case, for example, with Count de Gobineau, the Court
of Teheran regards French mediation very much as an
innocent amusement.

Valueless as French influence in the Persian capital
is as regards the Government to which it belongs, it
is very disturbing to European or Western interests

generally. As the absorbing of the whole Islam East by Russia cannot and may not once for all be justified by Europe—and hence the frustration of all the efforts of the Court of Petersburg tending towards this end is imposed as a primary duty upon every right-thinking European state—the mediating position of a French diplomatist in Teheran can ,alone be advantageous when the latter, combined with England and Turkey, is inclined to lead the Persian king to a course opposed tp the plans of Petersburg. Unfortunately, this one beneficial service is but little or rarely afforded ; not, perhaps, from a fixed inclination to Russian interests, but from want of a guiding principle at all. The representatives of the great nation like to be held in honour at any price. They are satisfied when they can send to Paris bombastic statements and highly important news ; they are enchanted at a hare sent by the sport-loving Persian emperor into the ambassadorial kitchen, and at other trifles of a similar kind ; and thus their vocation, consciously or unconsciously, is wholly neglected. French influence sometimes appears in favour of the Russians, and sometimes against the Russians, but always in an undecided tone ; we cannot, therefore, be astonished when the Persians, famed as they have ever been for intrigue and cunning, say of the French, "*Fransiz hitsch reng nedared*" (The French have no colour).

The English Embassy, who may be regarded here rather as the extreme outpost of India than as a regular representative, is required chiefly on account of the Afghan disputes; but in spite of the constant turmoils, the affairs of Herat, and the frontier disputes of Sigistan, it has never neglected to do its utmost towards the restoration of a better state of harmony between Turkey and Persia. John Bull walks always arm-in-arm with the Sunnite representatives at the Persian Court. This alliance exists sometimes secretly, as, for instance, in the time of Sir Henry Rawlinson, who, in order to please the Persians, forbade all open intercourse with the Sunnites; at other times it is quite free and open, as, for example, at the present day, when Charles Alison is called the Christian Efendi by the Persians, on account of his striking adherence to the Turkish Embassy. Of course personal interest dictates an *entente cordiale* of the kind, and it may almost be regarded as certain that English insinuations would not only produce peaceful feelings between Turks and Persians in the Persian capital, but would considerably support the latter in their progress in European civilisation, if Russia, who desires anarchy and strife at any price, and who has aimed at it from the time of Peter the Great up to the present day, did not here come forward and check our common task in the East.

That Russia behaves in such a manner will not appear new to any one; it is only surprising that the Persians, arch-intriguers as they are, Orientals innately accustomed to every diplomatic device possible, do not perceive the fatal character of this policy, when, not only at home and in every question, but even at foreign European courts, they appear in brotherly concord with the Russians, their future patrons.

Persia is represented in Constantinople, London, Paris, and Petersburg; in Constantinople the longest, and in Petersburg only recently. When I mention that Mirza-

Husein-Khan, the present plenipotentiary of the Shah on the Bosphorus, not only one of the most gifted, but decidedly the most gifted diplomatist the Persians possess, in spite of his residence at an Islam court, lives on terms of closer friendship with Prince Labanoff or General Ignatieff, than with the gifted Fuad-Pasha or Ali-Pasha, I shall be told that it is a usual custom for the ambassador to attach himself rather to his diplomatic colleagues than to the civil functionaries of the Government to which he belongs; still is it not a striking circumstance that a similar state of things exists in Paris, London, and Petersburg? Why do not the representatives of the Shah and the Sultan, at any rate, keep more closely together, when the preservation of their interests against a common adversary is involved? And why should the tall fur caps of the Persians be more seen in Baron Budberg's ambassadorial palace on the Seine than in the Rue Presbourg with Mehemmed - Djemil - Pasha? Why should the subjects of the Shah in foreign countries where there is no Persian representative, be consigned rather to the protection of the Russian Embassy or the Russian Consulate, than to a Turkish? It is remarkable that the Turkish and Persian ambassadors carefully avoid each other even at public soirées. I have seen with repugnance, both in Paris and London, how the representatives of the great Islam states, although meeting under the hospitable roof of the same host, intentionally avoid each other.

Without much political acuteness, it is easy to see that this outward behaviour is only a consequence of thoroughly hostile feelings. The Persian will vote and intrigue against Turkish interests whenever it is possible to him ; indeed, with sparkling irony he will place the Osmanli always in the shade that he may distinguish himself at his expense.

Yet, after all, is the conception of European civilisation greatly different in these two Mussulman governments ? What the simple, honest Osmanli understands by the expression "à la Franca" is tolerably well known from the recent changes in Constantinople ; from the institutions which have been formed there, and are yet to be formed there ; and, in fact, from all the works of the Turks which evidence a friendliness towards Europe : but what the Persians comprehend under that mighty elixir, "civilization européenne," is far less transparent, and it will not be superfluous to explain what it means. The Persian—the Asiatic who prides himself on his wit and genius, who was called even in bygone times, "le Français de l'Orient" (a title not very flattering to either) — like many other gifted scholars, without troubling himself with the elements of study, desires to be at once learned, at once European. Instead of acquainting himself with languages or other normal-school subjects, the military pupil sent to Paris wishes at once to study engineering and strategy, he wishes at once to become an able general ; and just because at any price he desires to be different in everything from the Turks, the forerunners of European instruction, we often meet with the strangest mistakes committed in this branch of study on the part of the Persian Government. Apart from the many thousand ducats which the otherwise penurious Government of the Shah expends in the establishment of looms, cannon-foundries, and glass-manufactories, which, however, soon go to ruin for want of workers and from a superabundance of fraud, the way is strangely blocked up in Iran to the introduction of European articles of industry. Thus, when on one occasion, in some military arrangements, the ministers found that, in consequence of certain commercial circumstances, the price of buttons rose too high, they despatched some Persian students to Paris to be instructed in the noble art of button-making. It was on my return to Trapezunt that I met these accomplished artisans on the Persian frontier. The Parisian student-life was still plainly apparent in them, and I could not refrain from laughing when the young Persians began to inform me of the spirited conduct of their Government, which did not spend money like the Turkish Government for the theoretic cultivation of its sons, but turned them into practical men — *i.e.*, button-makers. Similar, and still greater mistakes, are perceptible also in the native schools, in which the Persian youth, who are really naturally gifted, are said to be instructed in Western culture and science.

Persia is more remote than even China, in consequence of the difficult land journey which separates it from Europe. The number of European fortune-hunters is smaller here than elsewhere, and thus the choice of teachers, instructors, etc., is far more difficult. Shall we be astonished, therefore, if the Government employs many an honest artisan from the West as a doctor and district physician? if many a simple photographer here becomes a professor of chemistry? if many a brave and adventurous swordsman rises to be an engineer officer, or a general high in command?

Similar metamorphoses were to be met with throughout the East during our present century. They are not to be avoided at first, and they are only animadverted on among the Persians, because, unconscious that they are in the shade compared with other Mussulman nations, they consider themselves the first and best of their kind.

The observer of the differences between Persia and Turkey will not be surprised, if he has attentively followed the unbroken chain of provocation, hostility, and childish rivalry, to see by the daily press that the outbreak of a Turkish and Persian conflict is closely impending.

This outbreak is to be feared, as in ancient times, on the western frontier of Iran, just where it borders on the Pashalik of Bagdad, in that province which has been always one of the most sacred spots in the Ottoman State, and, moreover, the quarter in which the Ministry of the Interior in Turkey has committed most errors. Apart from the fact that the governors of Bagdad have to act sometimes with the Bedouin races, the Benilam, and the Montefidsch, who roam over the Arabian peninsula, and whose subjection under the Porte is much the same as the dominion of the Turkomans under the rule of the Shah, and that at other times they are entangled in open feud with the Kurds, those restless adventurers in the north, it is nevertheless the frontier disputes with the Persian Government which prove the most difficult to the administration. Up to the present day it has been almost impossible radically to remedy the evil. From the possession of unlimited power, the caprice and avarice of the civil functionaries in question have placed the Porte in constant embarrassment. When the idea was entertained of limiting their authority, and sanctioning all their arrangements from Constantinople, the immense distance and the want of communication appeared at once as an impediment. Gentle governors were just as quickly circumvented by the Persians as passionate and warlike ones, and even occasionally came into hostile collision. Thus the administration of the famous Serdar Ekrems Omer-Pasha was a true time of terror to the Persians. While the name Omer in itself was thoroughly hated by them, all possible malice against the Shiite believers was imputed to him as a renegade ; and although the Porte appointed after him as governor of Bagdad the sleepy, aged, and naturally inactive Serkiatib Mustafa Pasha, his successor, Namik-Pasha, a man passionate by nature, a fanatical Sunnite, and a Mohammedan zealot, was obliged to destroy every possibility of a good understanding in his efforts to repair the errors of his predecessors.

During the whole period of the rule of Namik-Pasha, who was summoned to Constantinople as Minister of War, not a month elapsed in which a diplomatic correspondence full of the grossest invectives did not pass between these two Governments through the Ottoman Embassy in Teheran on the one side, and the ambassador at Constantinople on the other. Sometimes the point in question was the violation of some frontier line, sometimes it was to excuse the irruption of some Kurdish hordes; sometimes an official or prince proscribed in Persia had fled to Turkish soil, sometimes a Turkish officer accused of theft or breach of faith had escaped to the Iran territory. These political renegades were carefully welcomed on both sides; in fact, they even laboured to surpass each other in munificence. Not inconsiderable is the sum which the respective Governments expend on such individuals in the form of a pension. The green book of the Persians which appeared in May 1868, and which was sent to the foreign ambassadors at Teheran (a ridiculous imitation on the part of a government which not only has no idea of a constitution, but not even of government generally), may place the matter in as strong an anti-Turkish light as possible, although neither of the two disputants can wash his hands of all offence; nevertheless, it is not to be doubted that the Court of Teheran alone, and its policy, instigated as it is on the part of the Russians, is unceasingly scattering the seeds of discord, and is endeavouring with its utmost power to effect an open outbreak.

All that I hear said of fortifying Teheran, of concentrating troops on the frontier, and, in a word, of warlike preparations, seems to me to be over-hasty. The youthful Nasreddin Shah, thirsting for laurels, in which his reign, moreover, is not very rich, may well feel some desire to compete with the Turks, a desire which will certainly cost him dear, owing to the miserable condition of his army; still the Turkomans, and the civil war raging on his frontier in Afghanistan, will preserve him from misfortune. If Russia were a second time to attempt to settle the Oriental question by a Crimean war, Persian neutrality would not be as certain as it was in 1854.

But it is not only in the recent disputes that I would lay the blame of disturbing the peace upon the Court of Teheran; it deserves this blame all through, and on every occasion. It is alone the fault of the Persians that the religious breach between the two sects has become a political cleft,

N

as we pointed out at the beginning of this paper. |ty This is best proved by the fact that Persians, who inunc;ilate all the commercial towns of the Ottoman Empire, are ᵥrot half so much hated by the Sunnite Turks as the Turks are hated by them ; for in Iran every subject of the Sultan is not only exposed to all possible ignominy on the part of the rude mob, but in many places is compelled to pay a shameful tribute called the Sunnite tax. Subjects of the Persian king live from Belgrade to Cairo, from Basra to Antivari, without any oppression or constraint; indeed, the simple Osmanli is far rather so friendly in his feelings to the Persian that he enters into relationship with him as far as his religion allows him. What would the Persians do with a Sunnite in Shiraz, in Yezd, or in Kerman, where the latter would be far from the protecting power of the Ottoman ambassador? Neither the magistrates of the place nor the Shah, nor any human power whatever, could protect him from malice and fanaticism; his continuance there would be an impossibility.   Is not this want of regard for equality of treatment in itself a crying injustice in political life ? Does not such a voluntary or involuntary intolerance sufficiently denote barbarism?   This arrogant behaviour on the part of the weak Iran towards the Ottoman Empire, which in every respect is more strong and powerful, plainly manifests the want of political maturity and sense of justice in the self-conceited ministers of the Shah. Yet we can bring forward a second and still more important fact, which must not be overlooked by the impartial observer of East Mohammedan affairs.   In the whole dominion of Islamism there is only one point at which it comes in contact with its foe, Christianity—only one point at which, weakened and humbled, it is exposed to the attacks of its powerful enemy. This point is Turkey. If only one spark of unity existed among the different Mussulman states, they would altogether, and with combined power, aim at the protection and guardianship of this one point; for they must know that if this bulwark received a breach, or was broken down, they would all be abandoned to the will of an invincible power. That Turkestan, Afghanistan, Egypt, Morocco, and the other infinitesimal states of Mussulman faith, have never thought of this, and do not wish to think of it, is injurious enough to them, but in their condition of barbarism it is not to be wondered at. All the more, however, is the fact astonishing on the part of Persia. Since that land possesses the oldest political tie of all, it ought most to perceive the common danger, and yet it most of all presses with hostile feeling against this one point, with which its safety is interwoven. I have before remarked that in the Crimean war, when the Western knights of the Cross entered the lists on behalf of the Crescent, the Persian sun and lion inclined rather towards the north, and were only with difficulty restrained from entering into a Russian alliance. But not only was this the case then, but on all occasions when Turkey is attacked by Christian foes we see the subtle but thoroughly infatuated Persians joining the enemies of the Crescent. Ever since the time of Peter the Great, Persia has directly or indirectly supported all Russian plans: it coquetted with Mehemmed-Ali at the time of the insurrection; it attempted to make common cause with every recreant vassal of the Porte; and I am firmly convinced, that if the Oriental question were to draw nearer the critical moment of its solution, the Persians would join those who voted most eagerly for the expulsion of the Turks from Europe.

Truly a laughable parody of Persian sagacity and diplomatic wisdom!

What the Turks lack refers not so much to Persia alone as to all other Mussulman states. Just as the rulers of the Osman house were speedily lulled into sweet sleep by the delicious sound of the waves of the Bosphorus when once they had held them in possession, giving up all vast political ideas, and only here and there seeking an alliance in Eastern Asia, as appears recently from a correspondence of Sultan Murad with the Sherbani dynasty in Bokhara; so, not from contempt, not from hate, but far rather from lack of governing principles and from cold indolence, they have made but few advances towards Persia. Only since the regular diplomatic alliance with Europe was entered into have they sent embassies in exchange for Shah-Benders (consuls); but even in this they have been too sparing. Iran has consuls and agents in Bagdad, Basra, Erzeroum, Trapezunt, Constantinople, Smyrna, Beirut, Alexandria, Belgrade, and Salonica; Turkey has only an ambassador at Teheran, a consul at Kirman-Shah, and this of the Shiite religion, and in Ispahan the shadow of an agent. Is not this a strange circumstance, showing in all its nakedness the sleepy character of the Osmanli? Indolence, therefore, and not an hostility on principle, must be assigned as one cause why the Persian disputes which arise from time to time are not at once adjusted on the part of the Turks. In Teheran the Persian authorities are occupied with empty intrigues, and with still more empty progress in civilisation; and·quietly dwelling in the interior of the continent, they seem to wish almost to ignore what the Turks have to suffer from the diplomatic communications of accredited ambassadors, from the momentous questions in Crete and Epirus, from their ever-increasing pecuniary embarrassments, and from compulsory plans of reform, &c. Turkey is fully occupied, whether it is her own fault or no. Truly Persia would accomplish far more in her own interest if she would guard as much as possible against the provocation of her neighbour, and would aim at peaceful unity. At present, thoughtful discretion may still avail; but if once the neighbour's house is in flames, it will assuredly be too late.

HERAT AND THE CENTRAL ASIATIC QUESTION (1869).

To speak of Herat is considered, in the eyes of the new political school of Anglo-Indian statesmen, as no longer seasonable, and, indeed, as utterly fruitless. The policy of Lord Auckland's time is condemned as narrow, in order to impart all the greater lustre to the more recent views of so - called indifference. To speak of Herat as the gate of Central Asia has become downright dangerous. I venture, nevertheless, to designate the old seat of the magnificent and science-loving Hussein-Mirza-Baikara by this epithet, and this simply from personal experience and actual evidence that the city on the Heri-Rud, forms on the one side towards the banks of the Oxus, the true gate to the vestibule of Turkestan, by which I mean the northern chain of the Paropamisus range and the Khanates of Meimene and Andchoi; and on the other side the true gate to the vestibule of India, by which I mean Afghanistan. Any one who has passed Herat on the way from or to Bokhara will have perceived this for himself. On the way from north to south, from Kaisar to Meimene, the ever-increasing ascent becomes more and more perceptible;

arrived at Murgab, the traveller has lofty mountains
before him ; and in Kale-No his path is impeded by steep
walls of rock and mountain ranges more than 8000 feet
high, on the summit of which the snow rests even in
the midst of summer. I shall never forget the fearful
evening which I spent on these heights, when I found
in September the snow of the previous year 8 feet high.
The declivity is equally rapid, and when from the foot
of the mountain the eye rests on the town and environs
of Herat, situated in a luxuriant plain, and enjoying a
soft climate, owing to its protection from the northern
winds by the gigantic natural screen, one readily agrees
with the natives when they say that God chose Herat
as a resting-place, both for those who are hastening
forwards to the toils of burning India, and for those
who are passing on to the torments of rude Turkestan.

It is true I have heard that fear of the Salar Turkomans has created this Central Asiatic highway over
these steep mountains, and that Herat can be reached
more quickly and easily in going from Meimene
towards the west. Yet, strikingly enough, we have no
historical data respecting this highway; for even in
past centuries, as the ruins of caravanseries sufficiently
testify, the road lay in its present direction.

Herat, however, is not a resting - place created by
nature ; but it has ever been a mighty emporium for the
commercial relations of Persia and India. When the
gates of Herat are closed, trade on the Indus, in
Bokhara, and in Ispahan will stagnate. To pass .
Merv is impossible, or at any rate most unpleasant,
not only on account of the predatory Turkomans, but
also on account of the barren steppes ; and I can well

understand how, at the time of the last siege of Herat
by Dóst - Mohammed, caravans preferred to endure a
quarantine of two years at Meshed, than, by evading
Herat, to choose another route.

However much, therefore, the before-mentioned diplomatists of the Anglo-Indian school, both in Calcutta
and London, have struggled against the acceptance of
this fact, the Orientals have always known this city as
possessing the characteristics we have denoted ; they
have perfectly seen its importance ; and how much the
neighbouring states have contended for its possession
is proved by the more than fifty sieges which Herat
has had to endure—sieges which have taken place not
so much for the sake of the rich soil that surrounds it,
as on account of the desire for conquest with which it
has inspired sometimes India and sometimes Central
Asia. With the exception of Baber, almost all the
conquerors of India and Transoxania have placed great
importance on Herat ; in a similar sense it forms at the
present day the apple of discord between Persia and
Afghanistan, or more justly, indirectly ¡that between
Russia and England.

It can therefore surprise no one if Russia, who is
quite Oriental in Asia, shares the same views with the
Orientals as far as regards the importance of Herat.
The contests under Mehemmed Shah, under whose
command Russian engineer officers actually took part
in the siege, are too recent for a recapitulation of the
events to be necessary. Ever since a strong interest
has been felt on the banks of the Neva for the city on
the Heri. Previous to 1840, the Russian ships of the
line had never felt themselves quite at home in the

southern waters of the Caspian Sea; at the present day a firm footing has been gained in Ashurada, and paid Turkoman chieftains have paved the way for Russian propaganda, not only among the Yomuts, but also among the Göklens. The Russian consul in Astrabad sends presents to the Kurdish chieftains of Kabushan, as well as to the grey-bearded sheiks of the Teke-Turkomans. And if armed bodies of Cossacks are to follow the pioneering propaganda, our self-satisfied English diplomatists will be utterly astonished to find in what a short time a Russian force landed at Astrabad can repair to Herat along the northern frontier of Persia. The distance from Astrabad to Meshed is reckoned generally as somewhat more than sixty geographical miles, a journey which can be easily accomplished through a fertile region within eight or ten days, so that even an army of more than 30,000 men need not be perplexed as to its commissariat. From Meshed to Herat a caravan goes in ten days, and an army travels the distance in eight days; here also there is no lack of food and water for the animals, and nothing but the unreliable character of the population, since it forms the highway for Turkoman attacks, renders it necessary that provisions should be taken for the two or three days from Djam or Meshhedi-No. A regular army, therefore, even if endangered by Turkoman hordes, can be transported within twenty days at most from the Russian vessels to Herat. Moreover, the transport is combined with less fatigue than on any other route in Central Asia.

From what we have here said it will probably astonish no one that the Russian diplomatists, not sharing the ideas of their English colleagues, consider Herat, this true gate of Central Asia, on the one side, as the advanced work of the difficulties to be fought with on the banks of the Indus; and on the other, they regard it as a secure starting-point for their plans on the south, besides being a strong defence against a possible surprise upon the acquisitions they have already made in Transoxania; hence it will not appear superfluous to any one to become better acquainted with the fate of this city since the death of Dost-Mohammed, to learn something of the political opinions of its inhabitants, and to consider the important part which is reserved for it in the future.

When in June 1863, Dost-Mohammed-Khan surrounded Herat with a rather considerable and well-equipped body of troops, the Shah of Persia had to be restrained by force—so, at least, the Persians would have us believe—from not hastening to the assistance of his oppressed vassal, Sultan Ahmed-Djan, with the forces kept ready in the neighbourhood of Meshed. It is true Sultan Ahmed was much devoted to the Court of Teheran. Nasreddin's name shone on the Herat coins; Nasreddin's name resounded in the Herat mosques at the prayer for the welfare of the ruler; the Shiite Persians carried their heads high in the old capital of Chorassan, the richest offices were in their hands; the King of Persia had therefore cause enough to stake life and property for Herat, which he already regarded as a rich pearl in his diadem. Notwithstanding, he did not do so. The conclusion of the Peace of Paris in 1856, according to which his actual participation in the Herat affairs was to be regarded as a *casus belli* against

England, kept back his army on the frontier at Mah-
mudabad ; and while Sultan Murad-Mirza, the governor
of Chorassan and the commander of the army of
observation, an uncle of the Shah, was sending alarming
information to Teheran of each small success on the
part of the grey-haired Dost-Mohammed, the ruler of
Kabul, at ninety years of age, was not only hardly
pressing the city on the Heri-Rud, but was even turning
his threatening glance to the banks of the Zerefshan.
He cherished a feeling of animosity against the father
of the deceased Prince of Bokhara—the son was to
suffer for it. Muzaffar - ed - Din early perceived the
danger that threatened him; he allied himself, therefore, with the Dost, but it was of no avail. The old
Barekzi had settled his own measures, and whether the
Emir liked it or not, he was very near crossing the
Oxus with Afghan bayonets. In fact, Herat, according
to the plan of the unwearied Afghan prince, was to be
the centre of new plans of occupation ; an Oriental at
ninety years of age, and forming new plans—what an
extraordinary phenomenon ! And yet so it was. Dost-
Mohammed actually designed to extend the Afghan
kingdom in the north not only eastward as far as Belkh,
but even westward as far as Tchihardjui — a plan
the execution of which had become all the more easy
as the minor khanates, such as Meimene, Andchoi,
Aktche, &c., were either disputing with each other, or
were already tributary to the Afghans. On the other
side of the Oxus he had thought of no solid conquests ;
his object here was to give a thorough rebuke for an
outrageous offence which the dissolute Nasrullah, with
whom he had once taken refuge at a time of misfortune,

had committed not so much against him as against his pretty beardless boy. It was known in Bokhara that this royal misbehaviour would have to be indemnified by heavy *lakhs* of gold ; nor did the old Afghan aim at anything more, for his eagle eye was resting on far other lands. He desired nothing less than to pay the King of Persia an armed visit ; all English dissuasions and threats could not shake him in this intention. He knew that as soon as he crossed the frontier of Iran, the gentlemen in Peshawur would withhold the yearly support in arms and money ; still Afghan vengeance is intimidated by no combination of circumstances, and his death was the only reason that prevented his invading Iran with a force far superior to the Persians.

It was evening when Herat, after a most obstinate defence, fell into the hands of Dost-Mohammed. On the following morning, at ten o'clock, he intended making his entry into the city, when death unexpectedly surprised him. A violent altercation which had arisen between him and a common Afghan soldier caused the slight colic which had troubled the Dost for some time to turn into a dangerous and fatal illness. He died in the early morning, in perfect possession of his senses, just as he was about to begin his morning devotions. Instead of making his entry on his splendid battle-horse, surrounded by a brilliant suite, he was carried in on his bier, and was followed by a mourning multitude. Had he entered the city alive, he would just as little, in consequence of the devastating balls of his artillery, have found a shelter there as now, when his corpse, for want of one uninjured mosque, was obliged to lie in the open street, surrounded by pious

Ulemas. It was hastily borne to Khodja-Abdullah-Ansari; and the last clod of earth thrown upon his grave may be regarded as the black seal which consigned to death for a long time, if not for ever, the future of a united and great Afghan kingdom.

Herat was taken, the power of the Afghans had reached its zenith, and the members of the family of the deceased Dost-Mohammed had not met for the funeral feast, the libations for the funeral meal were not prepared, when the ambitious son, grandsons, and great-grandsons began to kindle those sparks of dispute, the flames of which are still blazing destructively on the banks of the Hilmend and in the valleys of the Hindu-kush. At the time that I was in Central Asia, the dispute between Shir-Ali, the successor designated by the Dost, and Afzal-Khan, the governor of Belkh, or Turkestan, as it is called by the Afghans, a man never loved by his old father, and always regarded with suspicion, had already broken out. Not only did Afzal-Khan refuse to render to Shir-Ali the usual marks of allegiance, but he was even preparing for actual hostilities, by making war and devastating the Khanates of Meimene and Andchoi, in spite of his, Shir-Ali-Khan's, persuasions. Whilst the caravan route between Bokhara and Kabul was closed through Belkh, Herat merchants were allowed free passage through Meimene and Andchoi. In fact, Shir-Ali knew very well, perhaps even before his father's death, what his brother intended, and he would certainly have obliged him to act differently, if the *mesned* (throne) had not been so feebly in his grasp in other parts also of the Afghan kingdom. He desired first of all to come to an arrangement with the Persians. The report of the taking of Herat—a copy of which I happened to see with the governor of Meshed—was richly sprinkled with the customary rose-water, denoting hearty friendship; and although Persia could have known nothing definitely as to the continuance of the Anglo-Afghan alliance after the death of Dost-Mohammed, the authorities were moderate enough to accept the offered friendship. In reply to the report of the victory, the ambassador Mehemmed-Bakir-Khan was sent to Herat in the beginning of September 1863. Shir-Ali received him with great friendship; distinctions were conferred upon him such as had never been conferred on any Shiite by the wild Sunnite Afghans; and although the friendly ceremonials were interspersed with grand manœuvres and reviews of troops — the splendid Risalez troops and the martial Paltans being brought from Kabul in order to give the Persian an idea of Afghan power—still there was truly a great effort made to show the King of Persia that Dost-Mohammed's successor had adopted a different policy to that of his father with respect to Persia, and that at any rate he desired to remain at peace with that country. Sherbet, robes of honour, splendid horses, and reviews had the desired effect : Mehemmed-Bakir-Khan returned to Meshed fully reconciled; the Persian army of observation was recalled from the frontier; and Shir-Ali was secure from his most dreaded western adversary. After the termination of this successful strategy, he speedily returned to Kabul; and as a proof of the security he felt, he gave the command of the important frontier city of Herat to his son, Mehemmed-Yakub-Khan, a boy scarcely eleven years of age, whose amusing meeting with myself is well known to the readers of my " Reisen in Mittelasien."

After Herat was thus secured by the desired under-standing with Persia, by the neutrality of the Khanates Meimene and Andchoi, and by the officious service of the Hezare-Djemshidi chiefs, there only remained the Turkomans, who acknowledged no superiority, no com-pact, and no treaty of peace, from whose attacks the town and environs of Herat had to be protected; yet this was not done until after a combined predatory excursion on the part of the Tekke and Sarik tribes was repulsed in 1865 by the governor of Gurian. The marauders of the desert diminished, the commercial highways were more frequented, and Herat, which recovered from its wounds in an incredibly short time, soon raised itself from the miserable condition in which I had found it. The town and environs flourished, and this under the direction of the before-mentioned youthful prince, who, exerting mind and body, formed such an able champion in the frontier city that he speedily won a name in several battles as the right hand of his father and a skilful general.

Herat was now at any rate to be recognised as Afghan property; and such is still the opinion both of the Court of Kabul and of its neighbour on the other side of the Indus. Both of these regard the present *status quo* in Herat as a sufficient bulwark against Persia and Russia; but I will prove in the following remarks that both are mistaken.

That Herat, up to the present time, has not been able to distinguish itself by a strong adherence to Afghanistan, which for more than three centuries has been wooing it

—that indeed it has perhaps signalised itself, on the contrary, by the fact that it has ever desired to stand as an independent whole, and has wished to know nothing of the gentlemen at Kabul, rests rather on the ethnographical character of its inhabitants than on its political antecedents.   The Afghans are in a very small minority there : the whole tract of land stretching from the banks of the Murgab to Ferah, a tract almost seventy miles from north to south, is regarded by the Orientals as belonging to Herat; the inaccessible Hezerah range is considered by them as the eastern boundary, and that portion of land where the territory of the Shiite Persians begins as the western.   On this whole territory, forming almost the fourth part of the Afghan kingdom, there are few or no Afghans ; and the real population—that is, the inhabitants of the towns, who have received from the Afghans the name Parsivan, or, more correctly, Fars-Zeban, *i.e.*, people of the Persian language—are, from remembrance of the past greatness of Herat, most averse to Afghan rule, regarding, as they do, the Afghans as the main destroyers of their national independence, and in this they are tolerably right.   It is no wonder, therefore, that in spite of all religious hatred, the Parsivans, who are chiefly Sunnites, should incline to the Shiite Persians, their brethren in race and language; and this, moreover, from the fact that, in the first place, they feel themselves far more comfortable under the sovereignty of Iran than under the rude yoke of the Afghans ; and secondly, because Iran, which is really satisfied only with the shadow of supremacy, interferes but little with the autonomy of Herat.   I impute it to this circumstance that Iran's influence has been steadily increasing there for the last few years, and that several of the villages lying round Herat contain at the present day a considerable number of Shiites, who, on one side relying on Persia, and on the other cultivating intercourse with the Hezerahs, are the best emissaries in the service of the Shah.

Far higher, however, than their esteem for Persia is the value placed by the people of Herat upon those princes under whom they could enjoy a certain independence, although they may be of Afghan descent. Every one, even the simplest peasant, has somewhat to tell of one of these ; and I could enter into their feelings when, at the time of my sojourn in the city, I heard them speak with extraordinary reverence of Sultan Ahmed-Djan, and of his two sons, while they loaded the deceased Dost and his present successor with epithets of ignominy, although both were really Afghans, and were, moreover, related.

The ruins in the Mossalla (place of prayer) and the other parts of the neighbourhood called to mind too vividly that flourishing epoch of Sultan Hussein, the Timuride, and the powerful influence which he had exercised from his seat on the Heri to the borders of India on the one side, and to the shores of the Caspian Sea on the other, for the people of Herat to desire any foreign rule, however superior to their own. This convulsive clinging to political independence has passed in a remarkable manner from the people themselves to those princes, who, as has often been the case of late, have been sent here as vassals. This explains the circumstance that Herat has a history of its own, even under the Afghan rule forced upon it.

Immediately after the fall of Herat, the successor of

O

Dost-Mohammed had nothing else to do but to render the two sons of the deceased Sultan Ahmed-Djan—the younger of whom was named Iskender-Khan, the elder Shah-Nuwaz — harmless as regards his future plans. Shah-Nuwaz was at once sent to Kabul as a prisoner, and the people of Herat told me with tearful eyes of the heavy chains with which the son of their former prince was loaded. Iskender-Khan had time to escape; he fled to Belch, and from thence entered into the service of the Emir of Bokhara. He subsequently became notorious from the fact that he was the first Afghan who was faithless to his brethren in the faith, and who went over to the Russians. The fate of this renegade was not unknown in his native city, and most remarkably, as I hear, he was not in the least blamed; they imputed nothing else to him than that he had sworn allegiance to the Muscovites in order by their help to succeed in regaining his paternal heritage. And although the means were displeasing to a few wild fanatics, the majority of the discontented inhabitants of Herat, to whom the blessing of European rule had been known from the influence exercised by Major Todd, could not be angry at such a step. These two princes were, and still are, the idols both of the Parsivan population and of the numerous Persians who reside in the town and its environs, so that Azim-Khan might very easily have inflicted a great loss upon his enemy Shir-Ali-Khan by the seizure of Herat, if he had not been supporting one of these sons of Sultan Ahmed-Djan in the recovery of that city. That this did not take place, is, in the first place, to be ascribed to the want of sufficient confidence with which the children of Ahmed-Djan inspired the pretender to the throne of Afghanistan, on account of their well-known Persian sympathies ; in the second place, it was impossible to the rival of Shir-Ali, because on his march to Herat he had first to fight his way through Meimene, Andchoi, and many thousands of the nomad tribes there.

Yet the political combinations were not this time very favourable to the wishes of the people of Herat. The expelled sons of their last prince are still outside the frontier of their native soil ; and one, while I am writing these lines, is probably an object of admiration to the Russian ladies in Zarskoe-Selo, since General Kaufmann, as is well known, took him with him to Petersburg. The town and fortress of Herat have not only remained strictly Afghan, but they even became the refuge of Shir-Ali, when, driven from Kabul and Kandahar, he had to flee thither. The citadel, in consequence of this, has been completely restored ; the walls are renewed ; and if I am rightly informed, Dervaze-Irak, the gate opening into the highway that leads to Meshed, has been strengthened with stone breastwork like the Dervaze-Kandahar. In fortifications of this kind, as in all other matters of a military nature, essential use is to be found in the numerous Anglo-Indian Sepoy deserters who, both at the time of the Sepoy revolution. as well as after it, have fled over the Kheiber Pass and entered the Afghan service. Their number is considerable, and although they are inferior in capability to the European instructors in Turkey and Persia, they are of greater use ; for, as Orientals, they are better suited than Europeans for the training of Orientals.

Besides the fortification of Herat, still more strength

has been imparted to this portion of the Afghan frontier territory by a close league with Persia. Whether Shir-Ali-Khan has received actual help from Nasreddin Shah in resuming the civil war, I much doubt; still a kind of compromise has taken place between them—a compromise which was effected on the occasion of the visit of Serdar-Yakub-Khan to Meshed, when he met the Persian king there in the past summer. An unconditional cession of Herat seems not to have ensued: the Shah pronounced himself satisfied for this time with a portion of the Afghan Siistan; for, as is well known, the frontier line of Iran in this quarter was a very weak one, the nomad inhabitants, chiefly Beludjans, having sometimes joined one side and sometimes another. Neither Iran nor Afghanistan was a match for them; and if the latter, by the cession of this province, thought to make a trifling concession to the former, it was very much mistaken. Five years ago the Persians had scarcely ventured to set foot on the western territory of the Zare lake. At the present day Persia has already erected some forts on the east; and it can, if it pleases, by this position in the south, quickly threaten Herat by an attack on Ferrah, a matter which would have been very difficult without the possession of Ferrah. At the present day, while the way is being silently prepared for the great political events in Central Asia, and when Persia, in implicit obedience, stands waiting the watchword from the Neva, the ruler of the house of Kadjar will be cautious in taking a step which may even remotely encroach upon the Paris Peace. The friendly and cordial understanding will remain for some time undisturbed; yet, on account of the present calm (May 1869), we have turned our glance in that direction, and we will endeavour, in a few feeble sketches, to discuss the strategic and political value of the city—of that city which, without doubt, within the next ten years, will play a far more important part than was assigned to it in the time of the Afghan war.

In the year 1868 my readers may have seen in the English press the expression of indignation with which certain short-sighted politicians met the attempt of the Indian Government—an attempt, perhaps, not even seriously intended—to fortify and occupy Herat. The expense was computed at four million pounds sterling, of course a sum ridiculously exaggerated, and certainly only devised because by such a colossal amount it was intended to frighten the tax-paying public at home. The entire Afghan war, in which, five years before and five years after the outbreak, large subsidies and gifts in land and princes, had to be paid to the remotest environs, and in which an army had perished, had scarcely cost twenty millions; and now it was wished to make the world believe that the equipment of this town with a garrison would consume in one year the fifth part of the same amount.

I will therefore only express, that much as I was astonished at the computation mentioned, yet I was agreeably affected by the idea of such a project, and, unfortunately, it has hitherto gone no further. England ought and must retain Herat, of course in accordance with the Afghans; for the value of its possession is considerably greater than the gentlemen in Calcutta at the time of Pottinger and Todd imagined, and infinitely greater than the gentlemen in Calcutta imagine at the present day.

That Herat is the gate, in fact the very key to India, will be best proved by a glance at its natural position. 1. The two highways, both from the north and north-west, leading to the southern Hilmend and Indus, inter-sect each other here ; for, as we have already remarked, the road through Kabul is dangerous, and is but rarely taken. As the Persian and Central Asiatic merchant, trading to India and Afghanistan, rests at Herat, and considers Herat as the cross-road for caravans, so the army marching from the banks of the Oxus, or from the Caspian Sea, must halt here also. Herat is, I might almost say, the point at which the traveller has to undergo a change of climate in passing from the north-ern to the southern zone. This natural route has, more-over, up to the present day, never been avoided, and can never be so ; the eastern outlet would lead the traveller into the rude Hezerah Mountains, the western into the inhospitable districts of Siistan : for any one proceeding from north to south, nothing therefore is left but to take the old highway, trodden for centuries by caravans, free-booters, and conquerors, which has its starting-point at Herat. 2. Herat has the position of a place surrounded on all sides by nomadic tribes, and may for that reason be considered a secure rampart by the countries both to the south and north of it, as its possessors, by a wise policy, can obtain thousands, and indeed hundreds of thousands of nomad tribes, and other warlike elements, and this has actually been done by the distinguished princes of Herat in past times. It is easier than else-where to negotiate from Herat with the Turkomans, Hezerahs, Djemshids, and Özbegs of Meimene. The historical importance of Herat is plainly apparent to all these tribes; and the sovereign on the banks of the Heri who can make the chiefs of these nomad tribes his vassals, possesses a by no means despicable power against foes advancing from the north or east. 3. The richness of the soil, for which Herat was always famous, must not be forgotten. Djölgei-Herat (the plain of Herat) is justly famed as the granary of both Afghanistan and the northern districts; and it would be difficult to find a second place in the whole of Central Asia, not excepting even Persia, where a great, ay, a very great army, could be maintained with such little difficulty as here. Eastern historians tell us of the immense bodies of troops which, both under the Timurides and the Sefevides, and even in Nadir's time, had their winter quarters here. It would have seemed almost incredible, if the fact that I have myself observed—namely, that a great part of the Turkomans derive their supplies of corn and rice not so much from Sarrachs and Deregöz as from the plain of Herat—did not strikingly speak in favour of our assertion. Herat rice is sent even to Meshed, and to the shores of the Oxus; and without wishing to share the views of one of my former travelling companions, that even the pistachio plants in the neighbourhood of Herat were sufficient to satisfy armies, I cannot help regarding this town and its environs as one of the most fruitful storehouses.

Can England, after all that we have here said, look with such indifference on the possession of Herat? or does she fear, perhaps, that the expense of holding it would be too enormous? Upon this point, I think, the smallest scruples need be entertained. Taking for granted that an English garrison, with the consent of

Afghanistan, accepts here the post of a boundary guard, and that the occupation therefore is not one of force, but is undertaken rather in the interest of Afghanistan, the management of a town consisting of heterogeneous elements, and of a district accustomed to foreign rule, will be an easy task for England. The semblance of the brief British rule of 1838, for only a semblance can it be called, has not only not been forgotten in Herat, but even the most hostile Mohammedan extols this epoch as the happiest he remembers ; and an English rule would find here more support, or at any rate would meet with less ill-will, than in many parts of the Punjaub and of fanatical Bengal.

Many will perhaps call in question the readiness of Shir-Ali-Khan to take such a step, knowing, as they do, the value which Herat possesses in the eyes of the Afghans. I can in nowise share this apprehension. The sovereign of Kabul feels, indeed, that the city of Herat is a precious pearl in his diadem, but equally precious, perhaps, to him is its defence and protection ; and as the present sovereign is certainly as eager to conquer his rivals at home, and to consolidate the heritage bequeathed to him by Dost-Mohammed, as to maintain the *status quo* of his power in the west, he will not show himself averse if England, whose sincerity he needs not doubt, and certainly does not doubt, will take upon herself to garrison Herat, in order that he may devote his individual powers to the work of internal regeneration.

That Shir-Ali-Khan, or whatever Afghan sovereign it may be, not only will pay nothing for the acceptance of such a task, but expects to be compensated to a large amount for the service rendered, will not in the least surprise Anglo-Indian politicians. This is, of course, an anomaly in political matters. But we must not forget that this anomaly was called into being by England herself in former treaties with Afghanistan. The subsidies which Sir Henry Lawrence granted Dost-Mohammed in 1857, had been originally employed for the same object. The Dost struggled against bringing English troops into Afghanistan; he was satisfied with English arms and English money, for he was mighty in the interior, and Russia at that time was as far from the banks of the Oxus as her outposts now are from Herat. Shir-Ali, therefore, mindful of these circumstances, will not imitate his father in his obstinacy. The conditions required by him may be indeed greater as to the amount of arms and rupees to be given, yet I do not for a moment doubt his readiness to claim England's help in the protection of his outposts, unless he has already allied himself with the Russians, which is very improbable.

And Herat is worth a sacrifice. Russia's plans of attack seem still to hover before the world generally in the twilight of uncertainty; all eyes are now directed towards Bokhara, yet I feel persuaded that a diversion along the northern frontier of Persia is already secretly preparing. The Yomut-Turkomans, ever since the last Persian campaign directed against them, have stood on a far more friendly footing with Ashurada than before. Whether the route of march from Astrabad through Meshed to Herat is taken with the consent of the Persians or not, we have no reliable evidence; but that the strategic triangle of the Russian forces, stretching from the north towards the south, and from the west towards the east, will concentrate itself either at Herat or Belch, we may consider as certain.

Surprises in politics are just as disadvantageous as they are disagreeable; and the word of warning, "Keep a watch on Herat!" is just now not unseasonable.

SOCIAL TRANSFORMATIONS IN THE INTERIOR OF ASIA (1870).

IT is one of the chief excellences of the nineteenth century, that by its constant investigations and its unflagging watchfulness in all, even in the remotest parts of our earth, it is never especially surprised by any event, and therefore is not compelled to regard any political or social revolution, of whatever extent, with any great degree of wonder or surprise. It is not, indeed, to be denied that our view has been enlarged by the knowledge of certain regions to which our steam-vessels can far more easily procure us access than the staff of the traveller can do, as he wanders amid unspeakable hardships. Thus we possess information to the smallest detail of all that is going on in the old Zipangu, in the capital of old Cathay, and even on the banks of the Yang-tse-Kiang and Irawaddi. Any one who will take a little trouble can inform himself as well and as thoroughly from the copious literature relating to lands and peoples, upon the social, political, and hierarchical condition of the Burmese, Siamese, Chinese, and Japanese, as he can do with regard to the neighbouring European countries.

Distance by water has long ceased to be a barrier to European curiosity; it is alone distance by land which quenches the ardour of the investigator, for dangers and disappointments are here ever deterring the traveller from approaching the fount of knowledge. It sounds almost incredible, and yet so it is, that the seaport towns of Japan, China, and even the remote Mandjuria, are more visited by Europeans than many places in Persia and Arabia, which are comparatively so much nearer. Of Central Asia I will not even speak. We stand there at the same point at which we stood 300 years ago with regard to other parts of Asia. The inquiring spirit of the European has made more use of the sea, which has suited his yearning for adventure and his ungovernable desire to advance rapidly, and hence he has first visited the shores of the Asiatic continent. In the interior he has only penetrated gradually and step by step; he will, moreover, have only completed his task when he has reached the central point; hence Central Asia, which forms this central point, may be regarded as the keystone to that gigantic work which the Western mind has assigned to itself in the regeneration of Asia.

The opposite working of civilising influences is truly wonderful. While Central Asia is now ever more and more receiving the teachings and opinions of a new world by advances made from without, or more correctly, from the shore towards the centre, it was this very Central Asia from which, more than two thousand years ago, the old Parsi civilisation extended to all the four quarters of the Asiatic world of that day, like a stream from some mighty and gushing fountain. Sog-

diana, Merv, and Bactria, are, as the Vendidad tells us,
the original seats of old Iran civilisation; subsequently
its limits extended as far as Media in the west, while
in the north they reached to the banks of the Yaxartes,
where in recent times the ruins of old cities have been
discovered, and where archæological investigations
would assuredly meet with the richest success. This
Persian people, from whose centre in Bactria Zoroaster
sprang, must truly, even at that time, have reached no
inconsiderable stage of civilisation; it was they who
gave the impulse by which the Persia of the Pish-
dadians, the Keyanides, and the Sassanides acquired that
high culture, perhaps often fabulously exaggerated, but
which, according to Greek statement, must have, nevertheless, been far from contemptible. Ancient Bactria was the
cradle of the imaginative creations wrought out in the
historical romances of a Firdusi. In confirmation of our
views we have, indeed, at our disposal, no Assyrian-Baby-
lonian monuments, and no Egyptian works of art; still,
we think, the testimony of an Arabian author, who,
as the declared enemy of all non-Mohammedan culture,
would certainly indulge in no flattery, is of great importance. The famous Abu-Rihan, who wrote in the
first century of the Hegira, tells us wonders of Belch;
of the old Bactria of a thousand gates, as Justin calls
it, distinguished as the principal seat of astronomical investigations, and from whence the earliest computation
of time spread over other parts of Asia; of Khahrezm,
as the ancient seat of romantic heroic legends. We learn
from him that Kuteibe-Ibn-Muslim studied in the old
Khahrezm manuscripts the former history of the land
conquered by him, and that on the lower bank of the

Oxus, a single dynasty, the Shahite, beginning in the time of the Achæmenide, ruled, with the exception of a Turkish interregnum of ninety-two years, until the period of the Mohammedan invasion. What Bagdad and Damascus were in the first centuries of Islamism, that Belch, Samarkand, and Kermineh were, as regards civilised importance, several hundred years before the appearance of the Arabian Prophet. The fire temple of Nubehar spread its religious glow northward far beyond the Yaxartes, striking evidence of which is furnished us by the remains of Persian language among the Turko-Tartaric and Finnugrian races, and westward to the very shores of the Black Sea. It was said of the original fire placed there by King Djem, that model of Iran kings, that it burned continually, unreplenished, up to the time of the invasion of the Arabians. But a thousand years of stormy devastation on the part of the Scythian races, who poured in all directions through this part of the world, laid fallow the old Iran civilisation of Central Asia, and indeed annihilated almost every trace of its former greatness. Nothing but the unrestrained zeal and exaggerated religious fervour of Islamism, and not its intellectual culture, has penetrated here. Timur attempted, indeed, to carry to the banks of the Oxus and Yaxartes the arts and sciences from Ispahan, Kasan, Bagdad, Damascus, and from other provinces of Asia subjected by his sword; but the Muses are not to be forced in their love, and Central Asia has had to endure the sad celebrity of being, in our own time, the darkest point in the civilisation chart of the Old World, owing to the wild barbarism of its inhabitants.

It cannot, therefore, appear striking if we undertake a closer consideration of that period in which the light of a better future is beginning to dawn there. The regeneration of Asia is a difficult work: here, as in other places, the European mind meets with a hundred unexpected difficulties; more effort, more time, is required to produce one change, however superficial, in Central Asia, than is the case among Turks, Arabians, Persians, Chinese, and Japanese. Europe has to fight there not only against obstinate superstition, against tenacious and convulsive adherence to old and sacred customs and views, but—and this is more fearful and insurmountable—against physical elements. Where inhospitable wastes stretch for an immeasurable distance, and separate one land and society from other lands and societies, it is far harder to exchange the old course of ideas with a new one, than in regions where, from uninterrupted intercourse, new civilisation and new views are communicated like the light kindled by signal fires. Turkey has received glimpses of the light of the new era from Europe; Persia has received them from Turkey; and Afghanistan partly from Persia, and partly from India. The light has not been able to shine across the Hyrcanian steppes to the banks of the Oxus and Yaxartes; it has had to be brought nearer and urged forward with material force. The process of transformation is all the more rich in interest, both to the ethnographical investigator and to the historian of civilisation.

If we cast a glance, in the first place, at the ethnographical conditions of that inland region which lies between British civilisation in the south and Russian civilisation in the north, our eye is met by three races distinguished by different characteristics, physical as well as material. These are (1) the Turko-Tartars, who form the greater number; (2) the old Iran population, ancient Persians, by which collective name we understand the Tadjiks and Sarts, the Djemshids and the Parsivans; and (3) the Afghans.

The *Turks*, here as elsewhere inflexibly opposed to civilisation and to refined and peaceful habits of life, have hitherto—in spite of all the remains of the old Parsi civilisation to which they put an end in Central Asia, and in spite of all the efforts at culture made by the monotheistic Arabians, who could force upon them by the sword only the religious forms of Islamism, and not its subsequent spirit of culture— been only able to appropriate an outward appearance, and a feeble glimmer of that which we call civilisation. It seems as if this broad and flat skulled race had received from nature, from the first, smaller eyes, so that the brightness of intellectual enlightenment might dazzle them less; their heavy figures, their cold-bloodedness, and their extraordinary calmness of mind seem to have steeled them from the earliest beginnings rather for inactive nomadic life and its privations, and for ceaseless struggle against the influences of the elements. It is, then, scarcely remarkable that the whole history of this people, stretching from the icy banks of the Lena to the Danube, presents no single phase from which we may infer an effort after culture or any special mental capacity. From the "Kudatku Bilik," the first and oldest monument of the language of the Turkish races, which was written in the eleventh century, and the ethical pur-

port of which was intended to contribute to the dissemination of knowledge and civilisation, to the most
recent production of the Osmanli on the shores of the
Bosphorus, the excellence of intellectual endowments
has been ceaselessly proclaimed to the great race of the
Turkish family in all its branches. Foreign teachers
have employed every means to draw them into the circle
of the culture of the age. Yet what has been the result?
The Turks have not only never distinguished themselves
in any science or art whatever, but they have always
appeared as the destroyers of the arts and sciences, and
such, indeed, they have truly been! In vain may we
cite the brilliant period of the Ilchanis in Persia ; every
one must see that it was the great masses imbued with
Iran elements of culture who carried the Turkish chiefs
along with them, and not *vice versa*. Valour and honest
feeling, which were the boast of the earlier Seldjukian
princes, are not to be denied to the Turk of the present
day; enthusiasm or love for art and science is, however, a quality which is ever lacking in his national
character; in Central Asia of course to a still greater
extent than on the shores of the Bosphorus.

In considerations of this kind, we must not of course
lose sight of the fact that the Turks have ever shown,
and still show, a great predilection for nomad life. The
sovereigns of Central Asia prefer, even at the present day,
to live in the airy tent by the side of the ruins of the fallen
palaces which Persian and Arabian minds have erected.
The better classes, imitating the example of their princes,
feel themselves happy on the borders of a colony, and
even then not in the stone building which they raise for
animals and granaries, but in the circular, felt-covered

P

tent. Even the countryman chooses by preference the life of the cattle-breeder, and it is easier, as is well-known, to bring the nomad tribes under subjection, than to give them a fixed dwelling-place. So strong is the repugnance to a settled life felt among the Turks in the interior of Asia. We see that even centuries of vicinity to cultivated nations, such as the Persians, Arabs, and Greeks, were not able to improve the Turkish people very considerably in this respect. What has hitherto failed can only be attained with great difficulty in the future; and gloomy, very gloomy, is the prospect which we are able to form of the future civilised condition of the Turkish people.

The second ethnical element in Central Asia, namely, the original *Iran* population, is essentially distinguished from the other by its love of culture, and by its capability of appropriating culture to its own use. The Tadjiks and Sarts, the intellectual heirs of a people which has made itself famous through Bactrian and Khahrezmian civilisation, played, so far as historical tradition informs us, 1000 years ago, the same part among the Turkish tribes far into the East as they play now; they were merchants, peaceful husbandmen, and guardians of the arts and sciences. These characteristics distinguished the Iranians of Central Asia up to the brilliant period of the Bagdad Caliphate in the west and south of Asia. Just as, in the present day, the Asiatic is wont to combine the idea of industrial perfection with the name of Frengistan, so in the eighth, ninth, and tenth centuries of the Christian era, that only was highly esteemed by him and dearly paid for, which he obtained from Bokhara, Urgendj, or even from the remote Khokand. The Court of the Caliph at Bagdad, and the palaces of the great in Syria, Egypt, and even Andalusia, were adorned with articles of luxury, both in silk and leather, manufactured in distant Turkestan. Poor barbarous Europe, whose social condition at that time, compared with that of the Mohammedan East, occupied the same position as the present condition of the East does to our own, had heard but little of Turkestan through Marco Polo, who, as is well known, stayed there but a short time; yet all the stronger was the interest which this land enjoyed among other Mohammedans. With regard to science also, the Iranians of Central Asia were far in advance of their other brethren in the faith. Much of their intellectual capacity is unsurpassed even at the present day, and the mental activity ascribed to the Persians of the present time is to be found in a fuller and greater extent among their ancestors on the Zerefshan, the Oxus, and the Yaxartes. That which the Japanese are in the east of Asia, the Iranians may become in the west of Asia. I have constantly admired their capability of adaptation, and in recent times I have seen my experience of this still more confirmed by the fact that in the part of Turkestan conquered by Russia, it was the Tadjiks and Sarts who first made common cause with their foreign rulers. Less troubled with religious scruples, it was they who assisted the Russians, and allowed themselves to be placed in appointments as civil officers of the Czar; in fact, it was a Tadjik Mollah, who, in the ordinary Friday devotions, introduced the name of the orthodox Christian Alexander Romanow side by side with that of the first Caliph of Islam. It is, indeed, true that the nomadic Persians—their number is, however, but small—are very different to their settled brethren of the same race, for without adopting the virtues of the Turks, they have imitated them in many of their vices; still it is a settled matter that the Persian race of Central Asia will form the medium for the introduction of the civilisation of the West into the interior of Asia. We have now only to speak of the third element, namely, of the *Afghan* population.

This race, unimportant even in the time of the Gaznewid Mahmud, and inhabiting isolated valleys of the Suleiman range, has since that period absorbed into itself a great number of Indian, Turkish, and Persian tribes; in fact, to speak more correctly, it has obtruded its own nationality and language upon these tribes. Considered as regards its origin sometimes as a scion of the Jewish and sometimes of the Persian race, recent scientific investigations have placed its Indian descent beyond a doubt. These Afghan tribes have ever formed the most northern branch of the old Sanskrit civilisation; they were the rudest and wildest offspring of that old civilised land—in fact, they are so still; for, devoted to war, to plunder, and to a life of adventure, the true type of the Afghan race is just as incapable of civilisation, and is just as furious a foe to all culture and peace, as are the Turks. The best proof of our assertion is to be found in the disputes and difficulties which Shir-Ali-Khan has had to overcome in his reformatory efforts. A transformation of affairs in Afghanistan is, moreover, in no other way conceivable than by the complete annihilation of all the restless nobles, just as the Turks acted with the rebellious Sipahis in the Ottoman Empire. If the people of East India, imbued through

British dominion with European views, were not so inflexibly opposed to every innovation, as are the wildly fanatical Mussulmans of Sindh and Punjaub, according to the theory that mental transformations are communicated from neighbour to neighbour, a beneficent glimmer from the light of Western culture must long ago have fallen over the Kheiber Pass. Yet the stubborn obstinacy of the Mulvies, the wild fanaticism of the Wehabis, and, lastly, the anarchy of the Kheiberis, is too mighty a dam and too powerful a bulwark in defence of the social evils which centuries, and perhaps hundreds of centuries, have sanctioned. The hope of Anglo-Indian statesmen to produce in Afghanistan by means of English subsidies and encouragement, though without actual interference, a similar state of things as that which prevails at the present day in East India, rests on great ignorance of the internal condition of Oriental society. Life in Afghanistan at the present time is a faithful likeness of that in Sindh and Punjaub previous to the English invasion ; and if in the latter place it was not the amicable example, but the moral killing and enfeebling of the warlike aristocracy which could lead or will lead to the desired object, we must, indeed, be very short-sighted if we imagine that a similar result can be attained in Afghanistan in any other way.

These are, consequently, the chief of those national elements, which the European mind, while it seeks to free them from the fetters of opinions hundreds and even thousands of years old, desires to draw over to itself—of those national elements which, so to speak, form the medium between the Chinese and old Asiatic civilisation and that of modern Europe. Any one proceeding westwards from Europe will perceive that European civilisation decreases at every step. This is one of the most interesting observations which I made, as I journeyed from the Danube close to the western frontier of the Celestial Empire. A similar circumstance will strike the eye of the Chinese, as he travels from Pekin through the provinces of Shansi, Shensi, and Kansu, to Thien-shan-Nanlu and Thien-shan-Pelu, which lie in the extreme west. The finely-cultivated Chinese will at each day's march more and more perceive the decrease of ideas in affinity with his own mental world, the cessation of a taste for art, and the abatement of all desire for a luxurious and easy life. In Kashgar, for example, the life will appear to him just as it does to the traveller arrived from Europe. Central Asia, therefore, in spite of all the exuberance with which Arabian Mussulman culture was developed there in the Middle Ages, may justly be called the neutral ground of both civilisations. Can, therefore, the transformation now going on there pass by us unobserved ? The full force of our attention is, however, directed to these regions, because, while considering the civilising powers at work there, the question forces itself upon us anew — What power is truly the most beneficial channel for conveying Western civilisation to Asia ? Is it *Russia*, with her despotic government, with her national character impregnated with Asiatic vices, but with her pliable spirit ? or is it *England*, with her exalted ideas upon freedom, with her ceaseless yearning for progress, but with her cold and hard individual qualities ? We have in another place explained why the relations of these two nations, now playing such an important part in Asia, have assumed the form they have. We have observed, namely, that Russia, with her low stage of civilisation, with her outwardly European, but at heart Asiatic stamp, can far more easily associate with Asiatics, with whom she is so closely allied both mentally and physically, that she does not find them so discouraging, and that she does not seem so foreign to them as the son of Great Britain, who exchanges his damp, cloudy home for a tropical sky, his flourishing civilisation for the most primitive conditions of humanity, and the old seat of freedom for the old land of slavery. Just as little as I can extol the Russian Starosts, priests, and soldiers of the Cossack advanced posts for the easy way in which they become friends with Kirghises, Özbegs, Mongols, and Chinese, making common cause with them in their begrimed and stinking Kibitka, and in their filthy garments ; equally little can I blame the Briton, because he most unwillingly exchanges his roast-beef for the dish of rice with its aromatic spices, his ale and porter for toddy, his comfortable home for the dirty bungalow, his Manchester coat for the Futah and Tchoga of the Hindustanee. The Russian has a Czar, a religion, a past, all of which differ far less from the Asiatic notions of Padishah, Allah, and an Asiatic past, than do the English ideas upon State, Church, and History. Indeed, this question needs no further discussion ; history has shown us most clearly that Russia, in consequence of her original elements, can work far more easily in Asia than any other European nation ; yet our parallel has not so much in view the ease of the influence effected, as the utility of the influence itself. We do not ask who will attack the Asiatics best, England or Russia ? but we ask whose appearance is crowned with most success, to whom does the part of a civiliser most appertain, and whose influence is therefore most worthy of our sympathy and support?

There are philosophers who assert that the transition from old Asiatic civilisation to the views of modern Europe can alone be made possible by finding a medium stage like that of Russian civilisation. They say that the Asiatics, in order to become European, must first be made Russian; and in this sense the influence of Russia in Asia affords the surest guarantee of a brilliant result. There is, indeed, much that is just in this theory, yet we could only have accepted it as a good solid basis if Russia in her conquests hitherto had had in view rather the promotion of intellectual and material objects, than a mere Russianising aim. What use has it been to Europe, what use has it been to the Asiatics concerned, that within a period of scarcely fifty years more than twenty millions of Asiatics have been Russianised? The intellectual and material condition of these twenty millions has been little or not at all improved, for the Russian regime has not only not contributed to the advancement of culture, but in places where it has met with a race which has reached a certain stage of Asiatic civilisation, it has even exercised an injurious and paralysing influence. Who will deny the culture of the Transcaucasian tribes of Persian descent? Shamachi, Gendje, and Erdebil were places famous for Persian Mohammedan learning; their inhabitants cannot be denied a certain taste for intellectual effort and for industry; and what has Russia made of them after a rule of more than fifty years?

The Shiite on the other side of the Araxes, and on the west shore of the Caspian Sea, is more fanatical, more stupid, and more immoral, than his brethren by faith and race, who are languishing under the proverbial despotism of the Kadjar dynasty. What has Russia done for the Crimean Tartars? what for the Kasan Tartars? These people, gifted by nature with but little intelligence, are famed for their submissiveness and patience, and the Christian-Russian rule might have accomplished far more with them than the Sultan, so often inveighed against at Petersburg, could effect with his obstinate subjects.

Russianising is, as has been justly remarked, no civilisation at all; and although, when it lights upon utterly barbarous tribes, it can here and there bring about a peaceful mode of life by the introduction of social conditions and more fixed habits, no one can doubt that, where it comes in contact with the traces of an old and different civilisation, it ever leaves behind an injurious effect. The Kasan Mollah, whose ideal of culture is the brilliant period of Mussulman learning, and who still derives his refined notions and æsthetic conceptions from the old Mohammedan school, will scarcely be led to a better opinion by the half-European half-Asiatic Russian. Instead of regarding him as a teacher, he will feel towards him contempt, and perhaps even scorn; and one thing is certain, namely, that Tartars and Persians must first lose and forget the smallest trace of their earlier culture, and they must become thorough barbarians, if through Russian example they would receive Western civilisation. Judging by the spirit of progress which prevails at the present day in Turkey, the Moslems of the Ottoman Empire are near, far nearer, a radical change than their brethren in the faith under Russian dominion, although the latter are treated according to the spirit of the Christian doctrine, which has the reputation of promoting civilisation, and the former, on the contrary, are subject to the doctrines of the Arabian Prophet, which are decried as adverse to civilisation.

Yet, not only with respect to half-civilised nations, but even among wholly uncivilised nomadic tribes, I cannot ascribe so much advantage to the appearance of Russian civilisation as is generally supposed by those who, dazzled by the boastful tone of Russian champions of civilisation, regard the foreign powers working under Russian protection as native resources. We need only travel from Nishni-Novgorod to Astrakan—a tract of road which Russia has had in her possession for centuries—and see the dirt, the misery, the brutish existence of the Bashkirs, Kalmucks, and Kirghises who inhabit it, in order to be convinced of the assertion that Russia does not produce a very civilising effect through her example. These people still live in offensive Kibitkis; they wear clothes till they fall from them; they eat at the present day, just as of old, horse-flesh dried in the sun ; they kill, plunder, and sell each other to the Tchaudur-Turkomans just as they did a hundred years ago. Where is it better with the nomad tribes on the great steppes of the gigantic Russian Empire ? Where have they established flourishing and peaceful colonies ? Where has the primitive condition given place to one of order ? Nowhere, is the only reply any one accurately acquainted with the state of things can give. And if it is thus, is it not questionable whether it were not better for the interests of humanity to replace the Russian eagle in the old civilised soil of Turkestan by another civilised power more strictly European ?

In discussing these questions it has been frequently attempted to make use of a weapon forged from my own assertions—that is, the ruthless barbarity of the people of Turkestan has been given as a reason for the desirability of Russian intervention. It is indeed true that no one has desired a change more than myself, yet I have never been satisfied with the agents whom the consequences of this political state of things have placed here. That Turkestan, that nest of barbarism, should be cleared out, can be unwelcome to none ; yet it must not be forgotten that the banks of the Oxus and the Yaxartes, while on the one side they are the seat of unprecedented barbarism, form on the other side that point in the Mussulman world where mental culture may find the most fruitful soil. I know no point in Turkey, Arabia, and Persia, where I found so many establishments for instruction, so many richly endowed institutions, where the young flock in such troops to the schools, and where literary men would be held in higher esteem, than in Bokhara, Khokand, and in some parts of Khiva. At the present day this learning is limited to religious teaching, to explanation of the Koran, and to obsolete scholastic study. Nevertheless the schools exist ; the maxim that "knowledge is power" is established according to native ideas ; and a free-thinking and energetically advancing Government might, with earnest purpose, effect a work of great importance.

I ask now, will Russia, with the means standing at

her disposal, really call into existence a salutary epoch or not? Judging from the past, and from the true spirit of Russian conquests up to the present time, there is less to hope for Bokhara, Samarkand, and Khodjend, than for the civilised places on the Transcaucasian territory. The Ischans, the Mollahs, and the polite scholars of Tadjik and Özbeg nationality must renounce every hope of becoming acquainted with the teachings of the modern world according to the transformation theory of their Western brethren in faith and nationality. They must take a step backward; that is, they must become Russian, in order that then, in common association with the motley population of the empire of the Czar, they may take the way to the west, under the direction of the clumsy Muscovite. A terrible lot truly! We are scarcely to be blamed if, considering the choice yet open a few years ago, we should have preferred to see Western culture carried to the banks of the Oxus and Yaxartes by British apostles.

The German reader, who has thoroughly acquainted himself with the facts, will of course not agree with the aspersions which have been cast by America and France upon the influence of Great Britain in the East. We, too, have no wish to conceal the fact, that it would be better if the icy crust with which the British coloniser surrounds himself on his appearance among the people of Asia melted away, if he preferred to leave behind him the damp cold mists of his home; yet we cannot deny, in spite of all the individual defects of the English nation, that in China or Japan, in Siam or India, no less than in Persia and Turkey, it was the appearance of the English alone which brought about the hitherto unmistakable changes for the better. The people of Hindustan are beginning to see that the hated conquerors are seriously anxious for the civilisation of the country, and for the welfare of its inhabitants. So far as the climate allows, an activity of both mental and material industry has appeared on the banks of the Ganges and the Indus, such as has never before been known. The seed scattered by Elphinstone, Henry Lawrence, and Malcolm, is beginning to germinate and bear fruit. It is no unimportant event that the adherents of the doctrine of Brahma have cast aside the customs and prejudices which thousands of years have sanctified, and allow themselves to be led voluntarily by a strange people on the better path. Strictly Protestant England cannot indeed boast of winning over millions of souls in her colonies to the Anglican Church by the help of her missionaries, who cost her yearly many thousands. No ; Christianity will never triumph over the doctrines of Buddha, Brahma, and Mahomet, yet the fact is not to be mistaken, that the idols in recent times have been much neglected. In the temple at Djagarnath, where, according to an old custom, the Presbyterian Scotchman presents arms in the solemn procession to the carved idol monster, the number of pilgrims diminishes from year to year. The sacred Zebu oxen are yoked, the Fakirs find their business less lucrative, fear and horror of the sea diminish, self-mutilation is no longer regarded as a profitable business by the zealots, and the Hindostanee, who had formerly avoided the shadow of a European, are now opening discount-houses in London and Manchester. In fact, with the flagging of religious fanaticism, a new epoch must and will dawn in Hindostan—an epoch which

may not only be very advantageous in the distant future
to British masters, but which will redound to the honour
of that English policy, which is perfectly conscious that
it will hereafter be no longer able to guide, according to
its own will, the infant now in leading-strings.

Do we then need any further proof of the great difference existing between the influence of Russia and that
of England in Asia? I am far from assuming the position of a panegyrist of the Britons; yet, in the interest
of oppressed humanity in Asia, I cannot conceal my
delight when I see how the statesmen on the Thames,
leaving the course of a feeble policy, have been recently
preparing to extend their influence in earnest, though
indeed somewhat late, over the Kheiber Pass. Truly, the
British flag appears there under very different auspices
to those of the Russian double eagle in Turkestan. The
latter has given the Özbegs an idea of the new era by
devastating wars, by oppression, and by the imposition
of large contributions. The former has held out to the
Afghans the hand of friendship—a hand provided, moreover, with a well-filled purse. Shir-Ali-Khan is strongly
supported with advice and action; and the success of this
intervention is shown by facts which may not be lightly
estimated, namely, in the efforts hitherto of the Afghan
prince to bring his country into order, to break the
power of the arrogant chiefs, to protect trade, in one
word, to attempt to Europeanise his people. Moreover,
in spite of all the consequences of a former fatal policy, the
trace of English influence in Afghanistan has been long
unmistakable; the regular troops of the Afghans have
been drilled upon the English system; any one wishing
to appear fashionable has assumed the English dress, and

let his whiskers grow. Peshawur and Delhi have represented Paris and London, and we may regard it as certain
that the Oxus will speedily form the line at which British
civilisation advancing from south to north will meet
Russian civilisation progressing in an inverse direction.
This will be the first point at which the direct influence
of the two colossus powers of Europe will come into contact, an event which may not be so wholly desired by
the politicians on the Neva, because the free system of
the Britons, so helpful to national development, can
awaken no special love and adherence to the dominion
of the Czar among the Asiatics under the protection of
Russia.

I have not chosen to withhold these considerations
respecting the social transformations impending in Central Asia, from the fear that my remarks upon the political affairs of Central Asia may be regarded as an
anti-Russian expression of feeling arising from paltry
national apprehensions, and not as an objective view of
the subject. In truth, the moment in which a society
enters a new phase, in which millions of human beings
step forth from the despotic command of individuals
and enter another sphere of thought and existence, that
moment, in truth, is too important to be lightly passed
over.

THE POSITION OF RUSSIA IN CENTRAL ASIA, AND THE REVISION OF THE TREATY OF PARIS OF 1856 (1870).

THE appearance of Russia in Asia has been placed in varied connection with the most recent political events in Europe; so much has been spoken and written with regard to the last chess-moves of Russian diplomacy, that we cannot forbear casting a glance at those countries which find more attention in this publication than in other English and continental publications of a similar kind. The German reader must feel all the more connected with events in Central Asia, as the heroic contests and brilliant victories of Germany will exercise a decisive influence on the movements of the Northern Colossus in Asia.

On the part of Russia the desire has already manifested itself of revising the stipulations of the Paris treaty of 1856, a policy which at once transports us into the valleys of the Hindukush. That which Mac-Neil prophesied long before our time, and which from our own discussions will be now variously demonstrated by others, namely, that the Russian operations on the

Bosphorus no longer centre round Sevastopol and Sinope, but will and must make an actual beginning in the neighbourhood of Herat, is now a well-founded probability, which all the wisdom of the optimist English statesmen, and all the apparent stoicism of our own diplomatists, can with difficulty refute. With the exception of the gentlemen on the Bosphorus and their colleagues on the Thames, very few at the present day will doubt that the Russian troops stationed on the Oxus are the outposts which are to begin first and most successfully the probable contest for the solution of the Oriental question. All that is being carried on in a westerly direction from the Oxus to the eastern shore of the Black Sea, all that is being secretly prepared in Persia, Kurdistan, and Armenia, is closely connected with this object. In spite of the remoteness of these countries and the difficult access to them, in spite of all the secrecy of the crafty Russian statesmen, there can be no more surprises for us at the present day like those at the time of the last Persian-Russian war, when Paskewitsch's victories on the Araxes and the conclusion of peace in Turkmantchai threw the world into astonishment. These are not suppositions, but confirmed facts, which inform us step by step of the course of events. Turkey is arming, Russia, it is said, is arming also. Let us cast a glance at the remote East, that is, into the interior of Asia, and survey what has recently been taking place there, in order to convince ourselves whether the fruit is really ripening, whether the outposts mentioned are really in marching order, and whether the storm impending over the western part of Asia has begun in the thunder-like roar on the distant banks of the Oxus?

Q

We will begin with Bokhara. Here the state of things, which we before mentioned,* has little or nothing altered. The Emir of Bokhara, on one side intimidated by the unexpected success of the Russian arms, and on the other side placed in extreme danger by his own subjects, whom this defeat has provoked into revolt, could do nothing better than submit himself unconditionally to the victor, in consequence of this immutable decree of the powers of destiny. He maintained not only strict repose and quiet obedience, but, though he had formerly styled himself Prince of the Faithful, he took all possible trouble to cement a close bond of friendship with a servant of the unbelieving prince. I have reliable information that this policy was justified by none at the Court on the Zerefshan except the Emir and his immediate relatives, but was abhorred by all. Muzaffar-ed-Din was, however, right in persisting in it. Led by the chief of the artillery, and a few other high officers of Persian origin, who were more thoroughly informed with regard to the power of Russia than the obstinate Bokhariot fanatics, he succeeded, in the first place, in lengthening the term of his existence by some years; and, secondly, in subduing all those enemies who had not shared his views, and who would have plunged him into the greatest danger by unceasing resistance. To the latter belonged, as is well known, his own son and successor, who, longing for the soft white-covered throne, stepped to the head of the malcontents, with the pious intention of first overthrowing his own father, and then cleansing the sacred soil of Bokhara from the footprints of the unholy Russians—a pious desire, which of

* *Cf.* "The Advances of Russia in Central Asia," p. 67.

course could originate only in the mind of an immature youth. Prince Abdul-Melik or Kette-Töre (the Crown Prince), as he is also called, had already raised a small armed force. He appeared in different parts of the Khanate, everywhere attacked the troops of his father, and it was only when the latter perceived that his refractory son was placing him in serious difficulties, that he conceived the extraordinary resolution of consigning the rod of chastisement to the hands of the unbelieving Russian. The Russians, of course, did not refuse to accept the office. The rebellious son of the Emir had at that time already established himself in Karshi and Shehri-Sebz. A small body of Russian troops marching against him from Samarkand speedily, however, drove him away from these places. He wandered about without shelter, sometimes appearing among the Turkomans, and sometimes with the Khan of Khiva, until at last, doubting the success of his design, and wishing to procure a powerful ally, he fled to Kabul. Shir-Ali received him kindly, indeed very kindly. The *vena afghanica* of the sovereign of Kabul was touched. He had also really a twofold cause for rancour against the Emir of Bokhara. In the first place, his feeling of hostility against the power on the Zerefshan, which had always desired for the last 300 years to maintain its superiority over the other rulers of Central Asia, had been bequeathed to him by his aged father; in the second place, Muzaffar-ed-Din had actually offended him by always showing favour to his adversaries, and, in fact, he had afforded help to Abdur-Rahman-Khan, the most powerful and hostile of them all. The idea of undertaking an expedition against

Bokhara, in conjunction with the Emir's rebellious son, seems to have pleased him much. The guest was received with princely honours; in fact, as a delicate token of friendship, Shir-Ali-Khan offered him one of his daughters as a wife, and he accordingly married her. It would have cost Shir-Ali no great resolution to march with an army against the province of Belch, undermined as it was with Bokhariot intrigues, and from thence across the Oxus, if the matter had depended, as in former times, only on the two respective combatants. Now, however, on both sides a third party had appeared as a mighty arbiter. In Bokhara there were the Russians, who placed a curb on the independent conduct of the Emir, and allowed their vassal no freedom of action, in order that he might not forget that his days were numbered, and that his will could only be that of the Russian Emperor. The latter just now stood in the way of any agitation which could occasion a direct collision with the English.

A similar course was pursued by the English in Kabul. Shir-Ali-Khan, though not their vassal, derived the power of his rule from the Exchequer in Calcutta; it was therefore communicated to him in a confidential, but nevertheless firm, tone that he was to keep quiet—in fact, very quiet. England would be placed in the greatest perplexity if the Afghans, by their quarrel with the cat, were to draw the lion upon them; and the subsidies which were given him in arms and money on the part of Great Britain, were destined only for the consolidation of his own power, and not for the extension of his frontier.

The rebellious son of the Emir of Bokhara had therefore received no help from his father's southern rival. He was conveyed with honour to the frontier, and he then repaired, furnished with the cost of the journey, and with the prince's daughter, to Khokand, where he subsequently began a reconciliation with his father, and was to return to the capital on the Zerefshan.

So, at least, it was reported a few months ago. Recently, however, events have occurred which lead us to suppose that the rebellious son is again engaged in a conspiracy against his father's Government, for we hear reports of a great insurrection in Shehri-Sebz, that old seat of rebellion, an insurrection which the troops of the Emir of Bokhara were not able to quell, and the repression of which was again obliged to be entrusted to Russian arms. Judging from the telegraphic despatches, it must have been warm work in Timur's birthplace. The fortress of Shehri-Sebz, which stands in a marshy district, and the not inconsiderable forts of Kitab and Yamini, could not have been taken without danger to the Russians; nevertheless, peace was restored, and the whole territory will probably, as was the case with Kárshi formerly, be only for a time occupied by the Russians, and will finally be given up to the Bokhariots.

From these events it is therefore sufficiently evident that the Emir of Bokhara acted wisely in submitting to the unavoidable lot of Russian protection; but the Russians also will see that the policy of moderation which they pursued was far more expedient and salutary, than if, after the taking of Samarkand, they had rushed also upon Bokhara, and had once for all extinguished the feeble light of Bokhariot independence.

The Russian diplomatists can never be reproached

with want of circumspection and thorough perception of the state of affairs; the gentlemen on the Neva knew very well that a blow successfully given to Bokhara would intimidate the whole of Turkestan, and that the annexation of a single point would, sooner or later, bring with it the fall of the whole. Moreover, there was no especial hurry, and by waiting patiently for the fruit to ripen, it would probably fall all the more surely into their lap, and their plans for the future would be all the more successful. There are two grand advantages which Russia obtains by a cautious mode of proceeding. In the first place, she needs comparatively very small forces as garrisons in the conquered parts. On the march from the left bank of the Yaxartes to the Zerefshan, a distance of six or seven days' journey, it was only necessary up to the present time to garrison four fortified points at the most, namely, Tashkend, Khodjend, Yengi-Kurgan, and Samarkand; in fact, the whole army under General Kaufmann amounts at the most to 5000 men. While under such circumstances a considerable force can be employed in the east of Khokand, on the frontiers of East Turkestan, and another division can be used for observation in the direction of Khiva, the open towns are almost entirely devoid of all garrison. The people of Turkestan—I mean the settled inhabitants—are by nature more cowardly than other Asiatics, and they have not yet learned to revolt against the existing authority; they submit to their fate with lamblike patience. During the whole course of the Russian war in Central Asia, only one case of rebellion in Samarkand has come to light, and in this not Samarkandians, but the notorious madcaps from Shehri-Sebz took part.

During the absence of the Russian troops, these men attempted to storm the walls garrisoned by the sick and wounded left in the citadel, an attempt which was rendered impossible by the energy of the commandant, Major Von Stempel. Had the Russians not been moderate in the beginning, and if, instead of establishing Khudaya-Khan in Khokand, they had seized upon this Khanate as well as Bokhara, and had advanced as far as the Karaköl on the south, in spite of the most favourable circumstances this would have demanded an army six or eight times as strong. By the great extension of the frontier, united co-operation would, in the first place, have been far more difficult, and in the second, the Russian soldiers must have made head against the nomadic tribes remaining on the frontiers, which would, at any rate, have considerably impeded the execution of the Russian plans. As circumstances now are, the Khan of Khokand keeps himself and his people, amounting to about two millions of souls, not only quiet and still as mice, but he delights in being considered as the mercenary of the white Czar on the Neva, for he has until now kept the restless Kiptchaks in check; he has weakened Yakub-Kush-begï, his eastern neighbour, by constant hostility, and he has humbled him for the Russian arms. Almost similarly circumstanced is my proud friend, the Prince of Bokhara. Like a puppet, whose movements are directed from Samarkand and Tashkend, we see him hindering the plan of an alliance of the three Khanates, now restraining the Turkomans from a common attack, and then again, by resuming hostilities with the Afghans, opening a path to the south for Russian arms. He pays with praiseworthy punctuality the war tax imposed upon him; in fact, Russia stands at the present day just as securely on the Kermineh at his frontier as she does on the Araxes, the Black Sea, and the Amur, and she can with perfect security weave her further plans for the future.

The gradual extension of power has also greatly contributed to accustom the minds of the people of Turkestan to Russian supremacy, and to lead them, perhaps, in time to prefer it to native rule. There are few of the races in Asia who have bent beneath the Christian yoke of the West, amongst whom religious fanaticism bordering on fury has reached so great a height as with the people of Central Asia. Time and the advantages of the new position can naturally best eradicate this deep hatred. In Turkestan, subject as it is to Russia, there are now none of the tyrannical caprices of a sovereign to dread. The chicanery of despotic officers is scarcely to be felt in comparison with former oppression. Commerce and intercourse are now carried on with far more inducements than before; and since the Central Asiatic Mussulman has become convinced that the Russian does not disturb him in his faith, and that he protects his property more than the former native sovereigns, there is no reason why the greater part, and especially the merchant class and the peaceful husbandman, should not prefer the present state of things to the earlier. It is this feeling of security which makes the people of Turkestan from Tashkend to Kermineh more and more confidential with the Russians. The latter, too, feel themselves more and more at home in the conquered country, and if this quiet procedure were to last a few years longer, we may be sure that the foreign rule will not only not be regarded with hostility, but that in many places it will be desired.

No less advantageous for the political transformation on the other side of the Oxus has been this Russian policy of moderation, which in Turkestan is so serviceable to future plans. The gentlemen on the Neva have left the English free scope in Afghanistan. Shir-Ali was established on his throne here, as is well known, by English money, and this in considerable sums. It is now more than two years since English money and English arms have laboured to restore repose among the warlike race of the Afghans on the other side of the Kheiber Pass, unendangered by Russia's evident advances. It is, it is true, to be regretted, but we cannot leave the fact unnoticed, that imperious Russia with her forces has effected far more in the oasis-lands, than Great Britain has been able to achieve on the Hilmend with her love and expenditure. Afghanistan is still disturbed; it is still sapped by discord and disquiet, and not an inch is gained in the direction which England would so gladly see. On its north-east frontier, namely, in the province of Turkestan, the people are still wavering in the choice between the acknowledgment of the real sovereign and his rival. Even while we are writing this, Abdur-Rahman-Khan is standing ready to dispute the possession of this land with Shir-Ali. It is said the Emir of Bokhara has given this pretender to the throne the means necessary. Russia is full of resentment at this proceeding of the Emir; she threatens punishment, and nevertheless Abdur-Rahman-Khan with his army, the greater part of which is furnished with good Russian arms, which, it is stated, have been obtained through

Bokhara, will not withdraw from the upper stream of the Oxus. He calls Kundus, Belch, and Aktche his paternal heritage; and, in spite of all consoling reports in the Anglo-Indian official papers, there will be a tough collision here still, which will reveal many a surprise.

If we now glance from the north-east towards the west, we shall find that Herat, in spite of the heavy sum which has been expended by England for the security of this post, is attached by a very slight thread to the Afghan crown. In the first place, it is threatened and harassed by the Khan of Meimene, who pretends to be seriously offended with Shir-Ali; in the second place, the Hezerehs and Djemshidis, those voracious foxes who are set here to keep the geese, still behave in such a manner as if they were the masters on the Heri; in the third place, the Salor and Tekke Turkomans, in spite of all the rich presents which the greybeards and influential Ischans have received as a ratification of friendship, are still so ungallant as to extend their predatory excursions to the very gates of Gurian and Herat—in fact, it is not long ago that we received the tidings that even the district of the southern Ferrahs had suffered from their devastating inroads. Yet this is not merely the case with the Afghanistan frontier, but the central point of his power, in Kabul, in the family circle of the Emir, is no better off! Serdar-Mehemmed-Yakub-Khan, whom the readers of my "Reise in Mittelasien" will remember as that naïve prince who, with somewhat rough hand, attempted to remove my incognito,—this Yakub-Khan, who subsequently became a brave general, and rendered so much service in the contest for the crown, has now, according to the most recent reports, revolted against his own father, and has come forward in the south as a pretender to the throne, just as his nephew has done in the north. Even at the time that Shir-Ali travelled to Umballah, and Yakub-Khan, surnamed the Sword of the Kingdom, was left behind in Kabul, there were whispers on all sides of the coldness that had sprung up between father and son ; and when the former subsequently returned to Kabul, richly provided with resources, and rewarded his able son among the least of his servants, the embers slowly kindled into a flame. We find in the latter contests of the Emir the name of Serdar-Yakub-Khan but rarely mentioned ; and although the rancour between father and son was no secret, his rebellion in the neighbourhood of Kandahar, and in the city itself, where he has a strong party, has somewhat taken us by surprise. Anglo-Indian journals, which wish to see the smooth surface of political affairs in Afghanistan as little troubled as possible, inform us, indeed, as the most recent fact, that the difference between father and son is tolerably settled, and that Kandahar is out of danger. Unfortunately, however, this is not the case. The hostility of Serdar-Yakub-Khan to his father is the expression of an entire and powerful party, and arises solely from the preference which Shir-Ali shows for his youngest son Abdullah-Djan, whom he has designated as his successor, to the disregard of Yakub-Khan. It is this hostility between father and son which will yet demand many a mighty sacrifice from the country, and which may for years postpone the object which England hopes, through her subsidies, to obtain in Afghanistan.

It is true, on the Thames, Lord John Lawrence's policy

of inaction has been set aside, and there has been an effort made to stir in every direction; still the curse of unsuccess has weighed upon everything that the English diplomatists have hitherto attempted in Turkestan. Not only do matters look badly in Afghanistan, but in East Turkestan no advance is made in the alliance begun. Yakub-Kushbegi, the so-called Atalik-Gazi, in proof of his readiness to enter into diplomatic relations with England, received two private English travellers * with a courtesy and kindness only possible in Turkestan. He even sent an envoy to the Viceroy at Calcutta, who behaved with much tact, and returned the politeness by an embassy, which, in the course of last summer, set forth on the difficult way across the Kuen-Lun Pass under the direction of Mr T. Forsyth. Unfortunately, we now hear that this mission, after unspeakable troubles and hardships, reached Yarkend, and possibly arrived at Kashgar, but it was not received by the present sovereign. It returned to India after a short time, without having obtained its object. The failure of the whole proceeding is, on this occasion, again to be imputed to the inexperience of English statesmen. It is, once for all, difficult to make the Briton comprehend that Asiatics, and especially Tartar rulers, understand very little of diplomatic soundings. All that the sovereign of the Six Cities understood by diplomatic relations with England was, in the first place, money and arms; in the

---

* Messrs Hayward and Shaw. We have now to add, with regret, that Mr Hayward, in his scientific zeal to investigate the Pamir steppes, fell a sacrifice to his noble and high object on his way thither. He is said by some to have been murdered in Gilgit, by others in Yasin, by order of the ruling prince there.

second place, money and arms; and in the third place, money and arms. Beyond these his mind never reached. He urgently requires help, and, as a true Oriental, he would not have entered into a treaty until he were in possession of the *corpus delecti* of his wishes. With the Afghans, who, from a connection with the English of years' standing, are more accessible and intelligent, negotiations can be carried on in the ordinary way. With East Turkestan the course of proceeding must be different; for scarcely had Yakub-Kushbegi heard that the Frengi envoy was bringing in his travelling-pouch no cannons, guns, nor English powder, than he questioned the use of the empty pageantry of a reception, and the advantage to be gained from intercourse with a crowd of unbelievers, and he gave up the idea.

It will be readily explicable to any one that, on the other side, Russian diplomacy reaped its successes in the same measure as misfortune remained faithful to the efforts of the Britons. We have already spoken of Turkestan proper, that is, of Bokhara and Khokand; we must now cast a glance on each side, namely, on the position of the Russians in the extreme east, *i.e.*, on the Narin river and on the Thien-Shan range, and in the extreme west, *i.e.*, at Khiva and the eastern shores of the Caspian Sea. In the first-mentioned place, Russian diplomacy has not only hung the Damocles sword over the head of Yakub-Kushbegi, the successful conqueror of East Turkestan, but even over the Transili district, that part especially which is enclosed in the Governments of Semipalatinsk and Tomsk. All that is left to the Chinese here, from the gradual advance of the Russian outposts, extends over three poor districts—(a) the

southern one of Ili, the former penal settlement of the
Chinese, with its capital Kuldja, on the banks of the
river of the same name; (b) the central district of Kir-
Kara-Usu: it has a marshy soil and several lakes; (c)
the northern district of Tabagatai, with its capital
Tchugutchak. We find a line of outposts extending
along the Tabagatai range on the highway to Tchugutchak, from Sergiopol to Usdjar, and another chain
of outposts stretching from Kopal past Lepsinsk far into
the Ala-Tau range. Even at the present day, Lake
Zaizan, with its numerous springs, is in the hands of
the Russians, as is also the Lake Ala-Köl; and if the
new plan of crossing the two rivers Ili and Irtish with
steamers can be successfully carried out, Russia will
have succeeded in again finding a channel by which
here in the north-west she can penetrate into the very
heart of the Chinese Empire. Moreover, the possession
of Dsungaria itself is an advantage which is not to be
undervalued. Kuldja is scarcely sixteen miles distant
from the Russian frontier. Dsungaria itself is rich in
coal-beds, gold-sands, copper, and iron; and Russia has
been invited by the inhabitants, who have fled there, to
take their home under her protection, or rather into her
possession. In the year 1866, this conjuncture seemed
to Russia not to have yet arrived; she wished to give
a few days' respite to the motley population there
of Tarandjis (agricultural tribes of East Turkestan),
Kalmucks, and Chinese; yet, at the opportune moment,
the occupation of this important post will be an easy
task from Vernoi, and the Russians consider Dsungaria
even now as their future possession.

Similar, if not perfectly so, is the fate of East Turkestan. As we have before mentioned, the present ruler is using every precaution to avoid a collision, which, however, he will only succeed in doing when Dsungaria is safe under the wings of the Russian eagle; for, if once the Russians are masters in Kuldja and on the Ili, which they will be in a short time, there will be an end of the independence of East Turkestan. In Khiva and on the eastern shores of the Caspian Sea, hitherto the ground has only been cleared on the part of the Russians for future activity; preparations have been made, and the conquests themselves, on the part of the Russians, can all the more easily be effected. There is only one position in the west, running parallel with the outposts on the Narin, to be obtained, and they will penetrate from the inlet of Krasnowodsk to the Hyrcanian steppes. Russia has now three precursors of her power extending equally far into the south, namely, in the fort of the last-mentioned inlet, Kermineh, or, more correctly, Karshi, and the little fort on the Narin. At these three points she holds Turkestan, in the widest sense of the word, that is, the Turkish-speaking Mohammedan population of Central Asia, in her grasp; and the advantageous position she has already gained can very easily be turned into the complete establishment of her power. That Khiva for the present has not been disturbed is to be ascribed to the same cause as that which induced her to declare the ruler of Khokand suzerain, and to give the Emir of Bokhara a short respite, namely, the endeavour to avoid the necessity of a large garrison force and great expenditure, unless circumstances imperatively require them. When Russia once sees herself obliged to plant the banner of her dominion in the whole of Turkestan, the taking of Khiva, as well as the two eastern Khanates, will only be child's play—so skilfully has she hitherto placed the threads she is weaving !

It is clear that this advantageous position of Russia in the interior of Asia, that is, in Turkestan, imparts still more importance to the anxiety we have before frequently expressed with regard to her rivalry with India ; in fact, it could be easily asserted at the present day that Russia, even if she were animated by the best intentions and by the most sincere sympathies with Great Britain, can no longer hinder here the collision of mutual interests.   In spite of all the mean and selfish policy of liberal Albion, I am now exonerated from the duty of supporting with arguments the danger of the neighbourhood of the Russians in the north of India.   The difference between the present time and that three years ago consists in the fact that England confesses the existence of danger, is far more on her guard, and awaits the impending catastrophe with unmistakable anxiety.   It is true the apostles of peace of the optimist party on the Thames scream themselves hoarse ; it is true the Anglican Church throng round the orthodox double cross, and the ministerial colleagues, both on the Neva and the Thames, break forth in sweet expressions of friendship ; yet in Asia, on the field of action, matters are different on one side as well as on the other.   While General Kaufmann often pursues a policy which apparently excites surprise and perplexity in Petersburg, Lord Mayo in Calcutta equally acts in a manner which is in open opposition to Gladstone's official expressions.   Yet neither of the respective parties is especially to blame for this.   Russia is pursuing an object purposed for many years, and England is attempting to block up the way to her adversary on the chess-board of Central Asia by moves unfortunately made too late. And truly the Britons have now plenty to do, if they even indulge a dream of success. Russia, this Asiatic power *par excellence*, forestalls the Britons everywhere, but in Western Asia especially she has prepared the soil in such a manner that the threads of her plan are laid in an unentangled and unbroken line, and the smallest movement at the one end makes itself felt in violent convulsions at the other. Equal in importance with the outposts on the Narin, the Oxus, and the inlet of Krasnowodsk, is the Russian position on the Araxes, and the influence thus acquired in Persia. The sympathy with Russia has considerably strengthened in Iran within the last two years; the small Kadjar prince with his gigantic titles has paid a visit to a Russian Grand Duke staying in the Caucasus, and has received a return visit from him; and as the Russian sailors gave such hearty hurrahs to the Persian monarch, the latter permitted Russia in future to resort to Enzeli with vessels of war. The road from Enzeli to Resht passes through an extremely marshy neighbourhood, and is more perilous and bad than perhaps any other in the whole of Asia; and since this is the chief commercial highway to Russia for all imports and exports, the attempt has been frequently made in Petersburg to induce Persia to improve this road; in case of a refusal, Russia proposed to carry out the undertaking at her own expense. Until about four years ago Persia resisted this plan: she said, "Of course we can do nothing better than prepare the way for the Russians by which they can easily invade Persia with their arms and cannons."

This is perhaps a childish argument, which we meet with in many parts of Asia ; and yet we have recently heard, to our great astonishment, that the road from Enzeli to Resht is made, and, indeed, that this point on the Caspian Sea, so important for Russian trade, is speedily to be connected by a railroad with Teheran.   Is not this a success ?

We have in the West no idea of the strength with which the Muscovites have insinuated themselves into Persia, or how deeply their influence extends over the political and social relations of the land.   I will only make mention of Persian commerce.   About fifteen or twenty years ago, European manufactures arrived in numerous caravans either from Trebizond through Tebris, or through Bagdad, or from Bombay through Bushir and Ispahan, providing the Russian territory with such objects as they were obliged to import from Europe ; at the present day, the great change has occurred in the use of the commercial highways, which must be felt by the whole European commercial world, with the exception of Russia.   In the first place, on the Trebizond-Tebris road, ruined, as it has been, by Turkish negligence, where unfathomable mire and Kurdish predatory excursions frighten away the merchant in spite of the shortness of the route and established custom, the traffic has diminished in the same proportion as it has increased on the Russian commercial highway to Persia, that, namely, through Poti, Tiflis, and Tebris, and in the immediate future by railroad through Poti-Baku.   We hear already very rarely of commercial caravans passing from British India to Iran; the European import trade through Bagdad and Hamadan is also diminishing ; in fact, Russian sugar, Russian cloth, leather, iron, brass, porcelain, glass, and paper, have everywhere gained the market in spite of their inferior quality; and, in a commercial point of view, Russia is already a conqueror in the country. As regards political influence, it is certainly nothing new that the Persian desire of conquest in Sistan, and the hostile position of Persia towards the Afghans generally, the provocation given to the Osmanlis through the violent frontier disputes in Bagdad, and, indeed, even the useless intrigues of the Persians with the Imam of Maskat, which, though useless, were sufficiently disquieting to England, were all promoted by high commands from Petersburg. Russia's hand appears everywhere, in every act of policy, in the domestic circle of the royal palace, in the negotiation carried on with the Shah by the civil functionary respecting the administration of a province which he holds by lease, and even in the bestowal of a rich benefice on some Mollah. Everywhere this hand is apparent, and it can forge for itself in Persia a mighty weapon whenever the outbreak of the contest with Turkey should take place.

No less prepared for Russian plans do we find the land in a continuous line from the frontier of Iran to the Black Sea—plans which on one side extend to the Tigris and the Euphrates, and on the other through the whole of Anatolia. If the power, the greatness, and the aims of the White Czar are not unknown to the Asiatic in Java and Mollucca, in southern Bengal, and in the northern Punjaub and Cashmere, why should the simple inhabitant of the Armenian tableland remain uninfluenced by the actions of his frontier neighbour? The Armenians were long ago the main conductors of this Muscovite magnetism, and they are so still; for political freedom in Turkey affords free scope to their national intrigues. The Armenians in the north of Asia Minor are the best quartermasters of the Russian power; and from the fact that they have the capital of the country in their hands, they render their religious protector truly no insignificant service. And are not the Kurds also, those ambitious, predatory hordes, who hate the Turks only because they attempt to introduce respect for law and property—are they not always ready to be employed as Russian mercenaries? During the last Crimean war we have already seen the notorious chief Mehemmed-Bey of Toprak-Kaleh fighting under the Russian standard against the crescent. In case of necessity this may take place on a larger scale; and we are far from exaggerating when we assert that Armenia and the north-east coast of the Pontus, in spite of all the apparent authority of the Sultan, are already fast joined by a secret chain to Russia.

If Russia's policy in the interior and west of Asia is such as we have demonstrated it to be in the previous short sketch, it cannot and will not surprise the thoughtful reader that the Court of Petersburg is now striving to obtain the revision of the Paris treaty of 1856.

Let us inquire, in the first place, why Russia generally desires the revision. No one will attempt to persuade us that the slight manacles which the designer of so many trifles in Paris has forged for Russia, to the just indignation of Mr Kinglake, can have especially galled her feet. Does she want the right bank of the Pruth as a strategic point or as an integral part of the gigantic empire, since she may any day be occupying the Principalities? Or is it, perhaps, the prohibition to maintain a fleet of war in the Black Sea which is causing such regret to the sovereign on the Neva? It is indeed true that with such a maritime power Russia could far more easily attain her end on the eastern shores of the Euxine, and she would not have been obliged to feign so much friendship of late years to the Porte. She thoroughly misses the existence of the fleet; yet who does not see that the powerful and large commercial fleet which Russia maintains in the waters of the Black Sea could, in case of urgent necessity, be employed for other purposes? These vessels are for the most part well built, and have awakened thoughts of a similar kind in the Turks' whenever they pass the Bosphorus. It would require too much simplicity, and a mind too much prejudiced in favour of certain ideas, not to see that Russia's policy in her thirst for power on the Bosphorus has in view other vast and gigantic plans besides Panslavist and Greek hierarchical efforts. What Mohammed meant when he said, " The corner-stone of the empire of the world (of course the world of that day) is best laid by the conquest of Constantinople," has been first justly apprehended by the sovereigns of the House of Romanow. They know too well, and justly so, that in the possession of old Byzantium rests the final victory over the whole of the Islam world, and unlimited dominion over the whole of Asia. We shall be convinced of this if we answer the question, Why Russia, just at the present moment, desires the revision of the Paris treaty of 1856?

At the first sight, the existence of the favourable moment naturally strikes us as the befitting answer.

For Russia believes, and perhaps not wrongly, that, from the late political changes in Europe, she will meet with less enthusiastic champions for the crescent than formerly. Nor is Russia too sanguine in these expectations. There is probably no further need to fear the noisy promise and little result of French influence; indeed, from recent experience, we might rather assert that the want of French antagonism in the Eastern question may bring Russia more harm than good. Still Russian diplomacy will certainly not indulge the hope that the rest of Europe, especially England and Germany, will abstain from all interference in the solution of this question, and that the ambition of the Romanow House will find a *tabula rasa* in the East. What the Cabinets of Berlin and London will say to an outbreak of the great movement in the East is reserved for the future to reveal. It lies, moreover, beyond the range of our discussion; for, apart from such considerations, we will point out that Russia's desire for a revision of the kind not only stands in closest connection with European events, but also, and indeed perhaps chiefly, with the position she has recently obtained in Mussulman Asia. Let us only cast a glance at that which Russia has accomplished in Asia since 1856, and we shall find that the two extreme boundaries of the Mohammedan world, namely, Turkestan on the east and the Caucasus on the west, have bent beneath her power; we shall find that hitherto her advance has involved only partial contests, while common definitive action is still pending. Petersburg is ever pursuing the cautious policy of slowly annihilating the separate parts of the gigantic foe, and this by attacking the very arteries of her life. The power

of the Nogai Tartars was broken by the conquest of the
Crimea, their original seat; for, when the Girais lost their
independence, the last ray of hope of Tartar independence vanished for ever also. Circassia, which was so
much feared, and which cost so many sacrifices, could
only be subjected after the taking of the rocky nest
of Gunib; for, so long as Sheik-Shamil held out, the
bold Addighi still believed in deliverance from the
advancing Russian; yet, scarcely was the good and
honoured Sheik brought as a captive to the Neva, than
the Circassians on the shores of the Black Sea visibly
lost their courage, and allowed themselves to be hemmed
in by the Russian battalions. A similar process is to be
perceived in Central Asia. For more than forty years
the contest lasted which Russia had to sustain with the
frontier territory of the great Turkestan Khanate. In
one part there were Kirghises, in another Khivans, and
again in another Khokandians. Repressed in one direction, the resistance appeared all the stronger in another.
Russia advanced as far as Bokhara—Bokhara, which
was at all times the central point of the social and hierarchical life of Central Asia. Bokhara was successfully
vanquished, and by this step the enemies in Central
Asia were for a long time, if not for ever, intimidated.

What these central points which we have named were
to the separate states of the Mohammedan world, that
Constantinople is to the whole Mussulman world. We
should mistake if we called Mecca the centre of the
Mussulman world. It is of Rum, the old famous historical Rum, of which the Malay in the Indian Archi-
pelago, the inhabitant of Morocco in Western Africa,
the Turkestanian on the Oxus, and the Chinese in

Yünnan, speak with the same enthusiasm as of the
pride of Islam, the splendour of Islam, and the power
of Islam. So long as the crescent waves over the
seven-hilled city, the followers of Mohammed's doctrines
will not despair; yet should it ever be here crushed in
the dust by the double-cross of Russia, the fearful
tidings will carry alarm into the remotest distance.
Russia knows this well, and therefore she desires to
have Constantinople.

After such considerations, the question obtrudes
itself, in the first place — Whether our European
Cabinets are ready to yield to Russia the position of
the destroyer of Islam? and whether we shall permit a
power, which is so great even now in the commencement
of its dominion, to obtain such a gigantic influence? In
the second place, it deserves to be considered, with
regard to the present powers in Europe—in case the
West should not be agreed as to the utter extirmina-
tion of Islam — who is to utter the mighty veto to
Russian ambition? I hope no one will refuse these
questions the importance due to them. Had Europe
not recently shown that the time of crusades was long
past, and that the most Christian monarchs were far
rather ready to break a lance in support of the crescent,
it would not occur to any one to imagine that Europe
could entertain a feeling of sympathy or toleration for
the followers of the doctrines of Mohammed ; yet, thanks
to the progress of time, we are no longer in the age of
fanaticism, in spite of all the hypocrisy upon which so
many governments pride themselves. Whether Brahmin, Buddhist, or Mohammedan, it is all one, if a
religious society has only afforded clear proofs of its

vitality. So much has been written for and against the Mussulman faith in the last ten years; it has often been condemned with bitter asperity, at another time, again, it has been cherished with exaggerated tenderness. I, too, have been engaged for some years in practical and theoretical inquiries on the subject, and if my experiences with regard to it have not yet formed themselves into a fixed principle, and cannot at any rate be inserted in the narrow space of this paper, I can, nevertheless, express my opinion that I have found the West Asiatic world not at all wanting in vitality, and especially not wanting in vitality because it is Mohammedan. Up to the present day many European scholars have, by preference, contemplated old and interesting Asia by the feeble glimmer of theoretic light. A time will come when practical knowledge will be united with this learning, and then my conviction before expressed, as to the capability of civilisation possessed by the followers of Islam, will find universal acceptance.

As regards the European umpires, however, every one will naturally first turn to Great Britain, to that country which is more drawn to Asia by personal interests than any other European state, and which, so far as history teaches us, has not played there the part of a destroyer, but that of a civiliser. Yes, England, so it is universally said, is to utter her veto against the Russian eagle, in case this is found necessary; the task belongs to her, we also think. Still the sons of Albion seem lately to be too much engaged with the present; they wrap themselves up too much in the mantle of indifference to occupy themselves with a policy which extends beyond the limits of everyday exigencies. Moreover, England, so far as circumstances show, is no longer a match for her dangerous rival, and in the late Crimean war it was apparent that, in order to baffle the advance of the Russian army, a second, and even a third European power was necessary, although the object aspired after was not attained even then, when France combined with Italy assisted John Bull. At the present time, both powers are incapable of rendering this service, and as the very consciousness of this fact tickles the palate of the Russian bear, it becomes a matter of course that a vigorous and powerful European power is necessary to co-operate with England : this power seems to us to lie in united Germany.

Germany, to whom for a long while the position of a European umpire has been justly due, can and ought to effect all the more for the future of anterior Asia, as it contains within itself those civilising elements which are essentially lacking in the cold islanders on the one side, and on the other in the ardent but inconstant Romance nations. The name " Nemse," by which the German is known in the Mussulman East, has at present diplomatically penetrated only to the Court of Teheran, and at the most is only known in Asia among Turks and Arabians ; moreover, the ethnographical notions of the genuine Asiatic, with regard to the European nations comprehended under the common name of Frengistan, are too confused for him to trouble himself with the subdivisions of the unbelieving world, which is either hated by him or utterly indifferent to him ; still, in the places referred to, especially among the higher government circles, a better knowledge of these is never lacking. The French manner, outwardly so pleasing, which has insinuated itself into Turkey since the time of Sultan Mahmud, may suit some Efendis who pursue European amusements rather than European science in the capital on the Seine, better than the apparently heavy and serious characteristics of the German; the more sober, however, have had too much experience for the last fifty years not to entertain other opinions. I will only mention a few proofs of this in the organisation of the Turkish army. We find, for instance, in the lists of *instructeurs militaires*, that only German, and especially Prussian officers, have left behind perceptible traces of influence in the infantry regiments. The Turkish artillery, which acquired well-deserved fame during the Crimean war, has for almost twenty years been trained by a Prussian officer; and even among the later civil and military functionaries, those who have been educated either in Germany or England have been distinguished by the ability of their conduct. The cold phlegmatic Oriental can derive far more benefit from ant-like industry and patient, persistent effort than from the impetuous nature of the Frenchman, who, up to the present time, has pressed forward as the teacher in the East. And just because the national peculiarity of the German can render such essential service in the transformation of things in the East, it were most desirable that united Germany should now bring its political influence to bear in that quarter. In the East, as everywhere, when society is still in its infancy, only those are chosen as teachers, only the wisdom of those is admired, whose powerful position renders them the most imposing. Under the names "Nemse" and "Austria," the Orientals have hitherto only comprehended countries of

a very subordinate position; the recent results on the
stage of events will probably correct this impression, and
it depends only on the German diplomatists to teach the
gentlemen in Constantinople, Teheran, and Cairo where
true safety is to be sought for.

It is true, ever since the beginning of the French and
German war, a Prussian and Russian alliance has been
hitherto talked of; the expected advance of Russia is in
connection with this. Yet, in spite of the dissemination
which this opinion has found, we can scarcely give credence to it. The self-consciousness of the German nation,
and their high degree of civilisation, cannot allow that
their gigantic efforts should contribute to the prosperity
and increase of a more than half Asiatic and despotic
power. From the blood which was shed on the battle-
fields of France, the germ of a solid freedom must spring
forth; and from the altar on which thousands of the
noblest were sacrificed, the beams of a higher enlightenment must arise. Shall we, therefore, with such expectations, suppose that Germany's victories are only to open
the golden gates of the Bosphorus to Russian ambition,
and to establish the rule of the Muscovites over the whole
of Islam? Certainly not! Just as France found, unexpectedly, in the sons of Germany, a brazen wall, against
which her power was dashed to pieces; so the Russian
diplomatists will be brought to see, in their long-pre-
pared course of action, that a power has now arisen in
Europe which her intrigues and arms will not so easily
get the better of, as has been the case with former
adversaries.

THE LATEST ASPECT OF THE CENTRAL ASIATIC QUESTION—1871.

The Central Asiatic question stands in the same relation to the policy of Great Britain as the Oriental question does to the policy of Turkey. The Efendis at the Porte, the mildest men in the world, as is well known, cannot be ruffled more easily by anything than by starting discussions with them upon the *Question d'Orient.* In their eyes there is no Oriental question awaiting any decision whatever. They are of opinion that this diplomatic expression was devised by the enemies of Turkey, in order to procure a basis for the well-intentioned Cabinets of the West, from which that fount of friendly counsels was to gush forth, by which Turkey, out of pure love, is tortured to death. Is it therefore surprising if they wish to know nothing of the Oriental question? The relation of the Briton to the Central Asiatic question is pretty much the same. For not only would a cold chill seize the gentlemen in Downing Street, and at Government House in Calcutta, if they were spoken to respecting the political aspect of affairs on either side of the Oxus, but this is the case at the present day with most Englishmen. In the words "Central Asia" they

see the appalling spectre of the Afghan campaign of
1842, the loss of almost twenty million pounds sterling;
and, indeed, what is far worse, the approaching shadow of
the Northern Colossus, who will impose on the country
God knows how many more heavy debts,—apparitions
which can all place this now flourishing island-kingdom
in a very critical position.   John Bull therefore desires to
hear nothing at all of the Central Asiatic policy, with
Afghan, Özbeg, and Turkoman disputes.   Whoever
speaks to him of this subject, is hated by him in his
innermost soul ; hence the striking indifference manifested by the English daily press and periodical publications.   Hence also, for almost three years, we have found
in the latter no single discussion of Turkestan affairs,
and we shall probably still longer miss it.   We on the
Continent will perhaps not be blamed, if, as neutral ob-
servers, we pay more attention to the events in remote
Asia than the sons of Albion herself ; for these events
are, as we have already often intimated, too important,
both politically and historically, to be overlooked for
any reason whatever.   From the attention we have
hitherto bestowed on the subject in these sketches, we
propose now to give our readers an account of the events
taking place in Central Asia ; and thus, in our present
paper, we will discuss those incidents which, since the
appearance of our last article,* have occurred in that
portion of the stage of the world.

Only one year has elapsed since the above-named
paper appeared, and, nevertheless, much which we then
brought forward as political probabilities have come
before us as facts.   Alluding tò the powerful position of

* See page 240.

Russia in Central Asia, we then made mention of Serdar Mehemmed-Yakub-Khan, who, revolting against the authority of his father, was purposing to visit Afghanistan with a civil war. This conjecture has been, unfortunately, fully confirmed, although the rebellious son has recently, with a *pater peccavi*, been half reconciled with his father.

The cause of the quarrel between father and son is as follows :—The polygamy of the Eastern princes, which everywhere promotes family disputes, quarrels, and intrigues, brought very bitter fruit to maturity at the Court of the sovereign of Kabul. Shir-Ali-Khan has several wives, and by them he has two sons. When he ascended the throne, the mother of Yakub-Khan, a daughter of Khan-Aka, the Djemshid chief, enjoyed his especial favour, and her son, therefore, was always brought forward. Honourably taking part in so many of his father's contests, he was proclaimed Weli-Ahd (successor), without this act, however, as is the custom in Afghanistan, being made the subject of a public ceremony. In time, the affection of the Afghan king took another direction. The dark-skinned daughter of the Djemshid chief was removed more and more from the circle of his royal favour, and her place was occupied by an Afghan princess, whom the king subsequently married, but who was then already the mother of a boy eleven years of age, named Abdullah-Djan. Naturally this second lady, in order to secure the favour of her noble lord, had nothing else to do but to push her son forward at the cost of the before-mentioned Weli-Ahd, and to have her dear Abdullah-Djan proclaimed future sovereign of Afghanistan, to the disregard of Mehemmed-Yakub-

Khan. The king consented; and as his journey to Umballah was just then occurring, he took his young
successor with him, and introduced him to the Irish
nobleman then representing the Queen of England
there, as legal heir of the paternal dignities, and therefore and also of the British subsidies. This was oil in
the fire to the already furious Yakub-Khan; he only
waited the return of his father to give proof of how
deeply he felt injured by the occurrence. Without taking
leave, the injured son soon quitted the Court of Kabul.
At this Abdullah-Djan's mother rejoiced with all her
party, but not so Shir-Ali-Khan. He knew well the
irritable and wild temper of his elder son, and however
much they consoled him with the fact that Yakub-Khan,
pursuing the pleasures of the chase in the deserts of Sistan, had renounced all political ambition, he was ever
looking with anxious dread for tidings from the western
parts of his kingdom. It is true the government was here
in the hands of the Emir's m̄⁻⁺ faithful servants. Herat
was entrusted to Prince Fetn-Mohammed-Khan, own
nephew of the son of the famous Shah-Ekber, who assassi-
nated Sir W. Macnaughten; Ferrah was governed by
Afzal-Khan, Gazni by Khudah Nazr, and Kandahar by
Safdar-Ali-Khan, in whom the Emir placed full confidence. Shir-Ali-Khan was therefore tolerably secure
from treachery; Yakub-Khan could not even seduce his
own father-in-law into a breach of faith. None of all
this hindered the young prince in the least; the military
fame of his past years was mighty enough to gather
round him a small but resolute band, with which he one
day issued forth from the desert at Kain, and, on the
27th March 1871, besieged the important fortress of

Gurian. Scarcely had tidings of this arrived, than Feth Mohammed-Khan sent his own son, Serdar Aziz, to the help of the besieged with two regiments of infantry, two light cannons, and some howitzers. These, however, came too late, for Gurian meanwhile had yielded, and its commandant, Ali-Khan, had fallen in the contest. This success was of great use to the rebellious son, as the troops sent for succour, instead of entering into an engagement, passed over to the victor, and the officers could only with great difficulty escape to Herat. Soon after Ferrah also, which is only three days' march distant from Herat, fell into the hands of the aspirant to the crown. Herat was, it was said, under the command of a man who hazarded everything for his master's cause. He would not allow the enemy to approach, and he ventured upon a battle before the gates of Herat. This terminated, however, unsuccessfully; and while he himself found his death while fighting, the people of Herat, or, according to another version, the soldiers of Shir-Ali-Khan, opened the gates of the fortress to the rebellious son. The latter suddenly saw himself in possession of the western frontier fortresses of the kingdom, and master of a situation in accordance with his boldest expectations.

At that time, not the most exemplary order was prevailing in the different parts of the Afghan kingdom. In the northern province of Turkestan, the agents of Abdur-Rahman-Khan were making the roads insecure; in fact, it was said this aspirant to the crown himself, of whom we shall presently speak, was encamped with an army before Meimene, which latter small Khanate was not just then adhering with strict fidelity to the lord of

S

Kabul. In the south the Kheiberis, from their love of
plunder, had made it necessary to despatch a division of
troops against them.   Djemshids, Beludjans, Hezarehs,
and Turkomans, all were awaiting with surprise the outbreak of hostilities between father and son.   If the latter
had only made more energetic use of the means standing
at his disposal, he would have been even now established
as unlimited sovereign on the throne of Kabul.   The
state of things, therefore, in Afghanistan, was highly
critical, and it is only a matter of surprise that that
European state whom the affairs there most concern,
namely, Great Britain, only received tidings respecting
them when her neighbour's house was already in flames.
When some time ago, as a private correspondent in the
Times, I drew the attention of the English-reading public
to Yakub-Khan's intrigues, and the possible fall of Herat,
and Mr Eastwick inquired of the Minister of Foreign
Affairs whether there were reports similar to mine, Lord
Enfield, the Under-Secretary of State, gave an answer
in the negative; but three days after this occurrence,
official information arrived from Calcutta that Herat
had fallen into the hands of the rebel Yakub-Khan.
The English statesmen were now suddenly seized with
panic alarm.   One of my friends, closely connected with
the India Office, wrote to me that I should be astonished
if I had been a witness of the consternation which my
second letter in the *Times* with regard to the Afghan
disturbances had called forth in certain circles.   In fact,
they seem to have accurately dictated to the Viceroy
of India the line of policy he was to pursue.   He
immediately placed himself in connection with Shir-Ali-
Khan; and so we hear that the latter, who, on the 8th

May, was already prepared to march against Herat with
an army, and rejected with fury every attempt at an
accommodation with his son, that this Shir-Ali-Khan
has now accepted the position of a reconcilable father,
and is ready to forgive his prodigal son. Of course the
English subsidies have chiefly effected this, for Shir-
Ali-Khan, the prince of a poor, warlike, and neglected
country, is obliged to dance to every tune that is played
to him from Calcutta. Had he been able to pursue his
instinctive policy, Afghanistan would, at the present day,
be bathed in blood, and he would have lost his throne;
but the Britons saw soon enough the dangerous side of
an experiment of the kind; they counselled, therefore,
reconciliation, and so we hear that Serdar Mehemmed-
Yakub-Khan, in the course of the following June, made
his penitent entrance into Kabul, accompanied only by
a few faithful friends, without arms, as a repentant
sinner, with the Koran suspended from his neck and a
rosary in his hands. That a step of this kind on the part
of the son manifested peculiar boldness of character, any
one acquainted with Afghan, or with Eastern circumstances generally, will not deny, though he may find it
explicable. The son knows well that his father is not
scrupulous, that he could put him out of the way by a
little drink, a little powder, the accidental fall of a house,
or the going off of a gun; nevertheless he now stays
in Kabul, where he was openly proclaimed successor;
and since his deeply offended father cannot take the
desired revenge upon him, he wreaks his anger on his
son's adherents, making short procedures everywhere,
and giving their posts both in Herat and the country
round to Shir-Ali-Khan's own people. The army alone

of the rebellious prince has refused to join in the unconditional allegiance to their supreme master. The last
Indian post informs us that, waiting the return of Yakub-
Khan, they have shown themselves somewhat impatient,
and have declared that, if the prince does not soon place
himself at their head, they will hasten to the standard of
Abdur-Rahman-Khan at Meimene, as they have no
intention of swearing fidelity to Shir-Ali-Khan.

The refractoriness in this quarter is not, however, of
great importance. Yakub-Khan, meanwhile, in Kabul
is an object of lukewarm manifestations of friendship on
the part of the Court, and on the other hand is an
eye-witness of how his abettor, Ezlem-Khan, who was
brought to the capital loaded with heavy chains, and
was thrown into prison, has to expiate the hard punishment inflicted on him. The reconciliation between
father and son is, as may be well imagined, only external; for although the latter relinquished the advantages
he had acquired because he hoped to obtain everything
by peaceful means from his now intimidated father, yet
Shir-Ali only yielded in consequence of the orders from
Calcutta, and because, fearing the *principium juris for-
tioris* laid down by the English with regard to the Afghan
crown, he might easily expose himself to the danger of
allowing the yearly subsidies of Great Britain to pass
into Yakub-Khan's coffers instead of into his own. And,
indeed, on the part of England, there has been already
some communication with Yakub-Khan, although only
indirectly. My statement in the *Times* that the prince
was hostile in his feelings to British interests, was as much
defended by one part of the Anglo-Indian press as it was
attacked by another. Neither party, however, can help

extolling the valour and judgment of the enterprising prince, or drawing his attention to the great importance of a British alliance. In fact, one organ even proposes to him that he should take up his residence on the Hooghli as his father's plenipotentiary, so that, in the immediate vicinity of British influence, he could best fit himself for future duties.

Having examined the state of affairs in Herat, we will return to another point in our last paper, with regard to which our prophecies have proved themselves tolerably correct. We stated last year that, "on the Narin river, and on the Thien-Shan range, Russian diplomacy had not only hung the Damocles sword over the head of Yakub-Kushbegi, the successful conqueror of East Turkestan, but even over the Trans-Ili district, that part especially which is enclosed in the Governments of Semipalatinsk and Tomsk. All that is left to the Chinese here, from the gradual advance of the Russian outposts, extends over three poor districts—(*a*) the southern one of Ili, the former penal settlement of the Chinese, with its capital of Kuldja, on the banks of the river of the same name; (*b*) the central district of Kir-Kara-Usu: it has a marshy soil and several lakes; and (*c*) the northern district of Tabagatai, with its capital, Tchugutchak." Strangely enough, the Russian diplomatists have now induced his Celestial Majesty to amputate a limb from the middle of the body of his empire, and that at the personal desire of the latter; for, as the Russian semi-official organs have trumpeted forth in the course of last year, the Chinese might have called for the help of his Majesty the Czar in repressing the Döngen insurrection. From our preceding papers it will be known to our readers that East Turkestan, more than seven years ago, sundered itself from the bonds of Chinese dominion, and preserved its independence up to the present time under native princes. In the part called by the Chinese Thien-Shan-Nan-Lu, *i.e.*, the southern Thien-Shan district, or Turkestan, as we call it, Yakub-Kushbegi is still ruling. In the north, however—in the Thien-Shan-Peh-Lu of the Chinese, or in Ili, according to our denomination—the sovereign power has been seized by the Kalmucks and Tarandjis, with the latter of whom the Döngens—*i.e.*, the Chinese Mohammedans—have made common cause. As the first of these—the Kalmucks and Tarandjis—consist chiefly of nomad tribes, the latter, that is, the Mohammedan-Tartar fraction, who are settled and agricultural, obtained the ascendancy. The Tarandjis alone, according to Radloff, who visited this part of Asia in 1862, number about 6000 families. The Döngens are probably still more in number. The latter, moreover, both in a mental and material point of view, are far superior not only to the Kalmucks, but also to the Tarandjis. Until about two years ago, nothing had been heard of these Tarandjis and Döngens, but that the former had their principal seat in Kuldja, and the latter in Urumtsi, and that although not on very friendly terms, there was no mutual hostility between them. Subsequently, however, owing to the separatist zeal of the Döngens, the accounts from thence began to be somewhat doubtful. Their spiritual and temporal head, Daud-Khalife, became the rival of Yakub-Kushbegi; and although the report which reached Europe, through Forsyth, that the Döngens intended to assist the

Chinese in reconquering East Turkestan, has not been confirmed, still the relations between these brethren in the faith in the remote East increased more and more in coolness; and, in the year 1869, we find the ruler of Yarkend in the north of Turfan entangled in a war with these very Döngens.

Till the course of this summer little or nothing has been heard of the Tarandjis, whom one year of the Chinese yoke has sufficiently humbled. They had enough to do to maintain the *status quo* against the Buddhist Kalmucks; and in order to render themselves secure against them, they had intentionally avoided all trifling disputes between the Döngens in the East and the ruler of East Turkestan in the south; and under the spiritual and temporal direction of a Mollah, assuming himself to be Seid, they had lived happily at Kuldja. At length, in 1871, events occurred which dragged this tribe forward upon the stage of the world, owing, indeed, to its western neighbour; that is, to an outpost division of the Russian army, which was in possession of a guard-post on the frontier of the Semiretchinsk district, on the banks of the little river Uessüg, in order from thence, on the one side, to watch, or to protect, as it was humorously expressed, the Kirghises residing there under Russian dominion, but, on the other side, to have an eye on the newly formed Tarandji district; for, as we have said, the Czar had made it his duty to chastise the rebellious people of the Tarandjis, at the wish of his Imperial brother in Pekin. Whether General Kolpakoffsky, the Russian commander there, voluntarily entered into a quarrel with the sovereign or Sultan of Kuldja, as the Russians call him, or whether he was compelled to act on the offensive, is now difficult to decide, as only the Russian version of events lies before us; although, on the other side, the fact that the Russians, for the protection of the Russian-Chinese frontier, had extended the outpost division at the beginning of this year beyond Uessüg, the former frontier of the two empires, cannot be exactly regarded as a defensive measure. We know that a Kirghiz tribe, at whose head stood a certain Tasa-Beg, holding the rank of ensign in the ranks of the Russian army, had quarrelled with the Russian authorities, and their chief had then attempted with his tribe to escape to the Chinese territory, in order to join the so-called Chinese insurgents there. As the Russians tried to hinder the design of the Kirghises, the Cossack officer Gerassimoff was sent to the frontier in order to prevent the movement. Yet the ruler of Kuldja seems also to have been informed of Tasa-Beg's intention, for he had despatched people to assist his brethren in the faith. As the Cossack officer Gerassimoff was not able to cope with them, a company with two pieces of artillery advanced to assist him. These succeeded, it is true, in driving back the Tarandjis, and in occupying an abandoned fort on the river Korgas, but not in preventing the settlement of Tasa-Beg. With him hostilities really began. General Kolpakoffsky sent one messenger after another to demand from the Sultan of Kuldja—called by the Russians Abil-Oglan (?)—that the fugitive Kirghises should be given up, to which, of course, the Sultan would not consent. The *casus belli* was thus given. In the May of this year General Kolpakoffsky sent three smaller bodies of troops, consisting of infantry, cavalry, and some field-pieces, across the frontier to the Tarandji territory, in order to call the Sultan to order, as this could not be done by diplomatic means, and to discourage this restless neighbour for ever from attempting to endanger the interests of Russia. That these Tarandjis are no dangerous enemies, and that they bear the same proportion to the mighty empire of the Czar as the gnat does to the elephant, arises from the fact that the Central Asiatics, taken as a whole, are more cowardly than all other Orientals ; that the inhabitants of East Turkestan, that is, the brethren of the Tarandjis, are more cowardly than the Central Asiatics ; and that the Tarandjis, an agricultural and hitherto enslaved people, are far inferior in valour to their brethren on the other side of the Thien-Shan mountain. How, therefore, these unarmed peasants, the tenth part of whom had bad matchlocks, could venture a battle with the Russian army, well-disciplined as it was, and furnished with the most modern means of warfare, is certainly scarcely conceivable, and must have led to very comical scenes. Notwithstanding, we learn from the Russian report that Colonel Jelensky, who commanded one of the corps despatched, attacked by three thousand well-armed and valiant Tarandjis, repulsed the latter with a loss of two hundred men, after an encounter of five hours' length, while his own corps only numbered three dead and eight wounded. Of course, being on hostile ground, there was no choice but to press forward unceasingly : first, in order to procure provisions for the army ; and, secondly, in order to obtain the possession of some secure points from which the newly conquered territory could be defended. On the 18th May, the Russians conquered Fort Mezar, where an immense store of provisions and a considerable quantity of Chinese arms fell into their hands. Greater battles were fought by the Russians at Akkend on the 16th June, and at Alim on the 28th of the same month, where, according to Russian statement, they made themselves masters of the whole camp of the enemy, with twenty-three pieces of artillery. Soon afterwards, after the taking of the fortress Tching-di-cho-si, they utterly broke the power of the sovereign of Kuldja in a decisive battle before the fortress of Süding, which is about four miles from Kuldja. Nothing, of course, now remained for the conquered prince but to surrender at discretion. The following official statement respecting his submission was sent by General Kolpakoffsky to the Czar : —

"After the battle of Süding, the conquered Sultan of Kuldja sent to me with the request that I would permit him personally to repair to my camp. At the same time he gave up to me the renegade Kirghiz lieutenant Tasa-Beg, whose flight to the territory of the Tarandjis with thousands of our Kirghises was the principal cause of the campaign. Towards evening, the Sultan, Abil-Oglan, came to our camp, accompanied by several notabilities. He declared himself solely responsible for everything, and for this reason he surrendered himself to the Russian Government; he begged us to spare his subjects, and he promised that both he and his consort would unconditionally obey our commands. I replied to this, that it was the will of the Russian Emperor that our troops should occupy the capital of Kuldja ; for the rest, I promised him that his private property should remain unviolated, and that he should be allowed the choice of a dwelling-place. Upon this, in the presence of the Sultan and his high functionaries, our army set out for Kuldja, and was received with the greatest submissiveness by the inhabitants on the way thither. After our arrival in Kuldja, our army encamped in the garden near the fortress. I rode round the fortifications, on which occasion the Sultan presented me with the keys of the gate and of all the state treasures. In the citadel, besides military stores of all kinds, we found two hundred and fifty ure-oxen and six thousand pecks of wheat and barley. From the remotest districts of the country deputations of Tarandjis, Kirghises, and Kalmucks are constantly arriving, to notify their unconditional subjection."

Little as the brave general may have hurried to seize the half rusty keys of the miserable city, equally little were his cattle especially burdened by the transport of the treasures found in Kuldja. The whole neighbourhood, in the time of the Chinese, was very scantily peopled, and, as is easily explicable, it has suffered considerably more during the late disturbances and civil wars, so that the possession of the town, which in Radloff's time numbered about thirty thousand inhabitants, is of great, I might say incalculable importance to the Russians, not so much in an economical as in a political and strategical point of view. How far the possessions of Russia will by it be extended towards the east cannot be at present alleged with certainty; at any rate she stands now in the immediate vicinity of the Döngens, and not far from their capital Kir-Kara-Usu; and if the Chinese Emperor should demand the further obligingness of the Czar, she may, by crushing this second rebellious people, approach nearer the Gobi Desert, and all at once increase her possessions by twelve degrees of longitude and about six of latitude.

If these extensions of frontier are of great importance with regard to the future plans of Russia in China, they are of still greater weight as to the position' of the Northern Colossus with respect to its British rival in Central Asia. The Court of Petersburg, by the incorporation of Dsungaria, acquires the possessions of that valley district through which the most easy and hitherto frequented roads cross the Muzart range to East Turkestan, namely, the one leading in a south-west direction to Aksu, and that passing in a south-east direction to Kuldja. Hitherto when the highway to Turkestan through the Terek Pass led through Khokand territory, a comparatively mild language was used towards Yakub-Kushbegi from the Fort of Narin; at the present day, however, when the Russian eagle hovers over his head from the north, and can at any time pay him a friendly visit along these very roads, the Court of Petersburg will certainly behave differently to this successful pretender to the throne. He will henceforth be no more asked if it is agreeable to him to allow Russian caravans access to the markets of Yarkend and Kashgar, to receive a Russian consul in his capital, and so forth. Even without a hint from Pekin, the Atalik-Gazi may now receive a thorough lesson from the Russians. This will probably, moreover, not be long in coming, and if, in the next two years, I shall have to speak of Kashgar, the Russian flag will probably be hoisted there. This new acquisition has little or nothing in common with the powerful position of Russia in the western part of Central Asia. When

East Turkestan, through a Chinese Government of a hundred and fifty years, lost the three Turkestan oasis lands, Dsungaria was a thorough *terra incognita* to the Mohammedans on the Oxus and Yaxartes, and as far as I could judge from personal inquiries, they knew scarcely anything at all of its very existence. Moreover, it is not necessary for the new Russian acquisition to exercise any influence on the western part of Central Asia, for here the *status quo* of the last two years has made everything quiet, and has brought social ahd political life to such an extent into the groove of Russian notions, that the Government of Petersburg could scarcely even have desired a better result in such a comparatively short time. Khuda-Yar-Khan is happy to be able to vegetate under the shadow of the Russian eagle, and he punctually sends his yearly tribute to Khokand. With similar repose and blind resignation to the decrees of fate, Muzaffar-ed-Din-Khan, the Prince of Bokhara, demeans himself. I say prince, for even at the present moment his diplomatic envoy is at the Court of Kabul, while he himself, who a few years ago tried to impress me with the exalted position of " a prince of all the faithful," trembles more before an adjutant of General Kaufmann than a good Mohammedan would do before the destroying angel Esrafil. So also of late times not the slightest vestige of revolutionary zeal has sprung from the restless and fanciful minds of his fanatical Mollahs. They are probably expecting miracles from their saints.

But to the Russians also we must not give implicit credence, when they tell us that in Tashkend there appears a paper in the language of the country, and this, —for the Kirghises. That our journalists may not take

alarm lest some day one of their articles on Central
Asiatic affairs receive a reply from a Kirghiz politi-
cian, be it observed, for general comfort, that among a
hundred thousand Kirghises there is perhaps not one
able to read, and any one who is acquainted with the
Arabic written character will certainly prefer to read sen-
tences from the Koran and the life of Mohammedan
saints, than the sinful scribbling of Russian unbelievers.
The dissemination therefore of the Kirghiz journal is
not very extensive, for Russian culture will have ten
times more difficulty in making its way among the Central Asiatics than among the Tartars on the Wolga, or
the Kalmucks and Bashkirs on the steppes. Lastly, we
will observe that Khiva also has had its reprieve length-
ened. In the spring of this year, it was said, indeed,
that the Russians intended to punish the sovereign of
Khahrezm for breach of faith and outrage; in a word,
that they intended to pay him a visit. I do not think
that this prince, who showed me the greatest hospitality
during my residence in his state, is protected from the
power of Russian arms by my past benedictions (for so
long as I resided in the capital, once every day I had to
offer a prayer on his behalf). The Russians, moreover,
briefly assert that it is only the insurrection of the Kirghises of the Little Horde which withholds them for
the time from the annexation of Khiva. This Kirghiz
rebellion, at the head of which, according to the Russian
statement, a certain Sadik stands, only consists of a few
nomads, amounting at the most to three hundred families;
these wander about on the right bank of the lower Oxus
territory, because they will not pay tribute either to the
Emperor of Russia or to the Khan of Khiva. Some-

times it happens that the aged members of these wandering parties, when they are tired of roaming about, come
to an agreement with the Khivan authorities in one
way or another. They are allowed, perhaps, to give a
third or a half of the established tribute, and for this
they have permission to let their herds graze for a longer
time on the not especially fertile right bank of the Oxus.
Thus far and seldom further goes the connection of the
Khan of Khiva with the so-called rebellious Kirghises,
from whom, as Russian organs tell us, the flames of the
revolt at Khiva emanate, and for which the latter will
have to atone.

Putting together everything which has been said with
regard to Russian advance in Central Asia, who could
indeed assert that the Court of Petersburg has aimed,
not at the overthrow of the rulers of Central Asia, not
at the conquest of new tracts of land and new tribes, but
solely and entirely at the promotion of commercial interests? And yet it is just the latter statement with which
the adversaries of my political views in this highly important question make war against me.* Russia, they
say, has a civilising mission in Asia to fulfil, and this can
be best accomplished, they justly observe, by smoothing
the commercial highways, by regulating international
relations, and by the protection of her own subjects. As
regards Russia's mission for civilisation, I have repeatedly

---

* Among the different works which the Russian press and others have
recently brought out on this subject, I will specially mention the following
pamphlet. It bears the title, "Russia's Commercial Mission in Central Asia.
By Christian von Sarauw, Royal Danish Captain of Infantry " (Leipzig,
1871). The Captain writes, indeed, in the Russian interest, but not in the
Russian style, and his little work, which is free from the unpleasant language of Russian controversy, betrays much study on the part of the author.

expressed my opinions, and will not repeat them here; with respect also to trade, I will gladly allow that the Russians have already done much for the Oxus lands during the comparatively short period of their rule, and will certainly do still more. In consequence of a plan laid before the Privy Council last year, by the Grand Duke Michael Nikolajewitsch, and approved by the Emperor, two hundred German miles of railroad were to be constructed during the course of this year, two-thirds of which were undertaken for commercial and political purposes, and one-third from strategic considerations. The most important line of all is certainly that which is to lead from the west coast of the Caspian Sea along the southern slopes of the Caucasus. Poti on the Black Sea is the starting-point; the railroad from here to Tiflis, if I mistake not, is already completed; from Tiflis it is to be carried on to Baku, and this is to be connected by a steam navigation line with Krasnowodsk, a Russian fort recently built on the east side of the Caspian Sea; from the last-named place, the puffing steam-horse of modern times is to hasten on its iron road to the banks of the Oxus, across the sandy steppes and the plateau of Kaplankir. Although I consider the whole plan as far as Krasnowodsk perfectly practicable, and though I regard the communication between the dark waves of the Caspian and the yellow Oxus impossible, from the fact that the constant storms of sand might bury not only the rails but the whole railway train; still I will not deny that Russia will speedily bring into direct connection with the West, if not this point of Central Asia, at any rate others, which ten years ago were almost unknown to us. That the Russians are setting to work

in full earnest on the accomplishment of their railroad
project, is proved by the construction of the line of railway from Kursk and Rostow to the Don.   On the 13th
March 1866, the permission was given to construct this
railway, the length of which was a hundred and ten
German miles, and eighteen months afterwards it was
finished.* I will not deny further that Russia will contribute considerably in advancing the cultivation of the
soil and certain branches of industry in East Turkestan ;
for the investigation made during the last month by
a committee for the artificial irrigation of the steppes
near Djizzag will probably, if attended with success, be
repeated elsewhere ; and by the increased export of silk,
cotton, wool, skins, dried fruits, and other raw productions of the inhabitants of the Central Asiatic oasis
lands, the dwellers both on the Oxus and the Yaxartes
will speedily enjoy comforts of life of which they had
before never ventured to dream.   I admit all this ; for,
as my political opponents might convince themselves,
I have always pointed out the Russian conquests of
Turkestan as beneficial to the interests of that country, and, indeed, to humane objects generally.   Yet my
opponents forget that it is difficult, I might say impossible, to promote the trade and industry of any foreign
European power in Central Asia without obtaining the
position of a mentor there by political conquests and
actual extension of frontier.   Does not the recent past
history of Russia in the interior of Asia declare this ?
What was the cause of the almost two hundred years of
disputes with Khiva, if not the protection of trade as
regards the Russian fishery in the Caspian Sea ? Why

* Cf. the before-mentioned pamphlet by Sarauw, p. 37.

T

has Russia approached the Khanate of Khokand on the lower stream of the Yaxartes? why has she entered into lengthy political complications with Bokhara? why has she created the new province of Turkestan? and why, lastly, has she recently annexed Kuldja also, if not for the defence of commercial interests? Our European powers, like old Rome, have ever allowed the winged Mercury to precede the armour-clad Mars. The British joint-stock company which, in the year 1757, possessed only a few small factories in the Carnatic and Fort-William in Bengal, probably never imagined that their successors a hundred years later would be lords of the whole gigantic peninsula, with more than two hundred and fifty millions of inhabitants. Just the same were the motives of the French conquests in Algiers, and of the Dutch in Eastern Asia. Everywhere, but most of all in Turkestan, bales of goods are the best pioneers for inevitable armies and legal conquests. We will suppose Russia already in possession of the whole right bank of the Oxus; will she be able to refrain from crossing this river when Afghanistan and the Turkoman hordes are, as is well known, such restless neighbours? I put the question here, although Russia has given the answer from the beginning, by entering even now into political machinations with the Afghans without lawful possession of the whole right bank of the Oxus. It is now no longer a secret that Abdur-Rahman-Khan, the dreaded rival of Shir-Ali-Khan, is in high favour with the Governor-General of Samarkand, and that a yearly revenue is allowed him from Petersburg. Hitherto rumour has indeed anticipated the plans of Russia; for in India and Kabul the tidings were spread abroad that Abdur-Rahman-Khan had been placed by the Russians in the room of the present ruler of Bokhara, as the latter was in no wise equal to curb his passionate subjects. I repeat this is only an empty rumour; yet that Abdur-Rahman-Khan maintains a strong party on the left bank of the Oxus, and has a considerable body of troops in his pay, can only be ascribed to the loyalty of the Russian politicians, who, when time and circumstances demand it, will certainly make use of the Afghan aspirant to the crown.

That therefore the Court of Petersburg will sooner or later cross the Oxus, and insinuate itself into Afghanistan, is more than probable. Even English statesmen admit the possibility of this; yet they forget to ask whether Russia, when she has reached the Suleiman chain, will not, perhaps, enact the same political scene, and indeed be compelled, perhaps, to do so, which she performed on the Yaxartes, the Narin, and the Oxus? Russia, even if she were animated by idyllic peaceful ideas, can easily see herself obliged to take such steps. If, in the advance of an armed power, and in the ambition of a ruling house in Europe, it is difficult to anticipate the point of arrest, how much more so in Asia, where all circumstances and combinations are constantly impelling to further progress! They say that Russia and England will live together as peaceful neighbours; but in this assertion historical facts are disregarded. With which of her neighbours has Great Britain lived in peace, so long as she was mighty and powerful? She has not indeed declared war against the salt waves of the ocean; but wherever her Indian Empire has bordered on other states, she has never rested until these were either weak-

ened or incorporated, or had entered the list of her pro-
tection-seeking vassals. And will the British leopard
now live in peace and harmony with the Russian bear,
and pursue with common zeal the noble work of disse-
minating Western civilisation? No; it needs no specially
keen glance to perceive that the parties concerned do
not themselves think so. The long-dreaded combat for
rivalry is approaching nearer and nearer, and, judging by
the social transformations in British India, the chances of
victory for Great Britain are ever diminishing; for although
the catastrophe is still in the far distance, the agents of
the ruin are increasing rapidly. How doubtful are the late
observations of the Briton with regard to the relations of
the Mohammedans to their Christian protectors! I will
not here subject the view which Dr W. W. Hunter has
published in his work on this point to a strict analysis.
All that he tells us of the wild fanaticism, of the bitter
rancour, and the secret activity of the Mussulman subjects of the Queen is in no wise new. New alone is the
fact, that an Englishman can thus lay open the wounds in
his country's Government, and can sketch such a gloomy,
I might almost say, despairing picture of the future.
There is, indisputably, a wonderful difference between
the feverish activity of the Mohammedans of India and
the sleepiness and patience of the Hindoo population.
The Hindoo offers himself readily for every scheme of his
master; he allows institutions of a thousand years' standing, old established customs, and the most sacred super-
stitions, to be attacked, without bursting forth in fury
against the intruding stranger. He murmurs, sighs, and
frowns, yet he submits; for even the sepoy revolution of
1857 would never have become what it was without

Mohammedan ringleaders. The Hindoo is too indolent for him to excite himself into fanaticism, and he is too indifferent to risk his life for the sake of remedying political wrongs. And if the English do not disturb him, or if they let him rest unmolested in the shadow of his poor hut, the enthusiastic Brahmin may whisper to him as long as he likes, he will never become revolutionary by profession.

The Mohammedan is wholly different; in fact, he is the complete contrast to his fellow-countryman, from whose religion he differs. The wild fanaticism which helped the first Arabian intruders into India to disseminate the doctrines of Mohammed has continued here to the present day among the followers of this religion. Whenever I have observed at leisure the dark face of a Punjaubi, with his white or dark turban in strange contrast with his complexion, I could not sufficiently admire the expression of extraordinary excitement in his fiery and wildly rolling eyes. These people have in general far less religious knowledge than the Özbegs, Persians, Arabs, and Turks, yet the name of Mohammed and of the Mussulman saints transports them to the wildest ecstasy. Nearly one thousand miles from the banks of the Indus, not far from Herat, I heard a Punjaubi, after he had been praying for a good half hour in deep devotion, start up with a wild "Hai Frengi!" (Oh, you European!); and this hatred, which finds but feeble expression in the secret society of the Wehabites, animates all classes of the Mohammedans of India. We have already spoken of their seat in Patna; and although in Europe the proceedings against the principal ringleader, Emir Khan, in the late stirring times, were little talked of, his sentence of transportation caused great sensation there, and the adherents of the rebellious sect, instead of being intimidated, were excited by it to still bolder deeds. Thus, recently, Judge Norman, who represented the Chief Justice in Calcutta, fell a victim to the dagger of one of the fanatical Wehabis, who make a principle of the doctrine that the expulsion of the Britons from India is more necessary than fasting, praying, and other pious duties. Justice Norman was just ascending the stairs to the hall of justice, when the murderer, who had approached him under the pretext of wishing to present him with a petition, gave him two fatal wounds with a knife. The Judge, who was universally esteemed, died on the following morning ; and in the cry of horror which echoed through the whole English press, the same verdict, though variously worded, might ever be read, namely, that "at the next attempt to overthrow our (*i.e.*, British) rule in India, which sooner or later must happen, the Mohammedans would at any rate play the principal part "—certainly no rose-coloured conviction as to the future of the so-called Indian Empire. And, with such perceptions, will they, lulled in the sleep of security, await the approach of the Russians on the Indus ? with forty millions of restless spirits, who for the most part represent the proletariat of India,—for the lazy Indian Mohammedan has only to be idle under the native Mussulman Government, and nevertheless can live,—will they enter into a contest with such a power as Russia ? English statesmen might spare themselves the trouble of trying to persuade us to believe such fables. For that they themselves do not believe them, and that the fatal question presents itself to them with increasing distinctness, is sufficiently proved, partly by the adoption of secret preventive measures, and partly by the tone of mind prevailing among the Anglo-Indians themselves.

We will only mention the following instance in relation with this subject :—When, after the brilliant victory of the German arms in France, the clever satire of John Michal Trutz-Baumwoll, in the style of the "Battle of Dorking," appeared in the supplement of the Augsburg *Allgemeiner Zeitung*, and an English author produced in reply the clumsy work, "The Second Armada," the English journalists felt that they ought not to remain behind with seasonable papers, and consequently there appeared in the *Pioneer* a lively and cleverly-written sketch, entitled, "The Battle on the Sutlej." On the banks of the Sutlej, which, as is well known, is the boundary river between India and the Punjaub, the author depicts a battle between Russia and England, in which two hundred thousand Russians are engaged, consequently twenty thousand more than the whole Indian army. While British satirists of this kind almost always make the arms of Albion to triumph at last, the contrary is here the case. The Russian generals have at their disposal a skilled and numerous troop of horse ; and although John Bull fights with his northern rival with his usual perseverance and tenacity, the bad equipment and the treachery of the native troops give his enemy the advantage. Russia remains victorious, and annexes the Punjaub as well as Sinde to Afghanistan, which has long been in her possession. I repeat, the whole thing is only a jest, but it is yet characteristic enough of the future policy of the Anglo-Indians. That, nevertheless, a similar, though not yet open course of proceeding is aimed at by the Cabinet of St James, is evident from the lead which the Gladstone Ministry has recently taken in the construction of a railway communication between England and India. When Colonel Chesney, some years ago, came forward with the project of the Euphrates line, he was decried in England as an enthusiast. At the present day the Government itself is willing to promote the project of a railroad of 5311 English miles; and the press both in England and India speaks warmly of the whole proceeding. As Parliament sent out a committee to examine into the matter, detailed plans gradually came in, with estimates of expenses, the highest of which has at present been stated at £41,600,000 sterling. These expenses are to be borne, not by any single nation, but by all the countries generally through which the line of railroad would pass. We will speak of the ethnographical and political importance of this design in due time, in a paper given to the subject. For the present, we will only remark, that the execution of the gigantic project in England itself, although apparently for the promotion of commercial interests, would be in truth undertaken from strategic and political considerations. Russia, with her network of railways, is approaching ever more and more the Central Asiatic lands, and as England does not wish to remain behind in these regions, she is striving to shorten considerably the journey from London to Calcutta. Hitherto it has taken somewhat less than one month to arrive on the banks of the Thames in an uninterrupted journey from the shores of the Hooghli. Should the projected railway be accomplished, the same journey, according to the plan of Mr William Low and Mr George Thomas, could be accomplished in seven days, thirteen hours, and twenty-two minutes. In spite of the apparent repose and the sense of security displayed by London politicians, many things could be mentioned which evidence a perfect consciousness of an inevitable contest and timely measures of defence. Yet Russia also is not standing still, as we have shown. And when we again speak of the position of the Central Asiatic question, the reader will have no occasion to be surprised at the rapid progress of events.

A MOHAMMEDAN CONQUEROR IN ASIA
(1873).

PERCEIVING the manifold influence which the Christian West exercises on the adjacent Mussulman East in all spheres of political and social life, we must not be surprised if in Turkey, Arabia, Persia, in a word, in the whole of Western Asia, we look in vain for those dazzling apparitions, which, like a *fata morgana*, emerge from the barren monotony of Eastern everyday life. Our European civilisation, our mental and physical superiority, and, lastly, our restless temperament, which desires to penetrate and investigate everything, has once for all taken away from the Turks, Arabs, and Persians, and other nations with a famous past, all desire to revel on the field of political and religious adventure. These men with their broad, high, and thick turbans, with their melancholy and submissive expression and sad languishing looks, see themselves interfered with everywhere in all their movements, and in their whole mode of thought, by the European consular agents and missionaries who surround them. They lack the courage for any freedom of action. No longer the muse, boldly spreading its wings, soars upwards with bombastic song ;

no picture exuberant with metaphor is now created; and as no one any longer ventures to mount the unruly Pegasus of the Eastern Muses,—for the present poetry of Islam is a miserable echo of past melodies,—so no one has the courage to leave the rugged and worn-out path of prosaic everyday life, and through some extraordinary deed to attract the attention of those near and distant.

Only in the more remote depths of Asia, where our footprints are still rarely to be found, has the charm of a past mode of life still maintained itself; only there was it possible in recent times for a man to arise who has accomplished deeds extraordinary under the circumstances allotted to him, and who two hundred or even a hundred years ago would have found a place in Asiatic traditions by the side of Djengiz and Timur. In the village of Pishbek, also called Pisked, in the Kurama district, in a part of the Khanate of Khokand lying between Khodjend and Tashkend, about forty-five years ago, Mehemmed-Yakub was born, the son of a Khokand custom-house officer, or more correctly, of a clerk. Like all men of Iran descent, who, under Özbeg rule, are for the most part entrusted with the work of the pen, as the Özbeg considers himself alone created for that of the sword, Mehemmed-Yakub, in his earliest youth, held the office of a clerk, sometimes with one, and sometimes with another Khokand Sipahi. " Ability breaks through stone walls," says the Oriental ; and so it happened that he soon became remarkable by his intellectual quickness, and was promoted by the deceased Mehemmed-Ali-Khan to the post of a Diwandji (chief collector of customs) ; in 1847 he was raised by the Kiptchak

chief, Alim-Kul, to be Pansad Bashi (officer commanding five hundred men), and entered the rank of the
Sipahis. As he was called as a Tadshik to exchange
the pen for the sword, it is pretty certain that Mehemmed - Yakub had contrived to distinguish himself in
both mental and physical power, and nothing proves
the amount of confidence placed in him better than his
appointment as commandant of the fortress of Ak-
Meshid at a time when the Russian columns were
advancing on the right bank of the Sir, with slow but
sure step. Praise from an enemy is always the most eloquent, and so we give far more credence to the Russian
statement, according to which Mehemmed-Yakub-Beg
is said to have defended with rare heroism the fortress
entrusted to him, than to the Khokand report, which
reproaches him with having entered into forbidden negotiations with the Russians, and with having ceded to
them for 12,000 Tillah = 7800 pounds sterling, a lake
named Balik-Köl (fish lake) in the neighbourhood of the
fortress. After the Russians had taken the fortress in
question, Mehemmed-Yakub-Kushbegi seems notwithstanding to have enjoyed the undivided favour of Alem-
Kul, then ruler of Khokand; for as just at that time the
Endidjan Khodjas, led by Kodja-Buzurg-Khan, were
preparing for an expedition to East Turkestan, and
required, at any rate, the moral support of Alim-Kul,
the latter placed our hero at the side of the adventurous
Khodja, in the capacity of Kushbegi, or Grand Vizier, as
it is called in Western Asia. Before, however, we speak
of the march of Khodja Buzurg, and Yakub - Kushbegi to the eastern part of the Islam world, it is unavoid-
ably necessary to delineate in a few short touches the

positon of East Turkestan or Alti-Shehr (the kingdom
of the Six Cities) at that time, in order that we may be
acquainted with the scene of action open to the new
Asiatic conqueror.

As early as 1863, when I was at Samarkand, I saw
one day my travelling companion, Hadji Bilal, returning from the bazaar with pale face and troubled expression. He had received very gloomy news from his
home, and as in the course of our intimacy he had constantly told me of the fatal desire for conquest possessed
by the Khodjas, and had stigmatised these as the main
scourge, and, indeed, as the destruction of East Turkestan, I supposed from his repeated exclamations, " Those
miserable Khodjas! those good-for-nothing robbers! "
that another inroad had been made, or that a new civil
war had broken out. Nevertheless Bilal himself and I
also were greatly mistaken: the blow which on this occasion had struck the western part of the Celestial Empire,
emanated not from Khokand, but from China itself.
Islamism, the arch-enemy of the Buddhist doctrines,
which is ever more and more driven back by the mighty
influence of our Western civilisation in the west of the
Old World, whose period of power there has long ago
expired, and who only enjoys the bread of charity, this
Islamism will and must conquer for itself fresh territory
in the remote East, in consequence of the pressure in the
West. It recedes from the one part in order to gain
firmer footing in the other; and it is indeed extremely
remarkable how the sparks of the religious doctrines of
the Arabian prophet can still grow into a burning flame
even on the remote Chinese soil, where indifference in
religious matters has always prevailed. It is only lately

that we have become aware of the fact that China, in its western part, still numbers nearly forty millions of Mohammedans, who for the most part inhabit regions which have long remained concealed to the curiosity of the European traveller; for it is only most recently that, through the accounts of Baron von Richthofen, Mr T. T. Cooper, and the French expedition to the interior of China, we have been enlightened to any extent with regard to the influence, the powerful position, and the number of the Chinese Mohammedans. The revolution of the Taepings, which greatly undermined the already decaying structure of the Chinese state, must have served to encourage the rebellious inclinations of other non-Buddhist subjects of the Chinese Emperor. In the provinces of Kan-su and Shen-si there is scarcely one place of importance where the Mohammedans were not known as the representatives of prosperity, and as an active united body; in the south-west province of Yün-nan they were to be met with in numbers, and they constituted the greater part of the population. And although China is distinguished for its exceeding tolera-tion of all religions, and had certainly never interfered with these Islamites in matters of faith, yet considering the ardour of these Mohammedan fanatics, it appears remarkable enough that it was not till about the middle of the century that they rebelled against their Chinese masters, who, to the horror of the Mussulman, eat swine's flesh, worship idols, and commit other abomina-tions. In the year 1855, the elder of Li-Kian-fu sum-moned the faithful to arms; this summons was supported by the other elders, and speedily the insurrection spread over the whole western province of Yünnan.

That in an insurrection in the south-west, the true focus of it must increase in extent, and that the flames would spread to the north-west, where there was no lack of inflammable material, was to be foreseen. There had always existed a connection, both mental and material, between the Mohammedans of Yünnan and the Mohammedans of Shen-si and Kan-su. The latter, who, from a cause hitherto not satisfactorily explained, bear the name Dunganes or Tunganes, had, in consequence of their less settled life, and perhaps also on account [of the greater tract of country over which their dwellings extended, shown far less courage against the Buddhist Chinese than their brethren by race and faith had done in the remote south. The Dunganes, the greater part of whom were living in the towns of the old land of the Uigures, Komul, Barkul, Turfan, Urumtchi, Manassi, and Kir-Kara-Usu, were the true medium of the commercial relations between the Chinese and the East Turkestanians, as well as the true channel of the social intercourse between the rulers and the ruled ; the Mandarins could approach them on account of their Chinese nationality, and the East Turkestanians on account of their Islam faith. Moreover, the Court of Pekin could all the sooner employ them as civil and military functionaries, both in Alti-Shehr and in the eastern districts, as the Turkish-Mohammedan subjects could carry on business with them far more easily than with the Buddhist-Chinese, whose intercourse with the faithful was impeded by so many causes. That the Dunganes, conscious of their importance to the Chinese state, had ever been distinguished for a specially submissive character, we have never heard. In spite of the exceedingly peaceful disposition which has always characterised them, the Dunganes were, on the contrary, ever those who incited the East Turkestanians to reject one order or another given by the anti-Islam Government. Thus, for example, when the magistrates consisted of Dunganes, the picture of the Emperor was not exhibited for public adoration ; they winked at the prohibited growth of the mustache ; the Chinese might not let their swine go about publicly, and many other things of a similar kind. The Dunganes were, moreover, zealous, and indeed. fanatical Mohammedans. Without any knowledge of the Arabic language, there were many among them who knew the Koran entirely by heart. Their Mollahs cast the insulting epithets of "ignorant and unbeliver" as readily at their other Turkestan colleagues as the Bokhariot does at the Osmanli. And that they did not obey the religious law of the Gaza (war against unbelievers), and had hitherto taken no step towards shaking off the Chinese yoke, can only be explained by the fact that, like every son of the Celestial Empire who regards with contempt all who are not Chinese, they saw in the East Turkestanian, with his Turkish or Persian language, nothing but a barbarian and a being unworthy of their alliance. The case was quite different with their religious brethren in Yünnan, and not only because they wished to follow their example, but in the hope of possible help, the Dunganes, in 1864, rose as at a given signal in the towns of Urumtchi, Turfan, Kara-Shehr, and Kutcha (more correctly Kötche), massacred the Chinese authorities, who were present only in small numbers, and proclaimed the restoration of a Moham-

medan rule. That this insurrection could only have
been produced by contagion with the eastern provinces
of Kan-su and Shen-si, is beyond doubt, although we
are completely uncertain respecting the details of events
there. All that we know of the Dunganes' insurrection
relates only to the before-mentioned towns ; and the
first and most important of the successes mentioned is
the surprise of Kutcha, where about a thousand Dunganes fell upon the Chinese garrison, killing and plundering all who did not confess themselves Mussulmans. As
the political disputes in the west of the Chinese Empire
in this century had only extended to the frontier towns
of Yarkend, Kashgar, and Aksu, and this more remote
part had been spared, the Chinese functionaries, in their
sleepy carelessness, must have been all the more surprised by the Dunganes ; for nothing could resist the
excited current of the Dunganes' religious fury ; and in an
astonishingly short time they had seized upon the sovereign power in the territory at the foot of the Thien-
Shan mountain, as far as the " Six Cities."

In consequence of this unexpected success, the Dunganes were now obliged to follow suit with regard to
their behaviour towards the native inhabitants of East
Turkestan. If Yünnan had not been so distant, and
the danger of Chinese chastisement had not been so
near, a union of operations would certainly never have
been effected ; but the Dunganes on this occasion
thought better of it, and at the very outset drew the
Turkish population in that province into their interests
—in fact, in order to render them still more enthusiastic
for the success of the insurrection, they placed themselves under their command. In the Six Cities—for the

U

course of the insurrection was now to take this direction —everything remained in the greatest repose, for the fear of Chinese vengeance, after the unfortunate insurrection under Weli-Khan-Töre, still pressed heavily on the inhabitants of all these towns; and the East Turkestanians, a peacefully-inclined people, were, apart from the one fact of religious unsuitability, not so much dissatisfied with the rule of the Chinese as to expose themselves to the danger of a new insurrection. So the people thought ; but their leaders, the Khodjas, descendants of the Prophet in the true meaning of the word, and in reality temporal rulers, or, at any rate, aspirants to be such, were of a very different opinion. The thirst for power and the eagerness for booty in this class of idlers allowed no rest to the oligarchical rulers, veiled in the mantle of religion, and reverenced with idolatry by the simple people. Under the Chinese rule they had to be satisfied with the pious alms which pilgrims placed on the rich graves of their ancestors ; crowns and wealth were now hovering before their eyes ; why should they delay any longer ? Little enticement was required with the Khodja-Burhan-ed-Din of Kutcha on the part of the Dunganes, to induce the pious man to mount his horse at the mosque where the deputation found him in the deepest devotion, to unfurl the standard of insurrection at the head of the movement, and, in alliance with the Dunganes, to overthrow the Chinese dominion in the other Six Cities.

The pigtailed Mohàmmedans had indeed hit the right nail on the head. Led by Khan-Khodja (so the before-mentioned Burhan-ed-Din was called), the Dunganes continued their way from Kutcha to Kara-Shehr, and from hence to Turfan, which was taken in August 1863. Soon afterwards they proceeded to Aksu, where the peaceful inhabitants, for the most part Turks or Sarts, surrendered themselves after two days' resistance. The Chinese also in the citadel were speedily obliged to capitulate: Uschturfan met with a similar fate; and the victorious Khan-Khodja then repaired to Yarkend, where the citizens readily joined him, after having put to the sword the Chinese garrison, amounting to two thousand men. We have the particulars of the taking of this town from the English traveller Robert Shaw.* According to his account, the Chinese wished at first to come to an understanding with the Dunganes, and to arrange that they should retain a third of all immunities and revenues, with the exception of the supreme command. The Dunganes would not consent to this; and, as they had assured themselves of the sympathies of the inhabitants, they had only during the night to set the Chinese quarter of the town on fire in several places, in order to make the consternation and anarchy general. All the Chinese who saved themselves from the flames were pitilessly massacred. Nevertheless, the greater number succeeded in gaining possession of the citadel Yengi-Shehr, from whence they offered the most obstinate resistance. A successful diversion, in which about eight hundred Mohammedans lost their lives, was made; but at length the exasperation of the Mohammedans increased to such an extent that they did not shrink from the greatest sacrifices in the siege. The

* With regard to dates, Shaw differs from the other authorities. He places the insurrection of the Dunganes in the spring of 1863, while others designate the autumn as the time of the insurrection.

number of the Chinese meanwhile diminished more and more; and, as they were no longer sufficient to defend the walls, the fortress was taken by the infuriated Mussulmans. At the same time a frightful explosion was heard : the Amban (the Chinese governor) preferred to abandon himself with his people to destruction rather than fall alive into the hands of the Mohammedans. So frightful was this catastrophe, that some fragments of bodies were even hurled into the old town, and the atmosphere was darkened for hours by the whirling clouds of dust. After such heroism, Yarkend fell into the hands of the Dunganes, and remained almost a year under their authority.

Kashgar alone, the real capital of East Turkestan, in the midst of this universal insurrection, had never yet displayed the standard of revolt. It is true here also the Dunganes endeavoured to deceive their Buddhist countrymen ; yet the plans of the conspiracy were still kept secret, when the Chinese governor, feigning carelessness, and even friendship, invited them to the citadel, and had them all massacred there during the festivity. The cries and death-groans of the victims speedily found an echo in Kashgar; yet the inhabitants, humbled by Chinese supremacy, did not venture alone to attempt to loosen their fetters. The greatest influence had long been enjoyed here by the numerous descendants of the Khodja-Apak, usually known under the title of Hasret-Majesty. I have lived for months with a scion of this family, and am convinced of the feelings of hostility and rivalry which separate the Kashgar Khodjas from their so-called kindred in Kutcha. Had this not been the case, Burhan-ed-Din, after his success in Aksu, would

certainly have appeared here also as a conqueror; yet
the Kashgars would know nothing of him; and, in full
consciousness of their extremely critical condition, the
leading Mollahs, in conjunction with the members of the
Hasreti-Apak family, could do nothing else than secretly
turn to the Khodjas of Endidshan, and remain quiet till
their arrival. This is the reason that Kashgar at the
first remained spared from the flames of revolt rising in
all the other towns. In the midst of these expectations
from the West, a very different armed power unfortunately appeared in this direction. Kashgar is, as is well
known, situated on the spur of that high land which is
bounded on the north by the mountain range of the
Thien-Shan, and in the west by the lofty Alai mountain and the Pamir plateau. From times past these
valleys have been the resort of the cattle-breeding
Karakirghises, who, fond of plunder and depredation, like
the rest of their race, are distinguished, moreover, by
rare boldness. At that period Sadik-Bai was the most
important greybeard among them; and whether the
tidings of the threatening anarchy, or the demands of
some Kashgar faction may have determined him, at any
rate he attacked the Kashgar territory with his wild
horde, and indeed for several months kept the town in
a state of siege. And after the poor inhabitants had
had to undergo all the horrors of famine, and had become incapable of resistance, the wild nomads succeeded
in penetrating into the town and giving it up to the
most unprecedented destruction.

Under these circumstances, the Khodjas from Khokand were approaching the unfortunate Kashgar; and
here begins the active career of our hero.

How the restless Khodjas of Endidshan or Khokand, thirsting for adventure, and awaiting the invitation of their partisans in Kashgar, could have delayed till now to set out for East Turkestan, is inconceivable. Just at this time in Central Asia, from the rapid advance of Russia on the Yaxartes, and the successive defeats which the faithful had suffered at the hands of the Uruss, every one had been thrown into the greatest consternation. Khiva did not venture to stir, Bokhara trembled, and Khokand, where Alem-Kul held the reins of government, may even at that time have perceived its fate of dependence on the White Czar on the Neva as a dark phantom on the sky of its future. We do not wish to assert that a *sauve qui peut* was the order of the day; yet the conviction was universal that, to compete with the unbelieving Russian would bring no golden fruit. And as East Turkestan had ever been a profitable field for adventure, it required no special energy on the part of Khodja-Buzurg to penetrate with a small but courageous little troop across the Terek Pass into Kashgar, and there to try his fortune. Khokand, which had always supported these warlike descendants of the former Prince of Kashgar, was not now backward with advice and action. Alem-Kul gave arms and money, but the greatest help he afforded was in sending our hero; for not only Buzurg-Khan himself, but the whole troop of war-loving Kiptchaks and Khokandians looked with especial confidence on the person of Mehemmed-Yakub, who, experienced in battle, and skilled in artifice, had competed with the Russian, having such diabolical power at his disposal. He corresponded, indeed, at his first appearance, with the expectations placed in him. The Endidshanians had scarcely arrived under the walls of Kashgar than the horde of plundering Kirghises were driven back in wild flight. Their ringleaders fell alive into the hands of the enemy, and Sadik-Bei himself was amongst those executed. It was an enthusiastic reception which was given by the Kashgars to the brave little band of Endidshanians; for now for the first time in this western city of East Turkestan, with the feeling of freedom there was awakened also that of revenge against their Buddhist rulers. The ranks of the Endidshanians increased in a short time in a marvellous manner. At the tidings of the first success, stragglers had joined them from Khokand to the number of five hundred, most of them Kiptchaks; and Yakub-Kushbegi, who, it was said, had appeared before Kashgar with only eighty men, had, in the course of two months, such a force at his disposal that he was able not only to surround the citadel of Yengi-Shehr, distant from Kashgar somewhat more than a German mile, but to annoy the Chinese in every way. The laurels were now naturally not so easily gathered as the enthusiastic troop of Mussulmans with their leaders had imagined. The Chinese had never gained the reputation of especial valour, and least of all when opposed to Tartars; yet the pigtailed sons of the Celestial Empire now made an exception; it seemed as if they had a consciousness of the decisive nature of the contest—as if they had foreboded that these valleys of the Thien-Shan range would not so speedily see again the dragon standard; for they defended themselves with a lion-like courage, which would have redounded to the honour of the bravest in any nation. Fourteen months long, the Chinese garrison, oppressed on all sides, offered resistance. When the Amban saw the inevitable end of the drama approaching, he called his chief officers together under the pretext of taking counsel with them respecting the surrender of the place to Yakub-Kushbegi. The officers gave their consent. They were agreeing together about the presents which should be given to the conqueror, and the Amban, who, surrounded by his daughters, was sitting in his arm-chair smoking his pipe, ordered tea to be handed round by his sons to his assembled officers. The furious battle-cry, "Allahu ekber!" ("God is the greatest!") was already sounding in the ears of the company, already the wild outcry of the besiegers was heard, when the Amban composedly took his pipe from his mouth and shook the lighted ashes at the opening of a powder mine laid under his chair; this mine was in connection with the lower story, and with the powder magazine kept there. While the officers were taking counsel together, the mine exploded, and with it the house, the Amban, the family, and all present were blown up into the air.

With the fall of Kashgar, the most important, if not the largest town of East Turkestan, the triumph of the Mohammedans over the Chinese was quite complete. Buzurg-Khan, who assumed the position of a new ruler, was for a time satisfied with the government of the town and its environs, and political and military affairs were entrusted to the Kushbegi, who was no less crafty than he was brave. From the lack of hierarchical dignity, the sovereigns at all times, especially in Central Asia, could indulge in the unrestraint of a worldly life; and while Buzurg-Khan, giving himself up to every excess, caused himself to be honoured as a saint by the populace of

Kashgar, his energetic Vizier spared no trouble by examples of rare self-sacrifice, by generosity, and by a remarkable sense of justice, to secure the love and adherence of the better classes. From the uncertain and insecure state of East Turkestan at that time, it was evident that, if the direction of affairs were to fall into the hands of an energetic man, he would be able to effect extraordinary things. Yakub-Kushbegi perceived this state of things at the very outset; on his first appearance on the battle-field of events, the plan of his conquests over all the Mohammedans of the north-west of China stood ready in his mind. The band of bold Endidshanians were still lying before the walls of the Chinese citadel in Kashgar, when Yakub-Kushbegi set out for Yarkend with a few desperate soldiers, though on this occasion he only made himself master of the small town of Yengi-Hissars. Yet at this time he lacked a firm halting-point, for Kashgar was not yet taken; and continuous communication with the north of East Turkestan, where the Khodjas were still carrying on operations with the Dunganes in Yarkend, seemed too dangerous. Only when Kashgar was taken in the manner lately mentioned, did Yakub-Kushbegi begin to advance towards the realisation of his real design, by entering into open hostility with the Khodjas. If the latter had been strong enough to forestall the Endidshanians in Kashgar, the career of our hero would have become impossible; yet at that time the whole revolution along the northern chain of mountains from Komul to Utchturfan was in its earliest phase. The Chinese kept the Dunganes in check, and as the latter could not hasten to the assistance of the Khodjas in alliance with them, Yakub-Kushbegi found the field in the west open, and after conquering the Chinese, he turned his arms towards his Mohammedan rivals. The Khodjas naturally saw through the reasons of the hostility.

Scarcely had Kashgar passed into the possession of the Khokandians, than an army of Dunganes and Khodjas, joined also by several Yarkendians, was on the point of marching to Kashgar. At Khan-Arik, or, according to others, at the river Kizil, both Mohammedan armies met in battle for the first time, Yakub-Kushbegi gaining the victory, owing to the valour of his Kiptchak auxiliary troops, or, probably, to his own superior military ability. The Yarkendians, it was said, were the first to take flight; the Dunganian soldiers made a long resistance, and were enticed over to Yakub-Kushbegi's side by presents and other promises; in fact, they allowed themselves even to be used as tools, in inducing their brethren, who had remained in the Yarkend fortress, to surrender to the conqueror. This, of course, led to no lasting result, for the inevitable antagonism between the two parties who desired to succeed to the Chinese power in East Turkestan, namely, between the Khodjas of Kutcha and the Khodjas of Endidshan, was at this time an undeniable matter; both were thoroughly convinced that the victory of the one must bring about the overthrow of the other, and with this feeling the utmost possible efforts were made. Judging from the circumstance that the Dunganes were always considered as foreigners in the land, and that they were regarded as men who had yielded themselves as willing tools of the Chinese tyrants, their fate was sealed from the first. Yarkendians no less than Kashgarians could place little confidence in them, nor in their allies, the Khodjas of Kutcha, who, it is true, justly behaved as the national party, and had, indeed, acquired much merit in the expulsion of the Chinese. Kashgarians and Yarkendians all along awaited help alone from the west, and the able Yakub-Kushbegi had only to appear on the field, and secretly all were favourable to him. It happened, moreover, that, in his plan against Yarkend, he was secretly informed of the movements of the Dunganes by a certain Niaz-Beg, who held a prominent position in the fortress; it was no wonder, therefore, under such circumstances, that a month's siege placed him in possession of this largest city of East Turkestan. This was about the spring of 1865.

Master of the two most important places in East Turkestan, the bold adventurer of Khokand, whom success had made popular, came forward all the more freely in his efforts after sovereign power. Buzurg-Khan, of whom we have already spoken, was only the shadow of a king; he kept aloof from events, and was aroused from his careless life in the very first weeks of his arrival at Kashgar by the growing importance of Yakub-Kushbegi. And although he did not venture to interfere with his Vizier out of fear of being removed by violence, the latter nevertheless, to prevent possible disorders, set aside his master; he had him placed in honourable confinement, and subsequently, at the request of others, this was exchanged for free dismissal, with the condition, however, that Khodja-Buzurg, as became a pious descendant of the prophet, would prepare for a pilgrimage to distant Arabia. The Khodja in consequence, only accompanied by a few followers, quitted that land in

the dress of a Hadski which he had shortly before entered
with such plans of sovereignty; and although, instead of
going to the plains of sunny Arabia, he took a circuitous
route through Kabul and Bokhara to his home in Endidshan, there was a complete end of his sovereignty. The
Orientals have always been accustomed to recognise the
immediate accomplisher of power as the true possessor of
power. This, in earlier times, was the relation between
Timur and the Tchagataish prince of Samarkand; centuries later between Nadir-Kuli-Khan and the mock
prince Thamasp; and this relation existed all the more
between Yakub-Kushbegi and Khodja-Buzurg, as the
former was the real organiser of the army, the conqueror
of the foe, and the restorer of order. In this capacity he
was acknowledged not only by the Turkestanians, but
even by many of the former adherents, and even relations, of the Khodja; and had he not raised himself to
the throne after the taking of Kashgar and Yarkend, the
enthusiastic troops in conjunction with the Turkestanians
would have forestalled him in the choice of a sovereign.

Thus Yakub-Kushbegi was sovereign of part of
East Turkestan. In Khokand, of course, where Alem-
Kul meanwhile had been killed by his enemies, and
where Khudajar-Khan was endeavouring by the successes
of the Khodjas under his protection to recover from
the losses he had suffered from the Russians, Yakub-
Kushbegi could in nowise reckon on unanimous admiration. For apart from the fact that he would not
hear of any connection with the Mohammedan state on
the west, he had, moreover, by the deposition of the
Khodja, removed the channel of mediation, and was
now left to himself. It is not to be denied that, in

establishing his power, he not only employed extraordinary caution, but craftiness; and when circumstances required it, he even made use of unscrupulous
barbarity. In order to secure his position in the conquered towns of Kashgar and Yarkend, Yakub-Kushbegi had won over to his interest the greater part of
the Khokand Khodjas, by bestowing on them lucrative
appointments; he had drawn the natives to his side
by strict measures of public order and of jurisdiction,
and especially by adhering to the duties of religion. His
sovereign power was scarcely a few months old, when,
feeling himself secure in the rear, he could repair to the
south, to Khoten, to continue his conquests. Khoten, or
Iltchi, as the Turks call it, had likewise, towards the
close of the year 1863, thrown off the Chinese yoke,
and at the same time had chosen as its sovereign
a Khodja of high importance, named Hadji-Habi-
bullah. The venerable old man, eighty years of age,
had only returned two years before, through India, from
a pilgrimage to the holy cities of Arabia; and he had
striven heartily against his elevation to the throne, just
as much as he had against the modest badge of Islam
learning, the delight of the band of believers placed
under him. He it was who in 1866 gave such a warm
reception to the English officer W. H. Johnson, the
first European who had visited Khoten. The Englishman, who had been attracted by a love of adventure to
this south-eastern part of the Six Cities, had, it is true,
soon to pay for his rashness by a long involuntary
sojourn there, as the old Khan conceived the wonderful
idea of not letting him go until the English furnished
him with troops and arms against the attack he was

fearing on the part of the Chinese and Khokandians; but this, of course, was not done. Johnson returned home, happily; but the fears of the old Habibullah proved themselves, as regards the Endidshan, Yakub-Kushbegi, not at all groundless. Immediately after the taking of Yarkend, the latter entered into negotiations with the aged priestly sovereign, in which he still entitled him "pater venerabilis," and in this way allured him into his trap. For a time the old man resisted, in consequence, we are told, of the suggestions of his two sons. The matter was protracted for two years, and as Yakub-Kushbegi perceived that letters effected nothing, he repaired in person to Khoten, in order, it was said, to express his fraternal esteem for the great sovereign, but, in truth, to appear there as a conqueror; for, for this object he took with him ten thousand men, a suite in nowise necessary for a visit of courtesy. Compliments followed compliments, and when the good Habibullah was trustful enough to appear in the camp of his guest, he was at once arrested, and was made to sign in the camp, with the signet ring on his finger, the pseudo-summons to submit to Yakub-Kushbegi. A great part of the people obeyed. The Endidshanians meanwhile approached the town, took possession of it in spite of its resistance, and Khoten, with its seat of government, its treasures, and the numerous harem of the Habibullah family became the booty of Yakub-Kushbegi. It may be mentioned, as an interesting episode, that the women distributed among the conquerors revenged themselves terribly for the treachery committed against their aged master. They surprised their new husbands in the night, murdered them all and themselves—an act of vengeance which came very opportunely to Yakub-Kushbegi, for the poor Hadji Habibullah, with all his sons and principal relatives, under the pretext of being the authors of the treachery, were obliged to atone for it by their lives.

This inhuman act of Yakub-Kushbegi occurred towards the end of 1866. The result procured for the conqueror, at any rate, a considerable increase of power. For Kashgar, Yarkend, and Khoten numbered alone more than seventy thousand houses or families. And if Yakub-Kushbegi had even had the best intentions of remaining at peace with his rival in the north, the fact that the Khodjas of Kutcha, who desired to form the national party of the country, could in nowise consent to let their influence flag, stood in the way of any future peace. The conqueror had, as we have before observed, fully estimated this fact, and when he had completed his work in the south-east of Turkestan, and saw his rear secure from Kashgar to the lofty chain of the Kuen-Luen mountains, nothing else was left to him than to turn his arms against the Mussulman adversary in the south.

The contest which the new sovereign of East Turkestan was entering upon with the Khodjas in the north, was for this reason far more serious and more doubtful in its issue, inasmuch as it was no Gaza or religious war, but solely a matter of personal ambition. Yet a successful adventurer in the East knows how from the first to gain over the minds of others to his own advantage, and the faithful can often even incite to deeds which stand in the most direct opposition to the maxims of Islamism. Thus it happened that Yakub-Kushbegi met with the greatest assistance, and even with true enthusiasm, for his cause from the East Turkestanians. It seemed as if the old contest between the Montenegrinian and Montalbanian Khodjas, which raged in this region more than three centuries ago, was animated anew; for it need scarcely be said that it was the Endidshan strangers who were the most eager for the contest, and Yakub-Kushbegi was wise enough to turn this to his own advantage. Matters were not very favourable with the Khodjas. It is true the alliance which they had concluded with the Dunganes was still in full force; still the latter at this time were not their own masters, and they could not at all assist their western confederates. Burhan-ed-Din, surnamed the Khan-Khodja, was looking in vain on all sides for help, and so great was his hatred of Yakub-Kushbegi, that he did not shrink from even asking the assistance of the Russians. In 1865, at the time when the Khokand adventurer was employed in establishing his power, the northern priestly sovereign had perceived danger, and had sent a certain Mollah-Latif to the Russian governor on the Issikköl frontier with the understanding that he would in any way assist the Muscovite eagle, if he received some succour against his arch-enemy in Kashgar and Yarkend. Russia, who had not then perceived a fitting conjuncture for interfering in the affairs of the East Turkestanians, naturally refused to afford help, and the good old man was left to himself. Among the natives of the land, also, this so-called national party found but little concurrence. It was tolerably indifferent to the East Turkestanians in the valleys whether they remitted their taxes to Burhan-ed-Din or to Yakub-Kushbegi; and the Tarandjis in the Trans-

Ili district were just then too much intoxicated with
their recently-acquired freedom to desire to occupy
themselves with future plans. The two adversaries
therefore confronted each other alone. In the year
1866, Yakub-Kushbegi attacked the town of Ushturfan,
the west point of the territory of the northern Khodjas.
A certain Mohammed-Emin had provoked the inhabitants against himself by reprisals and by a dissolute life
—for these pious people, as is well known, are the most
notorious debauchees. They applied to Kashgar, where
the helper stood ready for combat, only awaiting the
opportunity. Ushturfan was soon taken; shortly afterwards Aksu also fell into his hands; and Burhan-ed-Din
had scarcely time to look round him before his enemy
was marching to Kutcha, his capital. It seemed as if
the northern Khodjas had placed extraordinary confidence in their armies, for they advanced half-way from
the last-mentioned place to meet the conqueror; but this
did not prevent them from being totally defeated in open
battle, and being obliged to retire in all haste to their
citadel. Yakub-Kushbegi followed them, and although
Kutcha was pretty strongly fortified, the one defeat had
taken from them the courage for further resistance.
They surrendered at discretion. Twenty of the highest
Khodjas were carried prisoners to Kashgar, where for a
time they were strictly watched over. Subsequently, if
report does not err, becoming reconciled with their fate,
they entered the service of the conqueror. Other restless minds preferred to go to Mecca; for the holy tomb
has been at all times the resort of those hot heads to
whom fortune has not been favourable in their earthly
career. The Dunganes' prince alone, Su-Mollah, who

X

would not surrender to the Khokand adventurer, withdrew to the eastern town of Turfan, where he died some years afterwards.

The power of the Khodjas was consequently broken. Yakub-Kushbegi had indeed no longer to fear the Khodjas on the field, but all the greater was his apprehension with regard to the Dunganes, who had still a considerable force in the north-west, in the neighbourhood of Urumtchi, and who, convinced that a collision was inevitable, were actively engaged in preparing for it. For three years, however, the peaceful disposition lasted. Yakub-Kushbegi had meanwhile more and more established his dominion in East Turkestan. His army, which received all those restless spirits who had lost all scope for their adventures by Russia's conquests on the Yaxartes and Zerefshan, had swelled to a great size, and from the circumspection, energy, and perseverance of the conqueror, had acquired a discipline superior to any that had for a long time existed in Central Asia. The Kiptchaks and Karakirghises of Khokand were paid troops. These received a salary of three tillas per month, and arms, clothes, and provisions both for themselves and their horses. On the other hand, they had to submit to the strictest subordination, and they were regarded as the choice troops of the new conqueror. The second part of the army was formed by the East Turkestanians themselves. Each family was obliged to send into the field one or two men, according as circumstances required ; these only received daily rations now and then, when the distance from home made communication impossible or difficult. This part of Yakub-Kushbegi's army had always been distinguished for

special devotion to its leader, and it is indeed remarkable how the East Turkestanians, who possess only a
small amount of military ability, could have been made
such serviceable soldiers. The third part of the army
consisted of former Chinese and Dunganese soldiers,
who, at the taking of Kashgar, Yarkend, and Khoten, had
been forcibly placed in the ranks under the conqueror's
standard, and were either employed as garrisons in the
towns or as frontier guard against Russia and Khokand.
The civil administration of the new sovereign also left
nothing to be desired. As after the overthrow of the
Chinese rule all bands were loosened, a strict and
indeed barbarous regime could all the less be avoided,
as the East Turkestanians had for centuries been only
thus kept in check. Yakub-Kushbegi gave this regime a
national Mohammedan air; and the Draco-like law with
which he treated all disturbers of the public peace, all
violation of the laws of religion, and, lastly, all disobe-
dience, is almost unprecedented, even in the annals of
Central Asia. For a long time the gallows at the gates
of the cities in East Turkestan had not been so active as
they were now under this national Mohammedan prince.
The stealing of a fowl, the neglect of a single prayer,
indeed the slightest refractory conduct, was punished with
death; and that the East Turkestanians did not stig-
matise such a despot as a tyrant, and did not abandon
the conqueror with terror, must be ascribed to the fact
that Yakub-Kushbegi was distinguished on the other
hand for strict love of justice and generosity. The
governors of a town or province had only to appear two
days later with the amount of tribute, and they were at
once deposed and their property confiscated, and fre-

quently they were even deprived of life. On the other hand, the slightest complaint of oppression was sufficient to subject the officer concerned to a strict examination, and woe to him who was found guilty ! Even the personal relatives and the first companions in arms of the conqueror —as, for example, Yunis Beg, the Dadchah of Yarkend —trembled before their master. As under such circumstances, in spite of the constant war with the Russians, peace and repose prevailed in the principal cities of East Turkestan, it is easy to imagine that the subjects, in perfect contentment, only bless the iron hand ruling over them. In the other Khanates also, with the exception of Khokand, the opinion was favourable with regard to the new conqueror. Khiva had sent three embassies to congratulate him on his military successes, while Muzaffar-ed-Din-Khan, the ruler of Bokhara, whom Russian bayonets had humbled, gave the new warrior of the faith (Gazi) the title of an Atalik, which corresponds pretty nearly to the European one of viceroy. This is the reason why the new ruler of East Turkestan received from his subjects, and indeed throughout Central Asia, the name of Atalik-Gazi, and thus he was also styled by the English in Europe. How the deeply fallen sovereign of Bokhara could give a title to a man far superior to him in power and importance may well surprise many ; yet we have already repeatedly drawn attention to his spiritual authority, and the ruler of Zerefshan, although fallen, still ever considers himself the prince of all the faithful in Central Asia.

At length the year 1870 approached. The Dunganes, who hitherto, from fear of disturbing commercial intercourse with the western part of East Turkestan, had remained in their defensive position, became increasingly anxious at the growing power of their enemy; and in the February of the year above mentioned, they set out from the towns of Turfan, Komul, and Urumtchi, with an army 7500 strong, and directed their march towards Kutcha.

When they arrived there, after some days of laborious march, they found the inhabitants of the place strengthened by a garrison from Kashgar; this, however, was thrown into disorder by the Dunganes, who, after having entered the city, remained there twelve days, during which time rapine and plunder held their orgies. A similar fate overtook Kurli, as well as the numerous small towns in the neighbourhood. At the time that Yakub-Kushbegi received information of these events, he was at Kashgar, and here he left his eldest son with a small garrison, and set out himself for Kurli. In April he entered the town with an army of eight thousand men, and remained there about eight days, in order to secure the commercial roads of the district; and on this account he promised the Dunganes to restore their property to them if they would grant him their assistance.

A reinforcement of five hundred freebooters arrived from the mountain chain of the Thien-Shan. Yakub-Beg was delighted with their help, as they possessed a thorough knowledge of the country, with which a great part of the inhabitants themselves were not acquainted.

On his further advance, Yakub-Kushbegi found Kara-Shehr desolate and forsaken; for Tocksun, which is thirteen miles distant from Turfan, was the first point at which the enemy had again collected its forces. Nevertheless Yakub-Kushbegi took possession of the town, and remained there fourteen days. As he meanwhile heard that the enemy was approaching, and was concentrating its forces, he fortified himself as quickly as possible, and as he perceived that they remained inactive, he assumed the offensive, and despatched two thousand men against them. As these were however repulsed, Yakub-Kushbegi set out with his central force, and after a hot fight, drove the enemy back to Turfan with a loss of eight hundred men.

Yakub-Beg advanced still further, and entrenched himself on the banks of the river Yar. After resting here for a week, he was attacked by a troop of Dunganes five thousand strong. At first the Sarts, forming the vanguard of the Kashgar army, took to flight, and it required all Yakub-Kushbegi's energy to induce them to turn back ; the remainder of the army however held their ground, and the Dunganes were put to flight. The latter were nevertheless not discouraged by this. After a pause of eight days, they again entered into an engagement, but were driven back, and were obliged to seek refuge in Turfan. In this battle the Dunganes lost about two thousand, and the Kashgarians about a thousand men. Upon this Yakub-Beg blockaded the town of Turfan, and both armies remained in their respective positions for two months. The fortifications were not so strong as was imagined, and the Dunganes made constant sorties. In one of these, in June, it happened that, under cover of night, they penetrated into the middle of the enemy's camp, but were nevertheless repulsed. The garrison meanwhile, which amounted to more than six thousand souls, suffered much from hunger; for this reason, Si-Yanshai, the governor of the fortress, was desirous to come to terms with the Kashgarians. Three times the negotiations were drawn up, and as many times set aside by the Sarts, although they had numerous relations in the Kashgar camp.

In this manner the siege was prolonged for three months. Yakub-Beg's troops were however accustomed to a hard life. Their food consisted of millet bread and occasionally boiled rice, and even this was served out to them only in small quantities. Notwithstanding they were satisfied, and thus proved their thorough discipline; and as Yakub-Beg had only to maintain his Khokand, Kirghiz, and Kiptchak troops, his success was sure.

When the Dunganes in Urumtchi perceived that the fall of Turfan could not be long delayed, they began to fear for their own safety, and all the more as the plundering bands of freebooters from the Thien-Shan became increasingly frequent. Yakub-Beg at once saw that now was the favourable opportunity for attacking his enemy with energy. He despatched a trusty officer with seven hundred men, in order to unite with the freebooters in a guerilla war. Their first encounter was at a village named Mambel. As it happened during the night, they could easily surprise the Dunganes, who were sleeping in the open air, and had no time to seize their arms. Many of the wives and children preferred suicide rather than captivity. About fifteen thousand head of cattle fell into the hands of Yakub-Beg; at the same time he liberated a hundred freebooters who had been taken prisoners by the Dunganian army. The Dunganes made several attempts to avenge themselves, and at last they rushed upon the entrenched camp of the Kashgarians in the mountains, and drove back its outposts, but they were attacked with violence, and were repulsed with great loss. Among the slain on the field of battle was the governor of the town of Manassi, who mistook the Kashgar camp for that of the Dunganes: after the discovery of his mistake, he defended himself with great valour, and was only with difficulty overcome. This was the last important event in this guerilla war.

As the garrison of Turfan now perceived their hopeless condition, they resolved to enter into an accommodation. After Si-Yanshai, the governor, had placed himself in Yakub-Beg's power, he was received with great respect, and was rewarded with the command of a fortress—a duty which he discharged with great zeal under the direction of his former enemy.

The taking of Turfan was a dearly purchased victory to Yakub-Beg. His loss amounted to six hundred men, while that of the enemy was three or four times as great. The moral effect of it, however, was such that the Dunganes in Urumtchi expressed the wish to come to terms with Yakub-Kushbegi. As the latter placed implicit confidence in Si-Yanshai, he was despatched as envoy to the fortress. He did his utmost to convert his countrymen and brethren in the faith, pointing to the army of his new master, which was twenty thousand strong, fourteen thousand of which had been sent by the Sultan to Kuldja; while Russia, he assured them, also promised help. Through these and other arguments he induced the Dunganes to surrender their fortress. Yakub-Beg consented not to transport any Kashgar troops there, and he was satisfied with their assurances of friendship. He however received indemnification for the merchants who had been interfered with by the pillage of Kutcha; this amounted to seven thousand jambus of silver (metal bars of the value of forty double ducats), two camels laden with gold, fifty-four with tea, and twenty with silk stuffs. He took [for his army seven hundred horses, an equal number of sheep and cattle, seven hundred sacks of flour, twenty waggons, and other property.

In order to prevent any dissatisfaction, Yakub-Beg entrusted the newly conquered province to Si-Yanshai, with the order to leave everything in its former condition. Turfan was, however, again fortified, and Hakim-Bei from Aksu, with a force of eight hundred Kashgarians, received the command; the same occurred also at Kutcha. Special attention was given to the fortification of Aksu and of the Muzart Pass, for at that time Russia had already carried her victorious colours into Dsungaria, and it was in expectation of such events that Yakub-Beg was constantly endeavouring to subdue the Dunganes, though without any permanent success; for, as the latest tidings inform us, a revolt has again broken out among them.

The restless conqueror of East Turkestan has, however, succeeded, if recent tidings are to be relied on, in repressing the second insurrection. It is possible that subjection will make a third and even a fourth attempt necessary; but at length the energy of this extraordinary man will overcome all difficulties, and his despotic command will undoubtedly extend over all the Mohammedans dwelling on the southern slopes of the Thien-Shan mountain, from the interior of China to Khokand.* The idea, carried out with such iron perse-

---

* This supposition is fully confirmed by the most recent events in East Turkestan. The Atalik has completely broken the power of the Dunganes, and has gained a firm footing in Komul.

verance, of concentrating all Mussulmans living between the frontier of the Buddhist Chinese and Turkestan proper, is the mainspring of that enterprise which Yakub-Kushbegi undertook in the winter of 1869 against the western territory of Sariköl. This region, in the northeast of the Pamir highlands, which is almost unknown to Europeans, is, it is true, not very fertile, and still less peopled; yet it forms a very important point for the defence of East Turkestan. And a single glance from Kashgar at this frontier, with its high walls of rock, will convince us that the possession of Sariköl, this mighty battlement of the great natural bulwark, may be of extreme importance. Babish-Beg, the last independent prince of this country, which was only partially visited by Wood, died in 1866. In the contest for the throne, one of his sons, named Alaf-Shah, fled to Yarkend. Yakub-Kushbegi assisted him in gaining the throne, and established him as sovereign; and as Alaf-Shah, as is usually the case in Asia, after he had regained power and influence, rebelled against his protector, the Atalik-Gazi had no choice left him but to conquer the country afresh, in order to subject it entirely to his sceptre. And thus the outposts of the fortunate adventurer are now stationed in the west, watching with keen eye the dangerous approach of the Russian columns, as well as in the north from Aksu to the opening of the Muzart Pass, where important and expensive fortifications have been raised, since the Russians have anticipated the Atalik-Gazi in the conquest of Kuldja and the whole Trans-Ili district. This pre-appropriation of the laurels on the field of conquest must, moreover, have been very unpleasant to Yakub-Kushbegi. Even in

1866, before he took the field against the Dunganes, he had begun to make advances to Abil Oglan and Daud-Khalifa, the temporary sovereigns of the Tarandjis and Dunganes on the northern heights of the Thien-Shan range. Yet he feared but little resistance there, and he wished first to get the better of his mighty adversaries near Urumtchi. The Russians of course must have had an inkling of this from the beginning, for Yakub-Kushbegi's army was still near Barkul when General Kolpakoffsky, under colour of the never-failing dispute between Kalmucks and Kirghises, surprised Dsungaria, and, as may easily be imagined, made a *tabula rasa* there—a real happiness for that district, for, as Radloff's recent paper in the Russian *Revue*, second year, No. 3, shows us, the country had presented a terrible appearance after the fall of the Chinese.

We are now arrived at the point at which we may reflect upon the political position of the new conqueror, and may take into consideration the possible prospects of his future plans.

As regards the former, it must above all be remembered that Yakub-Kushbegi, fully acquainted as he is through his early military career with the extraordinary designs of Russia upon Central Asia, and with the power of this Northern Colossus, on his very first appearance in Turkestan dreaded the disturbing interference of a foreign rule, not from the East, but from the North. It is indeed true that China, in former times, lost her possessions in East Turkestan repeatedly through revolutions, and, nevertheless, with her usual snail's pace, approached them and incorporated them afresh, and by strict measures secured to herself the dominion for a long period. At the present day, however, this is impossible to conceive, for the Celestial Empire has not as before to do only with barbarous tribes, but with a great and extremely strong European power. Russia, by her conquests in the Turkestan Khanates, by her position on the Narin, and, lastly, by her efforts to extend her commercial relations with the Government of Semipalatinsk, through Dsungaria and Kirkara-Usu, to the interior of China, can no longer see with indifference the political and strategetical designs of the Chinese. For this reason it was, as we have seen, that Kuldja was admitted into the Russian confederacy, although it was the Court of Petersburg which, for three years after the outbreak of the revolution in East Turkestan, had designated Yakub-Kushbegi and all the insurgents as faithless rebels, with whom no one would enter into negotiation, in order not to wound the feelings of his neighbour, the Emperor of China. How, after these events, the continuance of a friendly intercourse between the Chinese Court and the Russian Mission at Pekin is still possible, is truly an enigma; we can only suppose that the Russian occupation of Dsungaria is either utterly ignored in Pekin, or that it is regarded as the friendly act of a temporary possession. Of course Yakub-Kushbegi is of a very different opinion. He knows well that the Chinese will scarcely raise again the yellow standard of the dragon in this part of their former empire. But he knows also that his own interests are most endangered by this very power, which has diverted from him the danger of Chinese retaliation. He knows, and he has long known, that Russia cannot look calmly at the consolidation of a Mohammedan power in her immediate vicinity, that sooner or later a war is inevitable between the two, and he has in consequence, immediately after the taking of Kashgar, Yarkend, and Khoten, looked about for a third power, which has, it is true, also interests to defend in Central Asia, but which is hindered from making material conquests by the gigantic bulwark of a natural wall, such as the southern chain of the Kuen-Luen mountains. This power the crafty Khokandian has justly discovered in England. Had Yakub-Kushbegi's career occurred in the time of Lord Auckland or Lord Dalhousie, he would not have had to send various embassies to the banks of the Hooghli for the sake of entering into friendly relations. But the Great Britain of the present time seems to feel herself most comfortable in the sleep of indifference, and it was not till the Atalik-Gazi had received with ceremony in Yarkend Mr Robert Shaw, a private merchant, and had hospitably entertained him, and given him the most striking proofs of his desire to enter into friendly relations with England, that the Anglo-Indian Government considered it seasonable to enter into connection with this new conqueror in the remote Mohammedan East. It was desired, as is almost always the case, to promote in the first place commercial objects, and Mr T. D. Forsyth was sent to Yarkend, in the year 1870, at the head of a mission consisting of several Europeans and Asiatics. I repeat, the English felt themselves compelled to take this step. The act was obnoxious to them, and equally imperfect were the preparations for carrying it out, and the futility of the whole mission. Mr Forsyth, a distinguished judge of

Central Asiatic matters, and a diplomatist of the highest kind, left nothing wanting' as regards personal ability, but his hands were fettered in every possible way.

The budget of the mission — about £1416 — was ridiculously small. Moreover, Mr Forsyth was enjoined to speak only of trade, and not at all of politics ; and lastly, he received the order to stay in East Turkestan only for a definite time, and no longer—just as if express trains were returning over the Himalayas, or as if the Court of Yarkend stood in the same category with the Court of Brussels. Of course, Mr Forsyth, as already mentioned, could effect nothing ; for, as he could not wait, he did not even obtain an interview with the sovereign of East Turkestan ; and as he returned home without having obtained his object, the English turned away with indignation from the valleys of the Thien-Shan, as if the failure of their plans had not been their own fault.*

Russia, who ever goes more rationally and sensibly to work, has here also anticipated the heavy John Bull. In Petersburg, not in the least deterred by the temporary hindrance of the vague uncertainty which at one time hovered over the fate of Yakub-Kushbegi, the authorities acted just as circumstances might require : sometimes holding back, sometimes bold and energetic,

---

* At the present time, the Anglo-Indian Government is engaged in preparing a second embassy to East Turkestan, at the head of which Mr Forsyth is again placed, and as this time the whole mission is undertaken with far greater earnestness (£10,000 is the estimate of the expense attending it), the results may be all the more successful, as the Atalik himself took the initiative by the extraordinary embassy of his nephew to Calcutta.

and sometimes pursuing a policy which made its way with the sweet smile of friendship. Between 1864 and 1868, when the Russian position on the Yaxartes, on the Oxus, and especially on the Narin, was not yet satisfactorily established, Yakub-Kushbegi and his successes were almost entirely ignored. It was not till the end of the last year mentioned that Lieutenant-Colonel Reinthal received the order to repair to Kashgar with an embassy, under the pretext of claiming some Russian subjects who, fleeing from deserved punishment, had been hospitably received in Kashgar, but in truth to procure the right of having an agency business in East Turkestan—a right which had been conceded to the Court of Petersburg in the last treaty of peace with China. That the new sovereign neither gave a hearing to the one request nor to the other, and, without manifesting stubborn hostility, showed no special complaisance towards the Russians, is readily to be explained. Lieutenant-Colonel Reinthal remained twenty-one days in Kashgar in nominal captivity. He was scarcely allowed to leave his house, and he probably breathed anew when he was able to leave the city uninjured. This cold behaviour was, however, no open hostility, for otherwise Yakub-Kushbegi would not have sent Shadi-Mirza, his diplomatist *par excellence*, who superintended a regular courier service between Calcutta and Petersburg, to the latter city in reply to the first part of the mission. The Russians, who only feel aggrieved when it seems suitable to them to be so, entirely disregarded the cold treatment which Mons. Reinthal had met with. Shadi-Mirza was received in the most distinguished manner, and was everywhere fêted. He was shown all the remarkable objects, and, as may be readily imagined, especially the great armories and arsenals; in a word, everything which could make this thorough Oriental— or, more justly, his master—both astonished and afraid of the power of his Northern neighbour. All this was, however, quite superfluous. Yakub-Kushbegi had already long known the power of Russia. This was the main reason why he trembled at her hostility, and had always directed his gaze towards the south. As, however, as we have already related, he saw himself wholly deceived in his hopes with regard to England, and as, on the other side, since the taking of Kuldja, he believed that he could no longer avoid the embraces of the Russian diplomatists, the crafty Atalik-Gazi was at length obliged to yield, and at Russia's repeated solicitation, for the present, to sign a commercial treaty, according to which Russia was allowed to trade freely in the towns of East Turkestan, and to cross at will the country from one end to the other with her caravans. This treaty was concluded at Kashgar, through Baron Kaulbars, in May 1872. Soon afterwards an ambassador from East Turkestan conveyed the ratified document to the Governor-General Von Kaufmann in Tashkend; and Russia, without having shed a drop of blood, had secured to herself here almost the same advantages as she had obtained in Bokhara and Khokand only after obstinate fighting; and at the same time she had not only humbled the political influence of England in East Turkestan, but had inflicted such a blow upon her commercial interests that, however easily the optimist Ministry on the Thames might be able to suppress its vexation, the English tax-paying merchant would with difficulty do so. As we have thus touched upon the injured commercial relations of England, we may remark incidentally that Russia, by her late advantages in Central Asia, has inflicted a very sensitive blow on British commerce in all the three Khanates, and even in Afghanistan. Formerly, about ten years ago, in spite of the disputes in Afghanistan and the anarchical state of things on either side of the Oxus, there had always been a comparatively vigorous caravan traffic between the north-west commercial towns of India on the one side and the principal markets of Central Asia on the other. A great number of coloured cottons, muslins, and silk stuffs, besides cloth and iron goods, were sent from India, partly through Kabul and partly through Kandahar, to Bokhara, Barshi, Samarkand, and even to Khokand. At the present day this has much decreased; and any one who compares the commercial returns from the Punjaub ten years ago, which have just been furnished by Mr Davies, with those of the present day, will be immensely astonished at the great injury caused by Russian supremacy in Central Asia. Russia has not indeed been able officially to exclude the British merchant from Turkestan, and she will never do so. Yet the advantages of security and protection which she has procured for herself in her treaties with Bokhara and Khokand are specially intended only for Russian merchants and Russian travellers, and Russia will take care that these remain in exclusive possession of the monopoly.

But let us return to the history of our hero, the Atalik-Gazi, and let us examine what career is yet before this man, in case the Muscovite thirst for territorial aggran-

Y

disement does not stand in the way of his ambition. Such conflicts appear to us almost inevitable, as Russia's position on the Narin, at the Muzart Pass, and indeed throughout Central Asia, is one which makes all independence apart from her impossible; and, on the other hand, Yakub-Kushbegi can only with difficulty avoid a quarrel. There cannot, of course, be the least idea of a successful resistance to Russia, as even the ablest Asiatic conqueror, and the largest forces that are at his disposal, are nothing when opposed to the arms and strategy of the West. Yet for the moment Yakub-Kushbegi is absolute master of East Turkestan; his country extends from the heights of the Pamir steppes to the remote Komul, and is at least three times as large as France. The number of the inhabitants who obey his sovereign word can, at the boldest computation, scarcely exceed five or six millions. His army, however, taken all together, amounts to nearly 50,000 men, who, well armed, well disciplined, and thoroughly trained in the school of war, can make little or no impression on a European foe, but are most imposing to a native—*i.e.*, an Asiatic —adversary. Had the shadows of the icy north not yet touched the snow-covered summits of the Alaj and the Thien-Shan range, it would have been difficult to foresee how far ability, military success, and political combinations might have brought this new conqueror into the remote regions of Asia. In the west of China everything is out of joint, nothing but the loose tissue of the traditions of the past still, in some measure, sustains the Chinese rule; for although we may not care to attach to the independence of the new Mohammedan state in Yünnan the importance which is generally given to it, we cannot fail to see that the doctrines of Islam, oppressed and limited as they are in the West, are on the point of conquering a new soil for themselves in the remote East at the expense of Buddhism, and of obtaining new fuel for the expiring flame. Power, perseverance, but above all, enthusiasm, which is utterly wanting in the lands lying nearer to Europe, can still work wonders in those remote regions of the East not yet affected by the influence of the West. It requires only an animating mind and a vigorous spirit to make the flame burn brightly; in one word, a man who, smiled on by fortune, can constitute himself the leader of the Eastern Islam world. And such a man exists in the person of Yakub-Kush-begi. He possesses in himself everything which has helped the Asiatic conqueror of the past to the zenith of fame, and if the European advance so often mentioned did not stand in the way, it would be in nowise difficult to him, by uniting all the Mohammedans of Central Asia and Western China, and supported by a force of more than forty millions, to march with his standard over the steppes of Central Asia towards the west of the continent. Thus, at least, was it in bygone times; thus did the career of a Djengis, a Timur, and a Nadir begin. Yet at the present day all is changed, and as the mighty but prosaic Christian West, as we intimated at the beginning of our sketch, stands, directly or indirectly, in the way of all Eastern progress, and of all unusual display of power in Asia, even in the remotest corner of this old quarter 'of the globe, so the Atalik-Gazi will remain nothing more than the ordinary Turkestan Khan whom the fortunes of war have favoured. The age of mighty convulsers of the world is now once for all past.

THE RUSSIAN CAMPAIGN AGAINST KHIVA (1873).

I.

WHOEVER has given any attention to the events in Central Asia, must have come to the conviction that Russia can only completely establish her power in Turkestan, and her influence on the internal progress of Asia, when the intimidation and subjection of all the three Khanates is reckoned among acts accomplished. It is true the gentlemen in Petersburg have hitherto judged it prudent to annex only the valley of the Yaxartes, in the Khanate of Khokand, and only a part of the country on the banks of the Zerefshan, in that of Bokhara; and that a shadow of independence is left to the remainder of the two Khanates, is explained by the very admissible reason that, in the first place, the administration of this vast but thinly-peopled tract of land, apart from all dangers and difficulties, would bring less profit than was to be expected from the comparatively great expenditure. Russia, moreover, seems for a time to be satisfied with the aim reached, that, namely, of having procured a safe passage for her commercial relations, although the results hitherto shown do not wholly justify such an assumption. Mons. Rajeffski states in a paper published in the *Golos*, that Russian caravans and Russian merchants cannot always proceed unhindered in the so-called suzerain states—in fact, they are exposed to the same hatred and the same enmity as before.

Unquestionably this circumstance aroused in many minds the idea that the Court of Petersburg, by its conquests in Turkestan, has hitherto only desired to secure a kind of highway which was possibly to serve as a line of communication in acquiring greater extension of power, and also as a passage to the south, strategically and politically secure. Be that as it may, we cannot and will not raise the veil of possible future plans. It is for the present a settled matter that the Russians desire, directly or indirectly, to rule over all three Khanates. Russia, moreover, has a perfect right to do so; and since, as we have already mentioned, she has accomplished her plan in the north, east, and south, she must now turn her eye towards the west; to that west where, as is well known, a hundred years ago, her first beginnings were made, but where all attempts hitherto, either from ignorance of the country, or from insufficient preparations, have proved abortive.

That Russia felt herself, so to speak, compelled of late to adopt an aggressive policy towards Khiva, the reader will understand from the following circumstances. In the first place, it could not be supposed that after the humiliation of Khokand and Bokhara, the small insignificant Khiva should proudly stand with head erect, for such a demeanour would have been interpreted by the Central

Asiatics not as forbearance, but as weakness; they are accustomed to see in Khiva the warlike neighbour *par excellence,* and in their eyes the large number of Turkoman nomads between the lower stream of the Oxus and the Caspian Sea is regarded as a military force of no ordinary size. In the second place, the independence of Khiva is not only dangerous to the Russian power in Turkestan itself, but even the Russian authority in the north and east of the Caspian Sea is thus limited; for Khiva hospitably receives the seditious tributary Kasaks of the Little Horde, whom Russia has long ago admitted into the list of her subjects, and even seduces them to rebellion and unruliness. It is true the Russian authority over the Kirghises, and all other nomad tribes wandering on the steppes, is still very questionable, and is as doubtful as the relation in which the Arab races of Beni-lam and Muntefitch, in Mesopotamia, stand to the Turks, and many North African tribes to the French. It must not, moreover, be ignored that Khiva, just as much as Russia, has had for centuries a legitimate claim on the nomads mentioned. These poor people have, however, often had the good fortune of being protected by two masters—that is, they have been annoyed both on the north and south. Still, considering that Russian influence can certainly have a far more beneficial effect on their rude mode of life than that of Khiva, we in Europe must plead for the Russian possession of this people, and must designate as Russian subjects those groups of nomads who wander without a master from the Emba, on the west of the Sea of Aral, to the Uest-Yort, or from the left bank of the Yaxartes to the eastern shore of the Sea of Aral. Of course the

Khan of Khiva has no right to receive them hospitably as Russian subjects, but still less has he the right to incite them against the authority of his nomadic neighbour.

Russia can, moreover, justify her attack on Khiva, by the fact that this land, like all uncivilised Asiatic countries, is an impediment in the way of regular European trade, and, like all Asiatics, lays down the senseless principle: " My people may pass unhindered through your kingdom with their caravans and bales of goods; we can go in and out among you as it pleases us, but if you dare to set foot on our soil, you are the children of death."

If such an interpretation of international law would scarcely be submitted to by any other state, Russia of course would least of all see with indifference the encroachment upon her commercial interests, and the captivity of her subjects while following their peaceful employments. We will grant that the protection of the Kasaks, owning as they did a doubtful sovereignty, could afford no well-founded cause for a declaration of war; yet, on the other hand, it must not be overlooked that several Russian fishermen and merchants, venturing eastward into the country from the Bay of Guryef, or from some point of the Mertwikultuk, had been very constantly taken prisoners without any cause, and had been sold as slaves to Khiva. That the true delinquents— namely, some fugitive Kirghises, or tribes belonging to the Turkoman races of Tchaudor, Igdir, and Abdal—had as little to do with the dominion of Khiva as with that of Russia, and that therefore the prince of the former country could not be called to account for their crime, is

a question which Russia never undertook to examine
closely. It was enough that Khiva was guilty of having
purchased Russian slaves, and for this reason she was
to be punished. It would be difficult to bring forward
proofs that the Government in Khiva had seduced
the nomad tribes mentioned to commit this shameful
crime against Russia. Rapine and plunder have ever
belonged to these races, and the fact alone that the injured party was a *Kafir—i.e.,* an unbeliever—may have
given some encouragement to the nomads in their sense
of the public feeling at Khiva. The Government itself,
so far as I know, has carefully avoided all collision with
the Russians ever since the time of Allah-Kuli-Khan.
On the whole, however, these circumstances lessen but
little Russia's right of complaint with regard to the third
point, and this, therefore, may be designated as the most
cogent reason for inducing the Government of Petersburg to take energetic measures against Khiva.

That in Khiva itself, after they had been eyewitnesses
of the Russian successes in the East, they looked
forward with cheerfulness to the gloomy days of the
future, it would be difficult to assert. Eloquent proofs
of the sad tone of feeling, and even of the fear that
prevailed, may be seen, indeed, in the messengers who
in the name of the Khan of Khiva traversed Khokand, Bokhara, and even remote Turkestan, imploring
the sovereign for help, and gaining sums from the
people for the holy war against the infidel; no less is
this fear evidenced by the embassy sent to India, in
order to obtain from the English a friendly word in
favour of Khiva, or, what would have been still more
agreeable to the Khan, an armed interference. The

anxiety felt on the lower stream of the Oxus is testified also by the despatch of an ambassador to the Sultan of Constantinople. This ambassador last winter went in and out among the great dignitaries of the Porte on the shores of the Bosphorus, without, as is readily explicable, being able to obtain any real result to his endeavours. The fear with which the inhabitants of Khiva looked forward to the future was, moreover, well justified. Had the small province on the lower stream of the Oxus had at its head a prince of energy and judgment, the success of the Russian arms would certainly have been far more difficult than can be the case under the present circumstances. Khiva has, in the first place, 30,000 horse, recruited from the ranks of the Özbegs, the settled and ruling class of the land ; and although provided with the most primitive arms, they may still be called, to a certain extent, courageous and serviceable, and, indeed, they far surpass in bravery, if I may use the word, the Özbegs of Bokhara and Khokand. A wise prince, such as Allah-Kuli-Khan and Mehemmed-Ali-Khan, would have made the nomad tribes of the surrounding country enthusiastic for the cause of the land, and thus have placed no unimportant stone of stumbling in the way of the intruding foe. Among the nomads who belong to the dominion of Khiva, the northern Yomuts may be mentioned in the first place; their habitations stretched, in the form of a crescent at the back of the western part of the Khanate, from Kötsche to Hezaresp, and at the smallest computation they could send from 8000 to 10,000 horse into the field. These Yomuts belong to the Sheref-Djuni race, and form the branches of the Öküs, Solak,

Ushak, Podjuk, Mesprik, and Yimreli. In the second place, the Tchaudors deserve to be mentioned ; they inhabit the southern inland country between the Caspian Sea and the Sea of Aral, and they are to be found in the neighbourhood of Altürgentch, Buldumsas, and Köktchege. The best known names of their subdivisions are Abdal, Igdyr, Essenlu, Karatchaudor, Bosadji, Burundjuk, and Sheich; and the number of their effective horse is generally computed at 10,000 strong—a power considerable in itself, for the Tchaudors, as regards warlike matters, have no equal but the Tekkes among all Turkomans.

In addition to these nomadic forces, Khiva could also enlist the Kasaks in her cause, a considerable number of whom rove over the steppes without a master, wishing to avoid the tribute which is required from them as legitimate Russian subjects. There are, however, besides, several thousand huts, especially among the Mangishlakian Kasaks, which have long and openly acknowledged the supremacy of Khiva; and that they are not disturbed by the Russians in this disposition is best shown by the fact that they are the real medium of communication on the Mangishlakian highway, which, it is true, is but little frequented. In fact, if Khiva went to work with adroitness, she could win over to her cause the numerous troops of the Tekketur-komans in the neighbourhood of Merv. A united movement on the part of these different nomad races has hitherto, so far as history tells us, only taken place in the time of able rulers. These Turkoman auxiliaries really form the choice part of the forces of famous conquerors ; and I am taking but a very small number, when I assert that the Khan of Khiva, if he goes sensibly to work, can mount more than 50,000 of these nomads for the contest against Russia. If these 50,000 tolerably well-armed, well-mounted, and well-trained warriors are in themselves invaluable against an intruding enemy, only partially acquainted with local circumstances, on the other side, the territorial conditions of Khiva, whether in the south, west, or north-east, are no less valuable as a wall of protection, such as has stood at the disposal of no other Central Asiatic Khanate hitherto subjected. We will point out some of the advantages of this natural bulwark, by mentioning the highways leading to Khiva from the west, north, and north-east. 1. From the left bank of the Oxus to the shores of the Caspian there is a road of about 100 miles, leading on the one side to Tashkal (the "stone fortress"), or to the Russian Fort Alexandroffsk, and on the other side through Mangishlak to the town of Karagan, on the inlet of the same name. This highway, though frequented by caravans in very early times, cannot be called practicable for an army; for at one part there is a tract of land of more than three days' journey, where no drinkable water is to be met with; the country, moreover, is covered with countless swamps and morasses; and lastly, the snowstorms and the terrible cold in winter are as unsufferable as the torturing heat and killing thirst in summer. 2. From the Saraitshik station, on the lower part of the Ural chain, there is a road of a 1000 wersts in length, according to Wenjukoff, along which the unfortunate expedition of the Bekowitsch Tscherkoffsky passed in 1717, and which was also used by the Hetman Netchay in the seventeenth century. This road begins in the lowlands of the Sagish, and then takes a diagonal direction towards the plateau of Uest-Yort, through Barsa-Kilmez, along the western shores of the Sea of Aral, and terminates at Kungrat, and only for a third of the whole way is there any grass or drinkable water to be met with. 3. There is a road from Orenburg, on the upper part of the Emba, in the direction of Fort Embinsk, which was erected in 1839 against the incursions of the Khivans; and here, also, "little fodder, little water, no fodder at all, and no water," appear as items of the notices of various routes. This road is 1395 wersts long, and it likewise terminates at Kungrat, after going round by the Ay-bögürsee (erroneously called Aibugir by the Russians). 4. There is a road from Orsk to Kazalinsk, and from thence to Khiva, along the eastern shore of the Sea of Aral. The distance between the two first-named places is 739 wersts, and from Kazalinsk to the capital is considered 770 wersts—in all, 1509 wersts. This is, of course, a very indirect way; yet the traveller, so long as he keeps to the Bokhariot caravan route, is not annoyed by its circuitousness, as he is passing through a country greatly frequented by nomad tribes, and which, therefore, does not possess the character of fearful desolation. From Kazalinsk, moreover, as far as Görlen, where the road enters the Khanate, the traveller has to fight with all the difficulties and hardships of clayey, arid, or sandy steppes. Herr Wenjukoff, the learned Russian geographer, tells us that the unspeakable difficulties of this road were the main reason why the Russians have latterly tried to discover a new way to Khiva from Fort Peroffsky, or from the old Ak‑Mesdjid; this attempt, however, failed, for here also the district of Kütchki‑Tengiz (Little Sea), as far as Daukara, is filled with all the horrors of a desert country. Equally bad and unusable are the other roads starting from other points on the left bank of the Syr; for here we come upon the great sand steppes of Kizil-kum and Batkak-kum, or red sand and marshy sand—a designation which thoroughly accords with the nature of the soil; for I have sufficiently convinced myself of the horror of the steppes which separate the Khanates of Bokhara and Khokand from each other in the north, as it was my fate to travel through a southern tract of this soil in the so-called Chalata desert. The readers of my book of travel will remember the description of this region. Still worse is the aspect of things in the south-west. Here the Khanate of Khiva is protected by the Hyrcanian steppes, across which no highroad has ever existed, and which I myself traversed in its full length, and can only describe as a region where art and industry might in some measure alleviate the lot of the traveller, but which will ever be a tract of land subject to the curse of nature. Political enthusiasts of the future greatness of Russia considered it possible in time, perhaps in about three years, to bridge over these steppes with a railway—namely, from the Balkan range to the banks of the Oxus; and when I, from personal experience, turned this plan into ridicule, the Russian press assailed me with a storm of invectives. At the present day the subject is better appreciated, for the Russian scientific expedition of Messrs Stebnitzki and Radde has penetrated far into the country from Fort Krasnowodsk, and they also declare the project, as far as regards a settlement and future plans of commerce, as an empty phantom and as a complete mirage.

Khiva, therefore, in the strictest sense of the word, is a tract of country surrounded by dangerous and inaccessible steppes; and thus, defended as she is by natural bulwarks, she could all the more easily remain in the defensive, if she possessed the power of exercising a sufficient influence on the nomadic forces before mentioned, and if she could add to the dangers of nature those also of surprises on the part of the nomad tribes well acquainted with these steppes. Thus, for example, on the road to Mangishlak, the united army of the Tchaudors and Kasaks might not only extremely impede the movements of the Russians, but in some places they might render them impossible on the Hyrcanian steppe. Yomuts and Tekkes, by a flank attack, might place a numerous and well-drilled force, perfectly familiar with the tactics of war, in a very critical position. During the march an invading army of this kind would not only always have to proceed in thick masses, but with matchlock ready and guns cocked, if not with lowered bayonet; and how such a march could be accomplished, either in the freezing cold of the winter or in the burning heat of the summer, is not an easy problem. That in the north and north-east there is no great security for the Russian invading army is evident from the fact that the Russians would have in their rear a hostile though feeble power, and that, moreover, the Kirghises and Karakalpaks from the banks of the Kisil-Derya, or from the neighbourhood of Dankara, would scarcely take trouble to facilitate the Russian march.

As we have delineated the resources which the Khanate of Khiva could have at her disposal against the advancing enemy, we will now cast a glance at the offensive measures of Russia, and draw attention to those points at which her attack will be made, or perhaps is already made. Russia has occupied three strong points in opposition to the three Khiva bulwarks—namely, to the south of Orenburg, in the fortifications on the Emba, between the Caspian Sea and the Sea of Aral; secondly, in Fort Alexandroffsk, in Mertwikultuk; and thirdly, the position recently taken in the inlet of Krasnowodsk, and in Tchekishlar, which last-mentioned point, at the time of my journey, was known among the Turkomans as a favourite summer residence, at the mouth of the Etrek, and which was occupied by the Russians about two years ago, without obtaining the consent of Persia to the step, though the contrary is asserted by the notice of the secret treaty respecting the valley of the Etrek. To these may be added the fortified positions on the upper Zerefshan and in the valley of the Yaxartes, from which points a diversion might be made upon Khiva by going round by Bokhara. It is possible, and even extremely probable, that the Russians will attempt this way, though no prognostics of success can be held out to the enterprise; for the difficulties of communication, apart from the hostile nomads mentioned above, would hinder all movements. As regards the mental and material advantages which Russia possesses over her enemy, we must above all recognise the superiority of her arms and tactics, and especially the season at which the Russians will at three different points approach the little country situated on the lower stream of the Oxus. If signs do not deceive us, the attack will take place neither in midsummer nor in winter, but in the spring. The lesson of 1840, which Allah-Kuli-Khan, or, more justly, winter, gave to the invading enemy, has not been forgotten in Petersburg, and care will now be taken to prevent the loss of the several thousand men who at that time perished from cold and scurvy and other diseases. Across this part of the Uest-Yort, or on the plateau of the Hyrcanian steppe, the north wind blows with unfettered fury. Captain James Abbott, in his volume of travels (i. 230), speaks of this wind as follows: " Those only can form an idea of the bitter coldness of this north wind who have wintered on a vast continent. The human breath hangs in icicles from the pillows and coverlets even within the tents. Towels which are hung to dry in some small space by the fire, or in the open air by the sun, suddenly freeze, and water freezes at a distance of three feet from the fire." We do not doubt that the Russian infantry employed in this expedition would be able to cope with the severity of a hard winter. The terrible climate is rendered insufferable only because it has to be endured on a vast inhospitable steppe, exposed to an enemy accustomed to single contests. That Russia is now avoiding this season and choosing the spring, when many otherwise arid tracts are covered with grass, and when the rain is collected in natural cisterns in the hollows of the hard soil (*kak*), is the pledge of a favourable result.

Added to this, moreover, is the possibility that Russia may, perhaps, by intrigues among the Turkomans, win over to her side one or another race, or even branch of a race, by which she may perhaps not only completely break up the united band of nomad tribes, but may cast among them the torch of the bitterest hostility. The success of such a step against Khiva, of course, depends chiefly on the position which these nomad tribes are inclined to assume towards an invading power. Had we not learned by experience that the Turkomans could only exceptionally be gathered under one standard by great Mohammedan princes, and that in general they are split by constant feud and their power paralysed, it would, perhaps, be possible for them even now to arouse themselves at the threatening danger of total ruin, and to set aside the national character that pervades their race. Yet the Turkomans, who are but loosely held in the bonds of Islamism, and to whom the bright gold pieces of Russian subsidies are more alluring than the fluttering standard of a religious war, will be all the more easily bribed by Russia, as the present Government of Khiva has no authority over them, and, moreover, offers them no real decoy. Recent past events have shown that the Russians could win over to their own interests a grey-bearded chief of the Yomut race, and subsequently the influential leader of the Ata-Bai tribe.

The position taken at Tchekishlar seems, moreover, not entirely to have been accomplished by force of arms ; for although the Russian reconnoitring corps, in its expeditions to the south, especially near Etrek, meeting with opposition, was obliged to destroy the Turkoman tents, it is not yet proved that these were exclusively Yomuts, or that one tribe or another was not carrying on friendly relations with them. The case is the same in the neighbourhood of Alexandroffsk as in the vicinity of Krasnowodsk, and I repeat that, by partially obtaining the sympathies of the Turkomans, the danger which

z

might arise from these otherwise troublesome nomads will be considerably diminished.

After this general sketch, in which we have attempted to give the reader as distinct an idea as possible of the position of things, it is time that we should return to our starting-point of the Russian war against Khiva. We have already mentioned that this Khanate, after the successful issue of the Russian war in Khokand and Bokhara, did not feel herself entirely on a bed of roses. The youthful Prince Seid - Mehemmed - Rehim, now scarcely twenty-four years of age, who, if I am rightly informed, ascended the throne only three years ago, had, moreover, the misfortune, like many of his predecessors on the throne of Khahrezm, of being drawn into a war with the neighbouring Turkomans, especially with the Tchandor, Igdir, and Yomut tribes—a fresh evidence of how little he could have relied on these races in a Russian invasion. Like all Oriental princes, the young man is, moreover, eager for war, and is blindly submissive to the counsels of his chief vizier, Mohammed-Murad-Bai, who is always flattering him with the hope of speedy success. Towards the end of 1871, after the successful overthrow of the rebellious nomads, the unpleasant tidings reached him that the Russians had already advanced as far as the Sari-Kanish marsh, at the most two days' journey from the Altürgentch. This was the expedition of Col. Markusoff, which had extended its inroads to this point, after a march of fifty-two days from Krasnowodsk. Whether this Russian enterprise intended an attack or no, is for the moment difficult to decide. Col. Markusoff, who had advanced to the Ortakuja station (central springs) along the same road by which I travelled in 1863, was obliged to retire before the immense body of the enemy, and is said to have lost three hundred camels and several horses; yet the flash of the Russian bayonets in such threatening vicinity had frightened the Khan, and the fear of internal disorders induced him on this occasion, in spite of his youthful thirst for action, to adopt a reconciliatory course. At this time, a Turkoman named Nur-Mohammed, who was about to make a pilgrimage to Mecca, happened to be in Khiva. Nur-Mohammed, as an elder of the Tchandor tribe, is not wholly unknown to the Russian authorities at Alexandroffsk; for we are told he was once introduced to the Grand Duke, the Governor-General of Tiflis, and even to the Emperor himself. His character affords us a proof that the Russians may easily overcome any danger threatened by the nomad tribes— in fact, we meet with this pious greybeard again as a Russian emissary in the old capital of Khahrezm. How on a journey to Arabia from Astrakan, Khiva, which is quite out of the way, should be reached, is in itself unintelligible. Nur-Mohammed only wished to fathom the state of things there; and after he had succeeded in procuring admittance to the Khan, he contrived, by his influence, that two conciliatory embassies should be despatched to Russia to mediate a friendly relation on the part of Khiva. The one, which arrived at Alexandroffsk on the 27th February, old style, consisted of six persons, and was headed by Mohammed-Emin, the Kazi-Kelan, a high dignitary of the Church. The aim of their journey was Tiflis, where they intended to deliver to the Grand Duke the expressions of their master's friendship, with the promise that the Russian slaves now in Khivan captivity should speedily be set at liberty. Besides this influential priest, of whom it is reported that the Khan does not venture to sit or to smoke in his presence, there was in the embassy another man, Kul-Mohammed, a son of the before-mentioned Nur-Mohammed, who, like his father, has shown already many acts of friendship to the Russians, and was to promote the interests of Khiva with the powerful infidel as *persona grata.* The embassy numbered still some other notabilities, and although tolerably well received by Col. Lamakin, the officer commanding at Alexandroffsk, it did not obtain its real object, for it could not advance further than Temir-Khan-Shura, in Dagestan, and was obliged to return to Khiva without having effected its purpose. No better was the fate of the second embassy, which the alarmed prince on the lower stream of the Oxus sent to Petersburg, under the direction of Atalik-Irnazar, the governor of the Karakalpakian district. This envoy was the bearer of several presents for the Czar, among others, of a pair of excellent horses, valued at one thousand roubles, and he was likewise to promise that all the Russian captives in Khiva should be set at liberty as soon as possible. The embassy quitted Kungrat on thirty camels at the end of March; but it was detained at Orenburg by the Governor-General Krischanoffski, and Atalik-Irnazar, like his diplomatic colleague at Dagestan, was obliged to return without having effected anything.

What Russia designed by this harsh rebuff and decided rejection of all reconciliation, may indeed appear doubtful to many; yet we must be just, and confess that the Government on the Neva, or the executors of its power in the interior of Asia, acted with tact. The Russians have indeed not allowed themselves to be deceived as to the value of the promise of an Asiatic prince, and still more of one in Turkestan; for as the Khan of Khiva only disposed himself for friendly intercourse in his anxiety at the reconnoitrings from Krasnowodsk and the steppes of Batkak-Kum, so there was certainly no idea of any voluntary restoration of the slaves, and of the commencement of friendly or commercial relations, as soon as the Northern neighbour ceased from further threatenings. The circumstances which justified Russia in beginning a war with Khiva date from an early period. Formerly forbearance and delay were the result of circumstances; at the present day, however, it was wished to bring matters to a termination, an attack must be made, and the chastisement, and possibly the subjection, of Khiva must at length be resolved upon.

Such was the state of things at the beginning of November 1872. Khiva had also indulged in no further delusions; and while the Russians were employed in preparing their army of occupation in Orenburg, a troop of nine thousand men, chiefly Özbegs, Karakalpaks, and fugitive Kirghises, had extended their expeditions along the west shore of the Sea of Aral as far as the small forts on the Emba, while another troop, consisting of four thousand men, had taken the direction to Fort Alexandroffsk. These expeditions seem to have made the whole district from Fort Emba to the upper stream of the Irgis insecure, for at the end of November the post across the steppes failed to appear at Orsk for several days, and the delay was rightly attributed to a hostile attack. This informa-

tion comes to us of course from Russian sources, the
true facts of the case are therefore difficult to ascertain.
Yet from whatever side the attack may have come, so
much is certain that General Krischanoffski at once put
his army in motion, and despatched Colonel Kolotnischeff
with one thousand Kossacks across the Irgis, in order to
oppose the Khivan incursions. It was decreed by a council
of war that light cavalry were to be employed for a time
instead of infantry, owing to the advanced season of the
year; and in consequence the order was at once issued
to Kazalinsk (a fort on the south-east shore of the Sea
of Aral), that the Kossacks dismissed from Turkestan,
who were now on their way to Orenburg at the expira-
tion of their term of service, should at once be brought
back to the scene of action. So much is known to us of
the operations in the north. In the south and south-
east, the second corps, which at the lowest computation
must have been five thousand strong, was approaching
the left bank of the Oxus over a part of the way which
I myself have traversed on the Turkoman steppes, and
indeed the very same tract which it had reconnoitred in
the previous year. It was reported that this corps was to
be led in person by the royal Governor-General of the
Caucasus, yet this intention was departed from, and an
experienced general was placed at the head. He was
obliged to leave the steppes either at Kohne-Uergentch
or at Yilali, and a difficult task lay before him; for
although he cannot have begun his march until after the
before-mentioned partial co-operation of the Turkomans,
he was in nowise secured by this from a flank attack.
More than five thousand men belonging to the regular
troops stand at his disposal, and yet his task is most

difficult. As regards the third division, this was to set forth from the part of Turkestan already conquered—namely, from Samarkand and Khodjend—and after successfully crossing the Kiselkum, it was to reach the right bank of the Oxus, probably in the neighbourhood of Hezaresp or Shurachan, crossing this river on pontoons brought with it. According to a vague report, this third division was to be led by General Kaufmann himself, and was not to begin its march from Samarkand and Khodjend, but from Kazalinsk, or rather from the lower part of the Yaxartes. Yet whoever may be the commanding officer, so much is certain, that the three different divisions of the army, after having crossed the river, were to be concentrated on its left bank, in order that they might carry out the plan of subjection with combined forces. Until events have arrived at this point, any occurrence may cause a delay of the plan : yet there can be no idea of its utter destruction or frustration ; for it may with certainty be predicted that the Russian expedition against Khiva in 1873 will not be as unfortunate as that of 1840, and that the soldiers of the "White Czar" will bring this contest to a victorious issue.

II.

As regards the political and commercial value which Khiva can possess for the great Russian Empire, we will touch upon a few points as briefly as possible. Khiva is not only fertile, but it may be called the most fertile part of Turkestan. The excellence and the variety of its natural productions I have already pointed out in my "Skizzen aus Mittelasien." Judged from a commercial point of view, the opening of the whole Oxus river will be of an importance not to be too highly appreciated ; and as regards the scope for her political influence, Russia will only secure a sure basis for her position in the interior of Asia when she sets up her pillar of power on one side in the alpine regions of the Thien-Shan range, and on the other at the mouth of the Oxus. No one would envy the mighty empire for this favour of fortune. The campaign against Khiva might have come to a close, like all former campaigns, without making a great commotion in the political world, if by it a somewhat delicate international question had not been affected—namely, the position of the Northern Colossus with regard to her English rival in the south, who, by this recent movement, has been startled out of the slumber of indifference in which she has lulled herself for years.

By the dominion of Russia over Khiva, the Northern Colossus will have passed from the left to the right bank of the Oxus, and will have again a frontier territory before her, the exact definition of which is as difficult as was the case with the territory on the right bank of the Yaxartes previous to 1864. From that period to the present time England has always said that she may not, cannot, and will not disturb Russia in her new designs of conquest, since she brings wild anarchy into order, which is indeed no small service rendered to humanity,—since she opens trade and traffic, and enriches our geography and ethnography with the most valuable facts,—since, by her given word, she only intends to advance to the right bank of the Oxus and no further, in order to mark out Afghanistan, lying, as it does, between India and Turkestan, as neutral and unapproachable territory. So long as these statements met with general credence, and Russia gave no cause to shake this belief, the optimist politicians of Great Britain, and many like-minded politicians on the Continent, were tolerably justified in their opinions on this question. The recent movements, however, have necessarily produced a change of feeling, and each one now questions whether, if Prince Gortschakoff laid down the assertion in his diplomatic communication of November 1864, "that the fleeting grains of sand of the steppes are incapable of forming a frontier line, and that only the inhabited and arable part of the country is suitable for a solid line of demarcation," it may not now be further said that the Uest-Yort and the Hyrcanian steppes are likewise insufficient as a boundary to the south-west Turkestan territory, and that this must be formed by the mountainous northern edge of Iran from Astrabad to Merv and Herat? And truly Russia would justly defend such an opinion. If the government of the Kirghise hordes in the north of the Yaxartes is constantly impeded and endangered, how will it be possible to keep in check the hundredfold wild and predatory Turkomans, without enclosing them entirely? The Russians may talk as they please of the adventurous spirit of the Kasaks of the "Great and Little Horde;" these Kasaks are harmless people when we compare them with the Achal-Tekke Turkomans, with the Sariks and the Salors. To curb the latter, and to bring them to obedience, will be in itself a gigantic work, but it would defy every effort if Russia could not possess herself of a secure network of communication by a firm position on the Merv and in the neighbourhood of

Herat. Whether such a necessity is agreeable or disagreeable to the Court of Petersburg may indeed be doubtful for the moment; but that it justly awakens great suspicion in the English mind, and arouses misgivings which for years were purposely avoided, is beyond a doubt. It was in consequence of these misgivings that the London Cabinet, in December 1872, inquired for the first time of the Court of Petersburg respecting Russia's intentions towards Khiva. The report of this diplomatic step was for a long time persistently denied on both sides. At length, however, it proved correct; and in order, in some measure, to sooth the excited temper of the British leopard, Count Schuwaloff, the adjutant of the Russian Emperor, repaired direct to the Thames. As for his conciliatory words, they produced the best result with the Gladstone Ministry, disposed as they are to peace at any price. England can reconcile herself, as before, to the explanations of her rival.

No one will, however, take it amiss if we plainly declare that Russia, though she may be animated by the best intentions, is not able to fix the bounds of a " Hitherto shalt thou come and no further !" We have already shown that this halting-point is not possible in the immediate neighbourhood of Khiva; but that it is impossible also on the plain of Merv and on the banks of the Murgab will be proved by the immediate future. As hitherto almost everything has been fulfilled which I have presaged with regard to the Russian advance southwards, my last assertion will probably be realised also; for it is not only unrestrained thirst for conquest which impels the Russian eagle towards the south, but there are local, ethnological, and political reasons which prevent it from standing still. A power, although partially civilised, can with difficulty maintain the *status quo* when it has for its neighbour a barbarous state distracted by anarchy. Serious complications are not to be avoided with the utmost patience; and thus we have only the one alternative left, either entirely to withdraw from contact with a barbarous neighbour, which Russia will never do, or to stride over that neighbour until the vicinity of some civilised and well-regulated people affords a halting-point.

But let us return to Schuwaloff's mission, and see what turn matters have meanwhile taken on the Thames, and what has been obtained by the first alarm of the Anglo-Russian altercation. In the labyrinth of the various reports circulated with regard to the result of Schuwaloff's mission, that interpretation was asserted most obstinately which declared that the Gladstone Cabinet was satisfied for the time with the Russian promise that the whole expedition against Khiva had no other design than to give a little lesson to the Khan, and to induce him to conclude a commercial treaty; in a word, to compel him, if not to express feelings of affection, at any rate to enter into friendly relations with the Court of Petersburg. This was confirmed, moreover, by the purport of the official document recently published, which was laid before the English Parliament. How it can occur to any one in the world that this compulsory bond of friendship with the polar and shaggy beast of the North can aim at any lasting and positive result, and that Khiva, when she throws herself into the arms of Russia, will abandon herself to the slumber of repose and contentment, is indeed inconceivable. And yet the leaders of Liberal England seem now willing to walk on Russian ice, and to see in these protestations of the Muscovite that back-gate by which they can easily leave the oppressive demand for manly and decided conduct, and perhaps even for serious conflict. This self-deceiving policy, that marks the present Cabinet on the Thames, is equally unwise as it is unpractical, and it may bring the vessel of the British state on a sandbank of no ordinary difficulty. In the first place, Mr Gladstone and his colleagues would do better to weigh the value of Russian promises, and especially to recall to remembrance the historical course of those diplomatic negotiations which were carried on more than thirty years ago between Count Nesselrode and Lord Palmerston with regard to the Central Asiatic question, in which it was often enough proved that the words spoken on the Neva could not always be brought into perfect harmony with the actions of the representatives of the Czar in the East; in fact, they sometimes betrayed double-dealing and evident deceit. The not very enviable part which in dissimulations of this kind devolved upon General Simonisk, the Russian ambassador at Teheran, must repeatedly be accepted by Russian agents; and that treaties are only considered binding so long as circumstances require it, has been well shown by the revision of the treaty of 1856, a work of the most criminal compliance, and in which the English statesmen have the lion's share.

If, therefore, the confidence placed on Russian promises rests in itself on no granite basis, the fact must not, on the other hand, be forgotten that Russia in the present case, however much she may now be stimulated

by the noblest disinterestedness, cannot keep her promise of a subsequent evacuation of Khiva, and, moreover, dare not do so, unless she chooses to be obliged
by temporary re-occupation of the whole country on the
lower Oxus, and therefore by new and considerable
sacrifice, to procure the desired commercial intercourse
and peaceful neighbours. It was Russian diplomacy
and the Russian press which endeavoured to prove to
the world that treaties with barbarous states were only
of value so long as they could be impressed by the
direct influence of power—*i.e.,* so long as they were
compelled by force to adhere to the promise given.
This is a view, the truth of which no one will deny, for
the treaties with Khokand, Bokhara, and East Turkestan might have been confirmed by a hundred seals and
oaths on the part of the Özbegs, but they would have
been null and void if the mouths of the Russian cannons
on the Syr, the Narin, and the Zerefshan had not inter-
posed to inspire respect. The appreciation of the rights
of nations, the fidelity and sincerity which are not
found, nor are ever expected to be found, in Khokand
and Bokhara, under more regular governments—does
Russia expect to find these qualities in nomadic Khiva,
where there is really no government at all? and does
she persuade the English that by the subjection of
the Khanate, after conquering the Özbegs, the Turkomans, the Karakalpaks, and the Kirghises, she will at
once withdraw from all points of a land conquered with
so much blood and money, as soon as Khan-Seid-Me-
hemmed-Rehim has signed and ratified the treaty?
That the author of " Juventus Mundi," who has recently
manifested his love of the Homeric poetry, and therefore

of the Homeric age, can give perfect credence to such an innocent and primitive view of things, I do not doubt for a moment, and probably none will doubt who know Mr Gladstone and his writings. Equally little can it be held impossible that the Liberal English Ministry, which hitherto has shown sometimes a lamentable policy, sometimes a ridiculous one, but in most cases no Asiatic policy at all, will now be cautious enough to avoid the Russian snare. In order not to come forward in earnest, the Whigs will be satisfied with any evasion ; yet the English people as a whole may conceive this Central Asiatic question with their soberness and practical spirit, and may formally compel the Government to give no credence to the Russian promise with regard to the subsequent evacuation of Khiva, since the fulfilment of such an intention could never occur to the Russians, and never has occurred to them. With this chess move, if it is successfully carried out, Russia gains an important step in advance of her English rival; for, if she once obtains possession of Khiva, she will consolidate her entire position on the east coast of the Caspian, from Tchekihlar to the Todten Bay, which is now only provisionally the case ; and by a march against Chorassan and Herat, along that road which Burnes partly reconnoitred in 1832, on his return from Bokhara, and found traversable, she will procure herself a firm and lasting basis. The Russian army will then sooner or later be compelled by circumstances to inspire respect among the wild predatory Tekke and Sarik Turkomans in the south-east of the Hyrcanian steppes, to draw nearer to the arable land on the slopes of the Paropamisus—i.e., to choose at Merv, or perhaps still further to the east, a station suitable for holding a defensive position ; for, just as impossible as it is to induce the Khan of Khiva from afar to fulfil certain obligations, equally impossible is it to think of even guarding the possession of Khiva from Khiva. In order from thence to proceed to the eastern province of Chorassan, three different routes are at the disposal of the Russians : (1.) the road before mentioned along the northern frontier of Iran ; (2.) the road from Hezaresp to Deregöz, which can be traversed in ten or twelve days on camels through a sandy desert, in parts very bad, and void of water ; and (3.) the road of Kabakly or Karayap, chiefly used by the Khivans in their expeditions against Merv, which the English diplomatist Thomson took in the year 1843. This road has drinkable water almost the whole way ; it leads through Ilat (nomadic tribes), and it occupies with small marches no more than twelve days.

If, therefore, the Russian diplomatists succeed in persuading the English that the possession of Khiva is only provisory, and should this possible possession not be met from the first by preventive measures, it will be an easy thing for the Russian army to march to the northwest frontier of Afghanistan at a time when Great Britain, far from anticipating such a movement, is standing unprepared, and in the utmost calmness, on her line of defence on the Indus and at the passes of the Suleiman. I do not mean to say by this that Russia designs any surprise, and that England generally has to fear such an attack. No ; the result of this chess move will only be that Russia will arrive sooner on the true arena of subsequent events, and this precedence must not be allowed on the part of England if it is a settled fact that Russia's immediate vicinity on the north-west frontier of India is dangerous, and therefore, under any circumstances, is to be guarded against.

We have thus then reached the most important point of the Central Asiatic question—namely, a political state of things which once threatened with mighty fury, and at another time was regarded as a ridiculous nightmare —in fact, the troubled sleeper blushed at having shrieked so loudly—and which now again is emerging like a cloud, the fatal character of which few would dispute. We will therefore look at this question closely, and I am permitted in the columns of this journal briefly to explain again the reasons, already mentioned in detail, why I consider the immediate vicinity of Russia to India dangerous to the interests of Great Britain. (1.) In the first place, a government, whose ruling principle is extension of frontier, and which sees itself, so to speak, carried along in the rapid stream of conquest by local and ethnographical circumstances, called forth by this very principle, cannot come to a pause until some mighty hindrance bars the way, *i.e.,* the waves of Russian aggression, flowing from north to south, can sooner or later be checked alone by the dam of British power. (2.) Russia's mere approximation on the north-west of India is dangerous to England, chiefly from the fact that this part of the great peninsular empire is peopled by Mohammedan, and still more by fanatical Mohammedan tribes, who, sitting on the ruins of a throne of power and grandeur, but recently overthrown, breathe vengeance against their oppressors and against all unbelieving Christians. We in nowise assert that these Mohammedans, impelled to temerity by Wehabism, entertain the idea of a change of masters, and that they would give the preference to the Russian rule; all that these races care for is war and anarchy, blood and flames, and by whomsoever the helping hand were held out to them, they would grasp it eagerly, even though the new heap of ruins buried their last hope. (3.) Russia can use her threatening position on the Indus for the furtherance of her other plans with reference to the west of Asia, and England, who is also greatly interested in the state of things on the Bosphorus, in Asia Minor, and in Armenia, must not allow her rival in any place or in any manner to get the advantage.

These reasons could be multiplied three and fourfold, yet the duty of stating them ceases so soon as the English statesmen, having arrived at a just perception of things, as Schuwaloff's mission sufficiently indicates, no longer play the part of indifferent spectators of Russia's farther advance. It has ceased to be said, "We would rather have the cleanly-dressed, though only half-civilised Russian as a neighbour than the dirty and barbarous Afghan." It is no longer asserted that the two great European powers in Asia were only rivals on the field of geographical discoveries, of commerce, and of the dissemination of Western culture. It is now confessed that a contest with regard to supremacy is here involved, and indeed that a vital question is at stake : and for this reason we will, in the first place, mention the means by which the chances of a collision, which must be fatal to both parties, can be averted, and perhaps even entirely removed.

That the neutralisation of Afghanistan would best correspond with this object, as I pointed out more than

2 A

six years ago, is at the present day acknowledged by all the world, and the opinion has to all appearance taken root also in the Cabinets of London and Petersburg. Afghanistan is to be the centre of neutrality, and the intermediate body between the Oxus and the Indus, from which the two powers are to rebound in violent approximation. Had this country, which is for the most part mountainous, possessed more organised state relations than it does, if it had not been for centuries shattered by the most bitter internal feuds, and if its inhabitants, in consequence of this circumstance, had not become the most restless and warlike of people, the accomplishment of such an idea would be an easy matter. Yet we must take the Afghan country as it is, and we must not forget: (1.) That Shir-Ali-Khan does not hold perfectly undisputed the possession of his paternal heritage. He has a considerable number of nephews and uncles, who, as members of the numerous posterity of the old Dost-Khan, are not without claims, not wholly unjust, if not to the throne, at least to the government of some province, and who are always ready to over-throw him on the first occasion, or at any rate to cause him as much embarrassment as possible. (2.) The Af-ghans in themselves are the most disobedient and unre-strained people in the world. The chiefs of the different tribes have at no time willingly submitted to the supre-macy of one sovereign ; and as the land may in general be called poor, the sword has ever had more followers than the plough, and trade has been and is exclusively in the hands of the Persians and the Tadjiks, *i.e.*, of a foreign race. Repugnance to supreme authority is increased by the fact that Shir-Ali-Khan has attempted innovations, and has tried to put an end to anarchy; and this has made the true Orientals still more hostile in their feelings, and still more stubborn. He can therefore rely on them but little if at all, and we see that even his nearest relatives, indeed his own son, are always brooding rebellion and aspiring after the crown. (3.) The annexed provinces of Afghanistan are too loosely attached to the mother country to impart strength to it; in fact, they are even a considerable hindrance, and at a time of danger they would certainly far rather hold out a hand to the foe without than to the friend within. Herat, for example, where the eldest son of the king, Sirdar-Mehemmed-Yakub-Khan, is at the head of affairs, is attached to Kabul only by a very thin thread of dependence. There has been a dispute for years between father and son, and the fact that Yakub-Khan maintains a larger army than his father allows him, and indeed behaves in a most independent manner, was always unintelligible in Kabul, and has given cause for the most different conjectures. We will not give credence to the report spread abroad by the Afghans, that he even receives secret subsidies from Persia or Russia. Still the young man is at any rate not to be relied on, and he justly causes his father much anxiety. The small principalities of Meimene, Andchoi, and the country of the Hesarek and the Djemshids, are in connection with Herat. The former, situated on the highroad to Bokhara, and numbering about 300,000 inhabitants, has always wavered in its choice of a protector between Kabul and Bokhara; and since it only inclined by preference to the ruler on the Zerefshan, and the latter has now become powerless to carry on any foreign policy, it is always on the lookout for malcontents, in order to withdraw from dependence on Kabul. Aktche, Shiborgan, Khulm, Kunduz, Kulab, and Belch, known under the common denomination of Afghan Turkestan, also stand on no firmer footing of subjection to the successor of Dost-Mohammed-Khan. Here, for instance, the sons of Azim-Khan and Afzal-Khan possess a considerable influence, and the slightest commotion from without would be sufficient to sunder this important province from Afghanistan. Bedachshan and Wachan also, which the king of the Afghans at the present day calls his property, are very weak, and not at all attached to Kabul. His entire dominion over them consists in the payment of a yearly tribute of 15,000 rupees by the prince of this poor and mountainous country; and the land on the banks of the Pendje, the Surchat, and the Kohtche, the principal tributaries of the upper Oxus, may in truth be designated at the present day as without a master, as well as the whole of the adjacent district of the highlands of Pamir. It is true it cannot be denied that Shir-Ali-Khan's claims to Bedachshan rest rather on the force of arms than on the free choice of the inhabitants, for after the death of Dost-Mohammed-Khan, Djandar-Shah, the prince of the country at that time, wished to swear allegiance to the Emir of Bokhara, and I met the embassy sent for this purpose when I was at Kerki in the summer of 1863. Subsequently, however, Djandar's nephews acquired the dominion by means of Afghan help, and as they are still ruling in Bedachshan under the protection of Kabul, it is only just that Shir-Ali-Khan should exercise his full sovereign authority there.

That, under such circumstances, Afghanistan can

scarcely be transformed into a trustworthy neutral province, when its prince is being assisted in consolidating his own power, need scarcely be stated. For this office, this kindly service, has been undertaken by England when she entered into a sort of offensive and defensive alliance with Shir-Ali-Khan, and for the security of his throne and the regulation of his internal affairs, allowed him yearly the sum of £120,000 sterling, and considerable presents of arms besides. In the last few years, the jealous adversaries of Russia in England have, it is true, expressed the opinion that the British ought to cross the Kheiber Pass, conquer Afghanistan, and in this way form an advanced work as a defence for her Indian empire. This opinion, which is entertained by a small minority in England, and those chiefly belonging to the army, may however be designated as thoroughly erroneous, and it can and will in nowise be pursued by English politicians. England, made wiser by the fatal campaign of 1840, dare not and will not again march into Kabul as an enemy. Such a policy is opposed, moreover, to sound human judgment, for it would require immense sacrifice, and after all miss its object; since the Afghanistan country, subjugated by England, would not only not serve as a bulwark to India, but, on the approach of the Russians, would be far more dangerous than the Punjaub, Sind, or the whole of the north-west of India. The conquest and annexation of Afghanistan is, therefore, the most fatal idea for England that can be conceived. Afghanistan must be left in its independence if it is to be useful to English interests. . Such a proceeding, however, need not at all exclude precautionary measures; it does not render superfluous all improvements of the

position which England has to take along the whole
frontier line, from Peshawur to Karatchi. I must in this
respect agree with Colonel Sir Henry Green, or more correctly with General Jacob, and express my approval of
the opinion that the English frontier of Yacobabad ought
to be removed to the other side of the Bolan Pass, *i.e.*,
to the northern termination of this mountain road. If
we examine the entire north-west line, we shall find
that, judging from a strategical point of view, it is not
completely fortified. The valley of Peshawur, where the
English have as neighbours a hardy and fanatical mountain race, has at the present time a garrison of about ten
hundred men, who are quite sufficient for the place, and
are also able to guard the Kheiber Pass. Further to the
south, at the Pass of Kokat, the garrison consists only
of native troops. Further on, from Bannu along the
frontier stations of Dera-Ismail-Khan, Deregaz-Khan,
Radjanpur, Yacobabad, and Karatchi, a distance of
nearly twelve hundred miles, there is a garrison of
twelve thousand irregular troops, to which may be added
the guard detachment of two thousand men on the Sind
frontier, and the garrison of Karatchi. This is no inconsiderable number, and, moreover, if occasion required,
in consequence of the facilities of communication, it
could be greatly increased. In the selection of the different garrisoned places, however, a change ought to be
made as far as possible. It is readily conceivable that
it would be of great advantage to the Anglo-Indian
interests to remove the frontier station of Peshawur to
Djelalabat, *i.e.*, to the other side of the Kheiber Pass;
yet this would be connected with very great difficulty,
and might indeed almost be designated as impossible.

If England, therefore, cannot dispose of one of the so-called two principal gates of her empire in the north-west, she must take care to acquire possession of the key to the other, *i.e.*, the Bolan Pass. Here the object can be attained all the more easily as westward of Radjanpur is the home of the Belutjees, whose prince some years ago concluded an alliance with England for £5000 sterling, and whose subjects, from constant intercourse with the English, have learned to respect the power of their civilised neighbour; in a word, they are far easier to manage than the Afghans. No one would, therefore, raise an objection if the English were to appropriate to themselves the long mountain road of about seventy English miles, leading from Dadar to Quetta, in order thus to secure their position on the road leading towards the south from Herat through Kandahar.

But let us return to the question of the neutrality of Afghanistan, and inquire what are the means by which such an ardently desired object can be attained? In my opinion, which I in nowise wish to obtrude as advice, there are four measures which ought for the present to be pursued :—

1. The principle hitherto followed on the part of England, of forbearance and consideration for the prejudices and barbarous notions of the Afghans, must once for all give place to a distinct and vigorous policy. Above all, there must be an end to the consideration which excuses the Afghans for not wishing to see an Englishman among them, since the remembrance of Great Britain's former thirst for conquest makes them see a foe in the person of every Englishman. A friendly relation of nearly thirty years, during which

considerable sums of English gold have found their way
over the Kheiber Pass, and during which the Afghans
could not have perceived the slightest trace of English
antipathy or open hostility, ought by rights both in Kabul
and Kandahar to have been a sufficiently striking proof
of English sincerity. That this is not the case, is not
the fault of the English, and it will not astonish any one,
if these thankless protegés, of whose unruliness their
own king complains, were brought somewhat closer
within their benefactor's range. He who uses my purse
and my gun must not despise myself. In fact, the
British sacrifices just mentioned would then only be in
keeping with their true object, if English officers would
assist the aspiring Shir-Ali-Khan in the organisation of
his army, which would certainly not be unpleasing to
the Khan himself; if, moreover, a political agent assisted
him with advice—in one word, if the British merchant
and traveller in Afghanistan could feel himself more in
a friendly land than he now does, when an excursion to
Afghanistan by the Anglo-Indians is always regarded
as a dangerous undertaking. That this, in reality, is
not so difficult as is believed in London and Calcutta,
and that the Afghans could become accustomed to the
sight of a Briton in their native country, has been
recently sufficiently proved by Sir Frederick Goldsmith,
who travelled through Afghanistan when he went to
settle the frontier dispute at Sistan, and was everywhere
received with distinction. A beginning must only be
made, the importance must be assumed to which the
English are entitled, and friendly advances will not be
wanting. In this way alone is it possible to procure
a proper basis for English interests in Afghanistan ;

only thus will England act up to the duty which she has laid upon herself by her union with Russia for the pacification of Afghanistan, and only thus will the Viceroy at Calcutta, and through him the Cabinet of St James', be accurately informed of the Russian intrigues in Central Asia. The present circumstances of Afghanistan are thoroughly different to those at the time of the rivalry between Dost-Mohammed and Shah-Shedja, for without the British garrison in Bala-Hissar, the political agent, Sir Alexander Burnes, would not have fallen a victim to the dagger of a seditious rebel. Every Oriental is suspicious; safety, therefore, rests in the removal of all cause for suspicion.

2. The frontier of Afghanistan in the north and north-west ought to be definitely established, and ought to be liable to no change in future, even as regards a tract of land. Here, of course, considerable difficulties would have to be encountered with respect to districts and tribes; yet, in consideration of the great services which such a measure would render, a mixed frontier committee of English and Russian officers might set to work, and taking the *status quo* of the present Afghan frontier in the north as a starting-point, they might all the more easily arrive at a result than the Russians have done in Karategin, Bokhara, and Khokand, in coming forward with the principle, " *Hoc jubeo, hoc volo.*"

As the northern boundary of Afghanistan, the Surch tributary, already mentioned, might be taken, which beginning, so to speak, at the Terek Pass, encloses the Bedachshan province in the north, as far as Kurgan-Tepe. From the last-mentioned point, or where this river joins the Pendja, and under the name of Oxus flows in a direction from the north-east towards the west and north-west, *i.e.*, from the town of Hazreti-Imam, as far as Kerki; this latter river is at the present time actually designated as the northern boundary of Afghanistan. Yet we must not stop here, but prolong the boundary along this river as far as Tchikardjui; for apart from the fact that the petty Khanates on the upper course of the Oxus, as well as Kerki and Andchoi, may be regarded to a certain extent as belonging to Afghanistan, many disputes in Central Asiatic politics would be averted by the annexation of these restless little states. These points form, moreover, the main highway across the Oxus territory towards the south, *i.e.*, to India; and if Belch, on the highway over the Hindukush is in the hands of the Afghans, why should not Kerki be so also, through which the road to Herat passes, and which, from the political decline of Bokhara, has remained entirely without a master? From Kerki to Tchihardjui, the coast lands inhabited by the peacefully disposed Ersari-Turkomans might, without much difficulty, be subjected to Afghan authority; the only difficulty would be in the exact settlement of the frontier between Tchihardjui and Herat, as here, on the western branch of the Paropaneisus mountains, we are met by an inhospitable desert, and by the Kara, Alikli, Sarik, and Salor Turkomans, who rove over it; against whom a power like Afghanistan is no match, and who could only be intimidated by the black eagle of Russia. The settlement of the west frontier of Afghanistan, namely, the effecting of peaceful relations between the Afghans and Persians, a work of conciliation which has for two years been undertaken by

Great Britain, could now all the more easily be brought to a happy termination, if the Court of Teheran were freed from the obnoxious importunities of Russia, and were placed on a free footing. Iran is at the present time thoroughly Russian; yet we must not believe that this is a consequence of any peculiar affection for the Northern Colossus. Iran sympathy with Russia is the result of English indifference. The Government of the Shah must only be made to perceive that the independence of Iran is the aim of Great Britain, since in an independent position it can more easily remain neutral, and I do not doubt that the authorities in Teheran will endeavour to free themselves from the obnoxious tutelage of Petersburg. All that we have said as to the exact settlement of the frontiers of northern Afghanistan, as well as every security which Great Britain will give with regard to the consolidation of the interior affairs of this country, and which by her assent to Gortschakoff's diplomatic communication of the 31st January 1873, she has already given, can, however, only then answer the desired object, if England is not discouraged from the direct control of affairs on the other side of the Kheiber Pass, and if in these places, namely, Kabul, Belch, and Herat, she allows herself to be represented by agents who, enjoying due esteem, and acquainted with the Afghan character and with that of Central Asiatics generally, are able to procure British influence its full authority.

3. Russia must define her frontier on the north in such a manner that, exonerating herself from the suspicion of insatiable thirst for territory, she may quietly and leisurely proceed to that work of civilisation which,

according to her own assertion, she has undertaken in rude and uncivilised Turkestan. Her frontier in the south of her newly acquired possessions follows, at the present time, almost throughout, the right bank of the Oxus. Her position in Khokand, by which is understood the principality of Karategin, in Shehri-Sebz, and in the Khanate of Bokhara, is indeed such that she has not yet reached the yellow waters of the Amoor. Yet this will, sooner or later, be the case; it must, moreover, be the case, since it lies, indeed, in the interest of humanity that the Khanate, now only partly subjugated, should be entirely incorporated. By this, Russia will procure advantages for herself, for the present Russian state expenses in Turkestan are almost three times as large as the receipts, and it is undoubtedly just that a state should derive a certain benefit from her efforts for the civilisation of the interior of Asia, and this, of course, can only be obtained when the main point of the Turkestan trade, namely, Bokhara, is placed in the hands of Russia. Similar also are our views with respect to Khiva. We have before pointed out the probability that Russia, after a successful termination of the campaign, will not retire from the territory on the lower course of the Oxus; that, moreover, she cannot retire, and that she ought not. If we would have rest in the remote future, there must be a thorough setting in order in the present, and this can only be done when the anarchical state of things in Khiva is once for all terminated. A chastisement and provisory occupation of this country would only mitigate the evil for a short period. After the lapse of a few years, the present situation of things would be resumed, Russia would equip herself

anew, and England would be again suspicious. Is it
not, therefore, more expedient, if Russia at once, after
having accomplished the conquest of the country, leaves
behind a strong Russian garrison at several points, as,
for instance, at Hezaresp, Khiva, Görlen, Kiptjak, and
Kungrat, taking the southern line of demarcation formed
by the empty bed of the Oxus, which stretches in a
south-east direction from Hezaresp to the Balkan range,
terminates her possessions at Khiva, and gradually subjects the whole country to her sceptre? Whether difficult or easy, whether combined with great expense and
difficulties or not, the annexation and thorough conquest
of Khiva will, at any rate, cost far less trouble than the
repeated attempts to chastise the country. Much would
thus be cleared up, and the main result, namely, the
removal of English apprehensions, would be materially
promoted. Closely connected with such a policy is the
relinquishing of all those strong points hitherto occupied
by Russia on the east coast of the Caspian Sea. At the
time when she is engaged in war against Khiva, and in
its subjection, the maintenance of a Russian garrison in
Krasnowodsk and in Tchekishlar is explained, because
these are to serve as a basis for her operations. But
when once Russia has finished with Khiva, every glance
which the Russian eagle casts on the south-east shores
of the Caspian, could and must be suspected only as a
secret design upon northern Chorassan. No other object
could be pursued by Russia in this direction, in which
the island of Ashurada may be reckoned, and Great
Britain would be perfectly justified in conjecturing an
attack on Herat in every Russian movement on the
east coast of the Caspian Sea.

4. Persia, as we have before pointed out, must be strengthened and rendered more secure, especially in the mountainous parts of her northern frontier. The northern boundary of Iran must therefore be considered the banks of the Etrek, while on the east the left bank of the Murghab must be designated as the natural boundary, and by the re-annexation of Merv that frontier would be obtained which Iran possessed thousands of years ago, and which has been disputed only since the overthrow of the Lefides by the Turkestan hordes of Central Asia. It is true a great stone of stumbling in all these arrangements is afforded by the Turkomans, amounting to nearly 450,000 men, who render the great Hyrcanian steppes insecure in all directions from Andchoi to Astrabad, and from Hezaresp to Deregös. They can, and they will, moreover, for a time trouble the three contiguous states, and will much impede the accomplishment of peaceful harmony. Yet we must not forget that the wings of the Turkomans will be almost entirely broken by the powerful position of Russia in the Turkestan Khanates. Their principal means of livelihood, the main stimulus to their predatory excursions in the adjacent countries of Iran and Afghanistan, namely, the slave trade, would be entirely paralysed by a Russian occupation of Bokhara and Khiva. I hear that this horrible trade of human beings has recently already lost much of its lucrativeness ; and should it be subsequently repressed, even by a tolerably regular government in the Khanates, but few adventurers among the Tekkes, Sariks, and Yomuts would be found who, to the peril of their own lives, would make inroads into the above-mentioned countries,

stealing defenceless men from the plough and from their homes, and dragging them away as slaves. For his own use the Turkoman requires no slaves ; he scarcely finds bread for himself and his family, and he has hitherto practised his robber trade only in the service of the Khanate. And why should it not be possible to put down such a trade? Scarcely fifty years ago the Kirghises of the Central Horde were just as dangerous on the highway between Bokhara and Orenburg as the Turkomans, for their Barantas (predatory excursions) in Southern Siberia have cost more than one Russian his liberty ; and if the gradual advance of the Russian outposts brought order here, and transformed the Kirghises into harmless cattle-breeders, why should not this be the case under similar circumstances with the Turkomans? At the present day, these sons of the desert are the most restless, covetous, and unprincipled robbers in the world ; but a consolidation of the power of the state in Afghanistan, in Iran, and in the Khanates, must and will put an end to their infamous doings.

We should here have concluded our humble suggestions with regard to the peaceful settlement of the Central Asiatic question. We must however observe, that the measures proposed can only have the hoped-for effect if Russia seriously intends a peaceful settlement ; and if, relinquishing her desire for immediate vicinity to the British possessions in India, she is really striving only for the restoration of repose in the Khanates, and for the promotion of her own commercial interests. Nothing but a frank and honest policy, and an open and unequivocal course of conduct, can solve this fatal Central Asiatic question ; and as Great Britain desires no extension of frontier beyond the Suleiman range, and entertains no vast political plans in connection with this extension, it is Russia alone on whose behaviour the maintenance of peace depends, and who can avoid the mighty collision of the two great European powers in Asia, just as it also lies in her hand, to provoke it.

As the diplomatic correspondence just concluded between London and Petersburg with regard to the Central Asiatic question informs us, England still ever places perfect confidence in the words of her northern rival, and feels herself not a little flattered that Prince Gortschakoff has yielded to the desire of Lord Granville with respect to the difference of opinion concerning Bedachshan. The Russian Chancellor of State says in his despatch of the 31st January, " Russia consents to the demarcation of frontier at Bedachshan prescribed by England, because it is difficult to ascertain the state of the case in those remote countries ; because England has more opportunity of gathering accurate information ; and, lastly, because it is unnecessary to attach greater importance to this question than really belongs to it." Truly no insignificant proof of gentleness on the part of the Russian bear ! If a single glance at the map of Turkestan did not prove to us that Russia can hitherto have pursued only very secondary plans in Bedachshan, and that the west frontier of Afghanistan is of more importance to her, we might still justify John Bull's proud self-consciousness. But as matters actually stand, this pleasure is very childish, and at any rate unfounded. This whole line of demarcation, so far as it defines the northern boundary of Afghanistan, has too much the character of a provisory performance ; and as Russia in all probability, after the conclusion of the campaign against Khiva, will express herself definitively on the subject, we will postpone our reflections on the matter until that time, and will keep in view the progress of that campaign which Russia, as Count Schuwaloff affirmed in London, has undertaken with only four and a half battalions of regular troops.

THE END.

PRINTED BY BALLANTYNE AND COMPANY
EDINBURGH AND LONDON

WORKS PUBLISHED BY SMITH, ELDER, & CO.

LONDON : SMITH, ELDER, & CO., 15 WATERLOO PLACE.

ILLUSTRATED LIBRARY EDITION OF THE
LIFE AND WORKS OF

CHARLOTTE BRONTË

(CURRER BELL),

AND HER SISTERS, EMILY AND ANNE BRONTË

(ELLIS AND ACTON BELL).

In Seven Volumes, large crown 8vo, handsomely bound in cloth.
Price 7s. 6d. per Volume.

The descriptions in "Jane Eyre" and the other Fictions by Charlotte Brontë and her Sisters being mostly of actual places, the Publishers considered that Views would form the most suitable Illustrations of the Library Edition of the Novels. They are indebted for a clue to the real names of the most interesting scenes to a friend of the Misses Brontë, who has thus enabled the artist, Mr G. M. Wimperis, to identify the places described. He made faithful sketches of them on the spot, and has also drawn them on wood; it is therefore hoped that these views will add fresh interest to the reading of the stories.

NEW AND UNIFORM EDITION OF

MRS GASKELL'S NOVELS AND TALES.

In Seven Volumes, each containing Four Illustrations.
Price 3s. 6d. each, bound in cloth.

CONTENTS OF THE VOLUMES.

Vol. I.—WIVES AND DAUGH-   Vol. II.—NORTH AND SOUTH.
       TERS.   Vol. III.—SYLVIA'S LOVERS.

Vol. IV.—CRANFORD.

Company Manners—The Well of Pen-Morpha—The Heart of John Middleton—Traits and Stories of the Huguenots—Six Weeks at Heppenheim—The Squire's Story—Libbie Marsh's Three Eras—Curious if True—The Moorland Cottage—The Sexton's Hero—Disappearances—Right at Last—The Manchester Marriage—Lois the Witch—The Crooked Branch.

Vol. V.—MARY BARTON.

Cousin Phillis—My French Master—The Old Nurse's Story—Bessy's Troubles at Home—Christmas Storms and Sunshine.

Vol VI.—RUTH.

The Grey Woman—Morton Hall—Mr Harrison's Confessions—Hand and Heart.

Vol. VII.—LIZZIE LEIGH.

A Dark Night's Work—Round the Sofa—My Lady Ludlow—An Accursed Race—The Doom of the Griffiths—Half a Life-Time Ago—The Poor Clare—The Half-Brothers.

LONDON: SMITH, ELDER, & CO., 15 WATERLOO PLACE.